0.724

D0275749

COLCHESTER TOWN HALL
DETAILS OF TOWER.
Scale ¼ to the foot.

ELEVATION.

ELEVATION OF ANGLE.

ALASTAIR SERVICE

Edwardian Architecture

A HANDBOOK TO BUILDING DESIGN
IN BRITAIN 1890–1914

with 241 illustrations

THAMES AND HUDSON

In memory of my father and my uncle
D.W.S. and I.M.S.
and of my father-in-law
H.H.H.

Half-title: detail of screen, church of St Mary the
Virgin, Great Warley, Essex (1902–04), by Sir
William Reynolds-Stephens and C. Harrison
Townsend

Frontispiece: detail drawings of the tower,
Colchester Town Hall (1897–1902), by John
Belcher

Filmset and printed in Great Britain by
BAS Printers Limited, Over Wallop, Hampshire,
and bound by
Webb and Sons, Glamorgan, South Wales

CONTENTS

PREFACE AND ACKNOWLEDGMENTS 6

Part One The End of the Nineteenth Century

1 The Background to the Period 1890–1914 in Great Britain 8

2 Arts and Crafts Architecture – The House 14

3 The Free Style and Large Buildings 38

4 Public Buildings and the Baroque Revival 60

5 Church Architecture – Late Gothic and Byzantine 74

Part Two Edwardian Free Design

6 Free Design and the Edwardian House 88

7 Large Buildings and the Edwardian Free Style 102

8 The Edwardian Arts and Crafts Churches 118

9 Towards Rationalism – Offices and Factories 128

Part Three Edwardian Classicism

10 High Edwardian Baroque 140

11 The Beaux-Arts Influence on Edwardian Classicism 158

12 The Neo-Georgian House 170

13 Palaces of Prosperity – Variations on the Grand Manner 178

NOTES ON THE TEXT 188

SELECT BIBLIOGRAPHY 193

Leading Architects and Some of Their Buildings 1890–1914

197

INDEX 213

Preface and Acknowledgments

THE POPULATION of Britain quadrupled between 1800 (when it was 10 million) and the start of the First World War in 1914. The period of fastest population growth coincides with the period of architectural history covered by this book, the end of the nineteenth century and the first decade of the twentieth. In 1881 there were 31 million people in the United Kingdom; by 1911 there were 11 million more to house. These decades saw a time of unprecedented prosperity for Britain through her industry, through the resources of her Empire and through trade with the rest of the world. Despite continuing poverty for the working classes, that prosperity caused a rapid growth of the middle classes and – between about 1895 and 1906 – a tremendous boom in building. Within these years more houses, offices, factories and other buildings were built each year than ever before in the country's history. There was a proliferation of building firms, of speculative developers, of architects (both run-of-the-mill and talented) and of architectural styles. All of these developments were understandable consequences of the national situation, but they make this period of British architectural history a particularly complex one.

This book is the first concise study of the main, often conflicting, developments in British architecture between 1890 and 1914 – a period of high architectural achievement. The Arts and Crafts revival of domestic architecture, the attempts to create a new non-revivalist British style, the evolution of the Gothic and Byzantine styles in church architecture, the revival of the large-scale English Baroque of the age of Wren and Vanbrugh for public buildings, the introduction of the Neo-Georgian domestic style and the revival of a more refined French-influenced Classicism all produced buildings of great distinction. It was also a time when several new structural techniques were introduced to Britain and when the first, fascinating attempts of architects to adapt the exteriors of buildings to steel and concrete frame construction were made.

Clear-cut categorizations in this period can be misleading, especially with regard to the developments in British architecture after 1900. For example, in this book chapter five summarizes church architecture in general, chapters six to nine cover the various forms of free and non-historicist design, and chapters ten to thirteen deal with the Edwardian revival of different types of Classicism. It will be seen that this kind of breakdown cannot always be sustained, although I believe it is essentially valid. Thus, Sir John Burnet's Kodak Building may be viewed as a pioneering work of Free Style rationalism or as a commercial temple of Stripped Classicism. Equally, Charles Holden's early Neo-Mannerist buildings may be seen as Classical variations or as free compositions which happen to use some Classical detail. I have tried to indicate this ambiguity where it arises, for, as Sir John Summerson once wrote to me, tidy history is never true history in architecture.

In the space available, it is impossible to cover all the talented architects and fine buildings of the time. In the 1891 census 7,800 men gave their occupation as architect and this number increased to 10,700 in 1901. Readers may find some personal favourites given inadequate attention or even omitted. Admirers of John Douglas of Chester, C. E. Mallows, George Walton, the Barnsley brothers, Arnold Mitchell, William Flockhart, Niven and Wigglesworth, W. Curtis Green, Charles Reilly, Adshead and Ramsay, Walter Tapper, Charles Nicholson and F. W. Troup, for example, may well complain about the coverage given to their work in the text, though their work is summarized at the end of the book. All the same, I believe that I have fairly represented the architects who were most significant, either for the volume or for the quality of their work.

My thanks are due to many people. The manuscript has been read and constructively criticized by Richard Chafee, A. S. Gray, Robin Middleton, Nikos Stangos and David Walker, and it owes much to their suggestions. I have had a great deal of assistance from experts on individual architects; from Godfrey Rubens on Lethaby, Andrew Saint on Norman Shaw, Lynne Walker on Prior, John Brandon-Jones on Voysey, Richard Fellows on Blomfield, John Archer on Edgar Wood, Richard Woollard on Townsend, Alan Crawford on Ashbee, Rory Spence on Stokes, Mark Ricardo Bertram on Ricardo, John Warren on Rickards, David Walker on the major Scottish architects of the time, and from others. Sir John Summerson, Sir John Betjeman and Sir Nikolaus Pevsner have been constantly encouraging. Roderick Gradidge, Margaret Richardson and Gavin Stamp have provided many thoughtful and sobering comments. Venetia Maas has given invaluable help, as have the staff of the R.I.B.A. library and of the London Library. Louisa, Nicholas and Sophie have given hours of help with typing, checking and choosing pictures. They and David and Jean and many other friends have visited countless buildings all over Britain with me.

A note about the system of dating in this book is necessary. Where two dates are given (e.g. 1897–1906), the first is the date (where known) of the architect's design, the second the date of the completion of the building. Where one date only is given, the building was designed and built in one year to the best of my knowledge or, in a few cases, only one date is known.

ALASTAIR SERVICE

Photographic Acknowledgments

Annan, Glasgow 136; Architects' Journal (photo by Sam Lambert) 156; Architectural Press 57; Ashbee Collection, Victoria and Albert Museum, London 29; Geoffrey Broadbent 123; William Coles 79; Country Life 101, 112, 218, 239; Alan Crawford 27, 86, 163; Christopher Dalton 150; Eric de Maré 90, 137, 145–6; Greg Edwards 110; Glasgow Herald 80; Victor Glasstone 202; Terence Griffin 32; A. L. Hunter 157; David Irwin 152; Peter Joslin, Lancaster 193–4; A. F. Kersting, London 37; Bedford Lemere 197, 199; John Meacock, Clacton-on-Sea 174; Mewès and Davis 195, 198, 200; William Morris Gallery, Walthamstow 7; National Monuments Record 1–2, 61–2, 85, 95, 97, 108 (photo by Bedford Lemere); R.I.B.A. Library, London 127, 149, 161–2; Douglas Scott, Glasgow 133; Alastair Service 3–4, 8, 11, 15, 17, 19, 21, 24, 26, 28, 30, 33–4, 38, 40, 42, 45–6, 48, 51, 55, 58, 60, 65, 70, 72, 74–6, 78, 84, 88, 98–9, 102, 115–20, 122, 128–9, 134–5, 138–40, 143–4, 147, 153, 159–60, 164, 167–8, 171, 176, 178–9, 181, 185–9, 204–5, 208–10, 228–9, 231, 233, 236–7; Paul Shillabeer 148; Edwin Smith half-title; W. J. Smith 111; S. S. Summers 9; Colin Westwood, London 59, 64; Whyler Photos, Stirling 36. All other photographs supplied by the author.

1
The Background to the Period
1890–1914 in Great Britain

THE CURRENTS and cross-currents prevailing in British architecture at the beginning of the twentieth century reveal a situation of great complexity. The two main movements of the Edwardian period were the experimental work of the Arts and Crafts architects and their followers and, at the other extreme, the revival of the English Baroque manner of Wren, Vanbrugh and Hawksmoor. Yet there are many connections between these two opposing movements and many variations of both. For example, French Beaux-Arts Classicism was spurned by British nationalism during the Baroque Classical revival in the 1890s, then swept into fashion late in the first decade of the new century. Nor did either development fit neatly into the reign of British monarchs. The term Edwardian is useful to differentiate a distinctive architectural period from that of the buildings widely associated with Queen Victoria's name. But both Arts and Crafts architecture and the Baroque revival start well before Edward VII's reign (1901–10) and finish after it. The period covered by this book therefore runs from about 1890 – when many architects including William Lethaby, C. F. A. Voysey, Charles Rennie Mackintosh and Reginald Blomfield started active practices – until 1914 when the First World War put a stop to most building for several years.

By 1890 the most famous of the great Victorian Gothic architects were either dead or nearing the end of their careers.

Butterfield (1814–1900) was still in practice on a reduced scale, but Pugin (1812–52), the older George Gilbert Scott (1811–78), Street (1824–81) and Burges (1827–81) had died. Of the leaders of that generation, only G. F. Bodley (1827–1907) had much work still to do. The Gothic style continued to dominate church architecture but in all other fields a variety of freely mixed styles followed the 'Queen Anne' manner that had both grown out of and rebelled against Gothicism in the 1870s. Borrowings from different historical periods could be seen in the English buildings being erected at this time. Scotland, too, had its mixed designs, but there the almost pure Greek Classical revival continued to be widely favoured and became fashionable in Glasgow after 1850.

In London, the most successful architects of around 1890 were Alfred Waterhouse (1830–1905), Thomas Collcutt (1840–1924) and Ernest George (1839–1922), although Aston Webb (1849–1930) had a growing practice that was soon to become the largest of all. Such mixed-style buildings as Waterhouse's Prudential Assurance, Collcutt's Imperial Institute [1], George's Claridge's Hotel and Webb's Victoria and Albert Museum were the typical public buildings of the early 1890s. Meanwhile, in less publicized architecture, the great Victorian warehouse builders were still vigorous, vast country mansions in the tradition of Waterhouse's Eaton Hall [2] continued to be built and

1 *The Imperial Institute, off Exhibition Road, South Kensington, London (1887–93), by Thomas Collcutt. South front from east. Demolished 1957, except tower. A splendid public building of the early 1890s, in a mixture of historical styles.*

engineer-architects like Colonel Edis were putting up enormous eclectic office buildings. Grandiose hotels and flats such as those by Archer and Green were proliferating, and theatres in the light-hearted Victorian Classical manner of Thomas Verity were spreading across the country.

A reaction among architects to this undisciplined combination of historical styles was almost inevitable. They looked to Norman Shaw (1831–1912) for leadership in sheer quality of design, though Shaw always remained something of a historicist. And they looked to the writer and designer William Morris (1834–96) for their ideals, particularly as practised by Morris's architect friend Philip Webb (1831–1915).

The Arts and Crafts movement, so closely identified with Morris's name, developed from ideas formulated early in the Gothic revival.[1] In 1841 Augustus Welby Pugin wrote: 'the great test of Architectural beauty is the fitness of the design to the purpose for which it is intended.'[2] Pugin's Ramsgate studio produced textiles, metalwork and other craft products, as well as architectural designs. He constantly criticized the current bad taste in commercial artefacts and he called on designers to look to nature itself for inspiration. Pugin was not alone in his feelings and others, notably Sir Henry Cole, set up organizations to improve the quality of design. Cole started a firm which supplied designs to manufacturers of ceramics, furniture and cutlery in the 1840s and wrote about the need for an English nineteenth-century style.

The next important figures in the development of standards for English design were Owen Jones and John Ruskin. Ruskin derided Cole's efforts, especially his part in the Great Exhibition of 1851. It is with Ruskin that there first appears the contempt for machine-produced objects that was to remain a source of contention within the Arts and Crafts movement throughout its history. 'A piece of terracotta, or plaster of Paris, which has been wrought by the human hand, is worth

2 Eaton Hall, Cheshire (1867–80), by Alfred Waterhouse. West front. Demolished 1961, except clock tower. A country palace for the Duke of Westminster in the eclectic mixed-style manner which became popular after the High Victorian Gothic period.

3 Standen, near Saint Hill, East Grinstead, Sussex (1891–94), by Philip Webb. Garden front. Arts and Crafts originality, with stylistic and structural roots in Sussex vernacular building traditions. Webb's last great house, its influence can be seen in many later buildings by other architects.

all the stone in Carrara cut by machinery,' he wrote in 1849.[3] In this, as in many other ideas taken up by the Arts and Crafts movement, Ruskin was following the condemnation by the writer Thomas Carlyle of a society which had itself become mechanical.

It was, however, Ruskin's next book *The Stones of Venice*, whose first volume was published in the year of the Great Exhibition, that was to become a bible for the Arts and Crafts movement. Two undergraduates at Oxford, William Morris and Edward Burne-Jones, read it first in 1853 at a time when they were already committed to a revolution in British art and were especially stirred by the chapter 'The Nature of Gothic'. One of Ruskin's main arguments in the book was that buildings, decoration and decorative objects must *show* that they are man-made. Much of the book is fiery stuff: 'the great cry that rises from all our manufacturing cities, louder than their furnace blast, is . . . this, – that we manufacture everything there except men : we blanch cotton, and strengthen steel, and refine sugar, and shape pottery; but to brighten, to strengthen, to refine, or to form a single living spirit, never enters into our estimate of advantages.'[4] Here lie the seeds of Morris's lifelong work and of his close identification of political with artistic ideals.

Ruskin went even further in setting the pattern for Arts and Crafts practice. He called for craftsmen who would invent a new design for each article made, for painters who ground their own colours, for architects who worked in the mason's yard with the men, and for the distinction between one man and another to be 'only in experience and skill'. Ruskin taught at the Working Men's College, newly founded in London in 1854. He vigorously attacked capitalist industrialism and the rich in 1862

in a book that was dismissed with contempt by almost everyone except Carlyle, and himself started the St George's Guild in 1871 as an idealistic community attempt to adapt the medieval guild system. The attempt failed, but was the precursor of the important guilds which formed the backbone of the Arts and Crafts movement in the next decade.

The importance of William Morris was far more than that of a popularizer of Ruskin's ideas. Morris trained briefly as an architect in 1855 with the great Gothicist G. E. Street, became involved with the Pre-Raphaelite painters, especially Rossetti, and then in 1860 set about putting into practice the ideals he had gathered through the medium of a firm which used talents of men of similar ideas and became widely known as Morris and Co.

Morris and Co. practised in all the arts and crafts associated with building and decoration, and Morris himself did everything possible to spread his theories. He founded the Society for the Protection of Ancient Buildings in 1876 and in 1883 became an active Socialist when he joined the Democratic Federation. 'Real art is the expression by man of his pleasure in labour,' he said in 1879.[5] But it is the influence of Morris and his friends on architecture that is chiefly of concern here, and it was his close collaborator Philip Webb who translated the Arts and Crafts principles mentioned above into architectural practice [3]. Webb, in turn, inspired a school of architects of the next generation, of whom the most important theorist was William Lethaby (1857–1931).

Morris and Webb advocated the need for the architect to work out each design with reference to the particular site and purpose of a building – regardless of style. The architect must have knowledge of his materials and should work with his craftsmen, sculptors and painters as in medieval times; securing fine execution of the design in the best available materials, and keeping contact with local building traditions. John Sedding (1838–91), a talented church architect, played a significant role in preaching this approach in architecture.

From these ideas grew the Arts and Crafts movement of the 1880s, together with several organizations which served to forward its aims. By 1890 it was clear that members of the Art Workers' Guild and the Arts and Crafts Exhibition Society were developing a simplified and non-copyist architecture that did not, at the same time, ignore tradition. 'It is the power to embody the old principle [in] ever-new conditions, distinguishing and setting aside that which does not form part of the living thought of the time, which is the true objective of the architect,' declared Lethaby, chief founder of the Art Workers' Guild, in a talk to the Architectural Association in 1889.[6] Such attitudes were the source of the English domestic building revival of the 1890s that became world-famous at the time, and of the first attempts at a new national style for large buildings. During the early part of the period covered by this book, such attempts usually consisted of free versions of earlier, specifically English, styles. Later, architects like Townsend and Charles Rennie Mackintosh rejected all historical styles and tried to find a completely 'Free Style'.

Yet in the year Lethaby gave his talk, a London-Scottish architect called John Brydon addressed the same audience with a very different message. Brydon had recently built a Town Hall for Chelsea in the manner of Wren, and his 1889 talk was a paean to seventeenth-century English architecture. Inigo Jones and Wren, he said, had created an architecture that was 'English as distinct from, and in some respects superior to, even the Italian Renaissance . . . leaving it to us as a precious heritage to keep and to guard and, above all things, to study and maintain that we . . . may bring forth fruits worthy of the high ideal.'[7]

Brydon's lecture was certainly as much of a success as Lethaby's with the audience of architects and students. Wren's late Baroque work answered the need many felt for a truly British style as the British Empire approached its zenith of power and prosperity. Furthermore, the style allowed for the tradition of good craftsmanship and the integration of sculpture and painting into the fabric of a building – an Arts and Crafts ideal, though it led to a revival of flamboyant Classicism. This was to be followed by a reaction against its excesses and an attempt to bring back Classical good taste and a French elegance, led by Reginald Blomfield and Arthur J. Davis, after 1905.

During the course of the 1890s and early 1900s both these trains of thought – free design on the one hand, updated Classicism on the other – obtained strong followings. The object of this book is to trace their development in the various types of building: private houses, public and other large buildings, churches and cathedrals, and palaces of royalty, of government and of prosperity.

2
Arts and Crafts Architecture
The House

IT HAS BEEN SEEN in chapter one how the origins of the movement towards a new architecture in late nineteenth-century Britain lay in the ideas of Truth in Building of Pugin and other architects of the early Victorian Gothic revival, combined with the theories of John Ruskin. Several of the great Victorian Goths, notably William Butterfield, designed houses in a simple bold manner, almost free of Gothic style detailing. Some of the houses by George Devey (1820–86) built around 1860 adapt the old non-Classical vernacular style of their localities to contemporary needs [5]. But it was William Morris and Philip Webb, both emerging from G. E. Street's Gothic office, who were effectively the founders of the Arts and Crafts movement. For artistic and social reasons Morris wanted a return to idealized medieval days when artists were ordinary working men whose 'daily labour was sweetened by the daily creation of Art'.[1]

Morris had enough private income to allow him to get married and to commission a house that launched Philip Webb's almost entirely domestic architectural practice in 1860. Other designers gathered around Morris, and the firm of Morris, Marshall and Faulkner (later Morris and Co.) was founded in 1861 with the objective of reviving the declining standards of workmanship and design in all crafts since the Industrial Revolution. Webb's buildings were carried out by architect, builders, furnishers and de-corative craftsmen working as a team. His houses were designed to blend with their locality, using vernacular building traditions and materials. It was a small trumpet-call but its echoes were to spread through Britain and into Europe and North America during the next fifty years.

Another important architect followed Webb in the post of chief draughtsman to G. E. Street in 1858. This was the Scot, R. Norman Shaw, not a man of high political and artistic idealism like Morris, but one who possessed a talent for original design in architecture that outshone most of his contemporaries. Shaw and his friend Eden Nesfield gained recognition for the red brick architecture using Classical motifs, known as the 'Queen Anne' style. That style first showed architects how to grow beyond Gothicism in the 1870s, without losing the underlying Gothic ideals of truthful expression. Even Shaw could not find a way of harnessing the revolutionary achievements of Victorian structural engineering to create a new architecture for his time. But he did take a step towards freedom from tradition with the house he built for himself in Hampstead in 1875. His Hampstead Towers is certainly not Gothic and certainly not Classical [4]. Instead of

4 *Hampstead Towers, No. 6 Ellerdale Road, Hampstead, London (1875–76), by Norman Shaw. In this house built for his own use, Shaw composed a number of traditional English features into an asymmetrical yet balanced design.*

5 *St Alban's Court, Nonington, Kent (c. 1860–64), by George Devey. South front. An adaptation of the Elizabethan brick vernacular to the requirements of the nineteenth century.*

symmetry, the street frontage shows an irregular pattern of windows as demanded by the plan at each floor level, yet composed into an overall design that balances in a complex and delicate way.

Shaw was a man-of-the-world architect who maintained his own independent path of development while amassing a fair fortune from his practice. In temperament he was utterly different from his headstrong contemporary Edward Godwin (1833–86), artist-architect *par excellence* of the Aesthetic Movement with its interests in Japanese taste. Lover of the actress Ellen Terry, friend and architect of the painter J. McNeill Whistler, of Oscar Wilde and many other members of the Aesthetic Movement, Godwin soared through the Victorian architectural scene in the 1870s. 'If asked what style your work is, say "It is my own",' he told young architects at a

lecture in 1878.[2] In the same year he was designing houses in Tite Street, Chelsea – for Whistler and for another painter called Frank Miles – that certainly lived up to his own words. The White House for Whistler is well known (the building is now demolished), but the design for Miles was even more original [6]. As in Shaw's home, the elevation reflects the requirements of the rooms within and achieves distinction by accents of different weights that balance each other, dominated by the entrance porch and the high studio window. This architectural strength is relieved by sculpted bands and by the froth of green plants against the red brickwork that Godwin always showed in the sketches for his buildings. Unfortunately, the novelty of the whole design was too much for the landlords, the Metropolitan Board of Works, who forced Godwin to tone it down to the still remarkable design that survives today as No. 44 Tite Street.

The three streams of development beyond historical styles – the revitalized crafts ideal of Webb and Morris, the power of Norman Shaw's influence and the refined originality of Godwin and the Aesthetic Movement – came together in a number of ways during the 1880s. As the decade passed, other ideas, such as 'unity with nature' and 'the pursuit of simplicity', joined them to form the notable English domestic building revival of the end of the century. These ideas were by no means purely architectural ones, for they reflected many of the philosophical and scientific theories of the time.

During the 1880s a talented new generation of architects and designers was being trained and, one by one, its members went from the distinguished established offices into individual practice. From James Brooks's office there emerged Arthur Mackmurdo (1851–1942) and from Basil Champneys's there came Halsey Ricardo (1854–1928). A Scot, James MacLaren (1843–90), progressed from Campbell Douglas and J. J. Stevenson in Glasgow to Godwin in London before starting his own practice. John Dando Sedding's Arts and Crafts Gothic church practice produced both Ernest Gimson (1864–1920) and Henry Wilson (1863–1934), though Wilson had also worked with Beresford Pite (1861–1934) in John Belcher's prosperous firm. Charles Annesley Voysey (1857–1941) was articled in J. P. Seddon's Gothic office before, more significantly, working for a year under George Devey. Leonard Stokes (1858–1925) worked under two great Goths, Street and then Bodley.

Most important of all, Norman Shaw's famous office, understandably glamorous for young progressives, produced Edward Prior (1852–1932) and William Lethaby, chief inspirers of Arts and Crafts architecture after 1884, as well as Ernest Newton (1856–1922), Mervyn Macartney (1853–1932) and Gerald Horsley (1862–1917). These are the most significant names during the 1880s, though other

6 *First design of June 1878 for No. 44 Tite Street, Chelsea, London, by Edward Godwin. The design develops Shaw's asymmetrical balance into a frontage containing hardly any historical references.*

important designers appeared during the following decade.

It is no accident that Arthur Mackmurdo is mentioned first in the list above, for he was an originator who must be examined before and a little apart from the rest. He came from a prosperous and well-connected family, through whom he had contact with leading figures in the artistic world, including Ruskin, Whistler and the philosopher Herbert Spencer.[3] Under Ruskin's influence he visited Italy in 1873; under Spencer's he heard T. H. Huxley's lectures on the evolution of form in marine organisms. He knew the refinement of Godwin's houses, for he visited Whistler at the White House. He went to admire Philip Webb's houses, and was impressed by Morris's ideas and work.

In 1882 or 1883 Mackmurdo established the earliest of the guilds connected with the

17

Arts and Crafts movement, the Century Guild. It was a loosely organized body, centred around himself and Herbert Horne, a young architect friend. Other notable designers such as Selwyn Image contributed to its work and more importantly to its occasional magazine, *The Hobby Horse*. But the character of the Guild was predominantly that of Mackmurdo himself – and a very personal manner it was.

Mackmurdo's furniture illustrates his style most clearly [7]. The keynote in both

furniture and architecture is the ubiquitous mannered pillar, stretched to a slender vertical elegance and forming part of an essentially simple grid framework; functional, yet clearly linked to the Aesthetic Movement. Within that frame, the decorative patterns sway and billow in seaweed fronds, rather than featuring the winding garden or jungle plants of Morris or the pretty birds and flowers of Voysey's contemporary wallpapers.

The 1886 Liverpool Exhibition contained several remarkable stands by Mackmurdo's Century Guild and in the following year he designed his finest house of this period. The house is called Brooklyn and it survives in Enfield, a northern London suburb [8]. Again there is a use of elegantly stretched Classical forms to

7 Love settle and fabric design (c. 1886), by Arthur Mackmurdo. In furniture and architecture, Mackmurdo at this stage favoured a framework of elongated pillars. Here, his own sinuous fabric design contrasts with the straight lines of the woodwork.

achieve an overall design of extreme simplicity well in keeping with contemporary Arts and Crafts ideas. But the house sits like a small gem on its site, making no attempt to achieve an organic relationship with its surroundings; still less does it use any vernacular building traditions or materials. Mackmurdo remains a lone wolf in the early Arts and Crafts movement. His later buildings are much less interesting, though odd, and indeed he moved on from architecture to other interests in his long life. His career, however, does illustrate the range of new ideas from which the designer of the 1880s could draw.

The foundation of Mackmurdo's insubstantial Century Guild was followed in 1884 by an important and lasting organization of a similar sort. The name chosen after much discussion was the Art Workers' Guild, founded by the five pupils of Norman Shaw already mentioned who had been organizing regular discussion evenings for a year or more. The key figures were William Lethaby, Shaw's chief draughtsman, and Edward Prior, now an independent architect but still in close contact with the Shaw office.

The two men came from widely different backgrounds. Lethaby's father was a craftsman – a carver and gilder – in Barnstaple, active in Liberal politics and Bible Christianity. After a grammar-school education, Lethaby was articled to a local architect with craft interests, worked for a time in Leicester and then, in 1879, got the job of Norman Shaw's chief clerk on the strength of his drawings published in architectural magazines.[4]

Prior came from a well-to-do family. He went to school at Harrow, then to Caius College, Cambridge – where he won an Athletics Blue for high jump and hurdling – and so entered smoothly into the profession

8 Brooklyn, No. 8 Private Road, Enfield, north London (c. 1887), by Mackmurdo. The architect's most elegant house design, showing his liking for almost Mannerist pilasters. It is quite outside the Arts and Crafts tradition of vernacular roots in house design.

of his choice with a job in Shaw's office as early as 1872. His upper middle-class background must have been useful to Shaw in dealing with clients, yet Prior was to become perhaps the most extreme practitioner of Arts and Crafts architectural ideas of all Shaw's disciples.[5] He and Lethaby were to remain close friends and allies all their lives.

The original objectives of the Guild were clearly defined: they were to reverse the current tendency for architecture, painting and sculpture to drift apart and (in the words of a letter from Lethaby in 1883) to promote 'the Unity of all the Aesthetic Arts', especially in building. In addition to the five founders, there were twenty other original members and the number grew quickly. Early members included three respected architects of a slightly older generation – John Sedding, Basil Champneys and John Belcher – as well as many of the younger progressives already mentioned, notably James MacLaren, Voysey, Pite, Stokes and Mackmurdo.

Even more important, the Guild's members included notable men from other arts and crafts.[6] There were painters such as Henry Holiday and Walter Crane. There were well-known sculptors such as E. Onslow Ford and Sir Hamo Thornycroft, and the designers Heywood Sumner and Lewis F. Day. In 1888 William Morris himself became a member, as if to acknowledge that the Guild had become the London centre of the Arts and Crafts movement. This year also saw the foundation of the Arts and Crafts Exhibition Society by some members of the Guild, since the Guild itself refused to seek publicity or to exhibit.

It was at the weekly Guild discussion evenings that particular aspects of the new approach to design were put forward by a speaker, then debated (unfortunately, no minutes were kept of what was said) and, if a craft was involved, demonstrated. The exchange of thoughts and knowledge was immensely fertile and it is rarely possible to be certain who was the originator of each idea. Guild members also travelled together, seeking ideas from old vernacular buildings in various parts of Britain.

For example, there is the record of a visit by James MacLaren and D. S. McColl in 1886 to the Herefordshire villages and countryside around Ledbury – where MacLaren was building his first English commission.[7] McColl, a journalist and painter close to the Arts and Crafts movement, wrote:

we found, in a little Worcestershire village, a real survival of village industry, an old man who made rush-bottomed chairs, with no other apparatus than his cottage oven for bending the wood. MacLaren made him one or two

drawings, improving a little upon his design, but perfectly simple, and in the old spirit and got him to make a few chairs. When the Art Workers' Guild was formed, these chairs, known to some of its members, were adopted and passed from that into many houses.

MacLaren died young in 1890, but his work during the last five years of his life is of great interest and reflects most of the influences playing on the minds of the Arts and Crafts men. He followed the example of Philip Webb in using local styles as the starting-point for a free architecture. Thus he used half-timbering in Herefordshire, brick and tile-hanging in Sussex and stone or whitewashed rendering in Scotland.

In 1889 MacLaren built a series of farm buildings and housing around Glenlyon House in Perthshire, combining local building custom with geometrical simplicity and a powerful originality [9]. By contrast, some of the features of his London town houses (such as the corner cupolas and balanced asymmetrical elevations) were derived from Godwin, some from discussion with the other Arts and Crafts architects. Certainly they were to appear again and again in other buildings in the 1890s after his death.[8]

We can see similar Godwin influences in the work of others of the loose-knit Arts and Crafts group at this time, for example in the strong asymmetrical Flete Lodge at Holbeton in Devon, built in 1889 by Sedding with his young assistant Henry Wilson. The ideas of the leading Arts and Crafts designers were by no means always in accord, for these men were on principle experimenters and strong individualists. Partly through the influence of the great American architect H. H. Richardson (1838–86), many of them sought the 'organic' in building: that is to say, they tried to let the house grow from and blend with the ground with the help of local stone and other materials, by using craggy naturalistic forms and by experimental plans that followed the levels of their sites and were more flowing than the commonplace chunky grouping of rooms. But MacLaren's Farmer's House at Glenlyon had one particular feature that was to play a key role in the new architecture.

This component was a new sense of visual simplicity which contrasted with what most Arts and Crafts architects considered the overdecoration of the preceding period. Whatever the claims of others, by far the most important exponent of this simplicity throughout the next twenty years was Charles Annesley Voysey. Voysey's influential houses will be discussed later in this chapter. First, the more powerful and organic type of Arts and Crafts domestic architecture that sprang from the Art Workers' Guild must be considered.

Lethaby had outlined the architectural ideals of the Guild – they appear through the mists of his inspiring if not over-lucid prose in a paper he gave to the Architectural Association in November 1889.[9] Those ideals were, 'One, the "motive" or central thought in design. Two, that dignity in realisation we speak of as largeness, breadth, style. Three, the use and limits of a study of past art. Four, the reference to nature.' In the paper Lethaby went on to say that there are ancient architectural principles which should be adapted to ever-changing situations and to dismiss as irrelevant questions of 'pure' historical styles.

One of the recurring themes in much that was written at the time was that the 'past art' that might be used as a basis for a new architecture was essentially national in style, British rather than imported. For this purpose the architectural choice lay between a Free Style developed from

9 *Farmer's House, Glenlyon House estate, Fortingall, Perthshire (c. 1889), by James MacLaren. The architect worked in England and Scotland, and was an early Arts and Crafts practitioner. In this house the simplified and original forms of the design blend with vernacular tradition.*

Perpendicular Gothic, Elizabethan and Jacobean, or the English Baroque of Wren and his disciples. It was the broad strength of some Elizabethan domestic building that appealed to Lethaby, and to those under his personal influence, as a starting-point.

The first architects of the nineteenth century whose work used this stylistic inspiration were Anthony Salvin (1799–1881) and more particularly George Devey, who has already been mentioned at the beginning of this chapter. In the south front of Devey's St Alban's Court in Kent (c. 1860–64),[10] with its strong brickwork and stone-dressed multiple gables and windows [5], one sees something of the ancestry of Lethaby's first two houses. In some of Norman Shaw's houses in London, built when Lethaby was his chief draughtsman, there are the same powerful forms of brickwork with stone dressing: No. 180 Queen's Gate (1884–85) and No. 42 Netherhall Gardens (1887–88) [10], both now destroyed, were notable examples.[11]

A similar feeling of strength is evident in houses by Prior, Stokes and MacLaren in the second half of the 1880s. But it was only in 1891 that Lethaby was put in charge of a house under his own name for the first time. This was Avon Tyrell in Hampshire, built for Lord Manners who had sought Norman Shaw's advice in choosing an architect [11]. The plan, as in so many Arts and Crafts country houses of the 1890s, is long and comparatively narrow, an experimental development which goes back to William Burn's earlier work in Scotland and to George Devey's in England.

It is interesting to compare the design of Avon Tyrell with the four points its architect had picked out in his paper two years earlier. Lethaby's 'motive', or central idea, seems to have been the long shape

10 No. 42 Netherhall Gardens, Hampstead, London (1887–88), by Norman Shaw. Demolished c. 1937. A good example of the type of strong brick forms, with stone dressing, developed in Shaw's office at the time when William Lethaby was his chief assistant.

22

under one roof, with a series of bays and gables terminated at both ends by massive protruding accents. The multiple gable row is a feature used earlier by Devey and by Philip Webb at Standen (1891–94) [3], which was built at the same time as Avon Tyrell. Largeness and 'breadth' of style are obtained by the overall proportions and those of each part, and by the use of the brickwork firmly gripped by stone dressing. 'Past art' is referred to in the free adaptation of Elizabethan windows, chimneys and other detailing. Finally, there is a harmony with 'nature' in the careful siting and in the way the brick and stone style of the house is carried through into the walls and terraces of the garden. In this last respect, Lethaby was never as extreme as his friend Prior in 'organic' building. Avon Tyrell has a certain amount of external sculpture (and used to have more). Lethaby did not pursue the use of relief sculpture of foliage on the exterior surfaces of his later houses; though it appears that the use of this decorative motif by other Arts and Crafts architects, such as Wilson and Townsend, was inspired by Lethaby's 1891 book Architecture, Mysticism and Myth, which will be discussed in chapter three. But as with all of Lethaby's buildings, Avon Tyrell is pervaded by his originality and by a particular magic atmosphere. To visit it is to feel the reality of the 'art of the future' of which he wrote.

Lethaby's next house was called The Hurst, designed and built near Birmingham in 1893 and now demolished [12]. Like Voysey's Perrycroft of the same year, the plan is L-shaped, but the similarity ends there. Again, Lethaby used extremely strong forms in brick with stone dressing, and here in one bay he punched out one of his own individualistic stone patterns from the brickwork. The same type of design was used two years later in a well-known house

11 *Avon Tyrell, Thorney Hill, south of Ringwood, Hampshire (1891–92), by William Lethaby. Garden front. His first commission after leaving Shaw's office. Lethaby's own ideas and individualism are already evident in the design.*

13 *Redcourt, near Haslemere, Surrey (1895), by Ernest Newton. Garden front. A Lethaby-influenced house by one of the Art Workers' Guild founders, who was later to become a chief exponent of imaginative Neo-Georgian domestic design.*

12 *The Hurst, Four Oaks, Sutton Coldfield, Birmingham (1893), by Lethaby. Garden front. Demolished c. 1960. Another strong design in brick with stone dressing. The **L**-plan was an early example of many experimental Arts and Crafts house plans of the 1890s.*

23

by another of the five founders of the Art Workers' Guild, Ernest Newton. Later, Newton became a leader of the Neo-Georgian domestic revival, but in this house, Redcourt in Surrey, he followed Lethaby's influence with only details hinting at what was to come [13].

The fourth key point mentioned in Lethaby's 1889 lecture, 'the reference to nature', was used with restraint in his own buildings. As will be seen in chapter three, other Arts and Crafts architects emphasized this aspect much more strongly in larger buildings. But in domestic work the search for ways to blend a building with its site and surroundings, for organic expression in architecture, was the particular pre-occupation of Edward Prior, the other great original theorist of Arts and Crafts architecture.

Prior's approaches to this matter developed first through the use of local materials, then into experiments with irregular ground plans and with broken compositions of masses. According to Lynne Walker,[12] Prior had experienced Norman Shaw's preference for local building materials as early as 1877, when he was Shaw's clerk-of-works at a house in Yorkshire. He made drawings of vernacular work in Yorkshire and North Wales and probably studied Philip Webb's work at that time. In his remarkable terrace of houses at West Bay in Dorset (1885) [51] he originally planned to use 'local rubble' and 'local stone or concrete roughcasted', but for unknown reasons (perhaps economic), Portland stone from further east in Dorset was eventually used.

The first written account of Prior's feelings for texture and for organic and vernacular building is given in a paper he gave in 1889 in Edinburgh.[13] Here he talked lovingly of 'the velvet thatch, the soft warm tile, the silver splashed lead, the hoary roughness of stone ... how charmingly these lie in the lap of the countryside.' And this is how he wrote of nature:

There are Nature's own Textures for us to use ... We may borrow from her and show the grain and figure of her works, the ordered roughness of her crystallisations in granite or sandstones, or the veining of her marbles. But it is to be noted that our work in each must take a character from the material ... as evidence of our delight in texture, we may leave our wood or stone as it comes from the chisel or the saw, to show the fracture the tool has made ... our plaster may show the impress of the loving hand that laid it, our iron still ring under the hammer that shaped it.

Prior's attitude towards nature was probably influenced by the ideas of Herbert Spencer and T. H. Huxley which have already been mentioned in connection with Mackmurdo. Such ideas echoed and developed those of Ruskin, and were in harmony with the general philosophy of the Arts and Crafts movement. Another influence on Prior was doubtless the slightly earlier work of American architects whose houses, blending with their countryside sites, were much publicized in England during the 1880s.[14]

It was in the 1890s that Prior started to express his feelings fully in his architectural practice and to experiment with both plan and massing of forms. As regards the former, it seems possible that Norman Shaw's Chesters in Northumberland (1889–91) sowed the seed of Prior's idea: the possibilities of variations on the **X**-plan. At Chesters, Shaw added a curving Baroque mansion to a smaller old house and the plan was an expression of the Baroque style [63]. Prior's use of the **X**-plan was, however, very different and one can only interpret his numerous versions and variations as a deliberate attempt to blend a building with its site by avoiding the imposition of a man-made rectangular form on nature.

The first known Prior design of this type, often referred to as 'butterfly plan', was shown as a model called 'A Cottage in Dorset' at the Royal Academy in 1895. Prior and Voysey were next-door neighbours in St John's Wood at this time[15] and there is a story of Voysey helping to touch up the model's roof with a paintbrush on the day before the exhibition opened. The roof of Prior's model swept up from near ground level on each side, then dipped before rising again to its highest point. The plan was for a steep site, broken vertically as well as horizontally, with entrance door, hall, bedrooms and kitchen at ground level on one side under the day-rooms, which were at a higher ground level on the garden side.

The model design was not commissioned by a client, but it probably led to Prior's next building: a house called The Barn beside the sea in Devon. This was completed in 1897 and is one of the masterpieces of Arts and Crafts free architecture. The plan is a simplified version of the 1895 model and solves the problem of handling the junction of the angles with masterly ease [14]. As Halsey Ricardo commented in 1897, 'by the plan given with the Exmouth house we see at once how much the surroundings outside the house have been considered – how much they and the house have played into each others' hands and to their mutual profit.'[16]

The interiors of The Barn are pleasing and ingenious, but it is above all the unity of the exterior with its site that makes the house so breathtaking to visit. It is placed in such a way as to make the most of the position, with views down a long garden

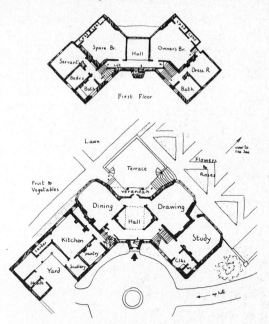

14 *Plan of The Barn, Foxhole Hill Road, Exmouth, Devon (1896–97), by Edward Prior. This type of experimental plan fascinated Prior from 1895 onwards and influenced many other architects. The intention was to break up the conventional block of a house and to create a closer contact with nature.*

15 *The Barn (1896–97), by Prior. Garden front. Like the plan, the building materials and the silhouette of the house tried to give the impression of an almost natural extension from its site.*

16 *Model of a stone house designed by Prior, exhibited at the Royal Academy in 1899. The house was not built, but it was clearly intended for an area of Britain with a vernacular tradition of massive masonry.*

17 *Stoneywell Cottage, Polybott Lane, Ulverscroft, Leicestershire (1898–99), by Ernest Gimson, with Detmar Blow as executive mason. Originally thatched. The composition is rooted in the great chimney which grows from the upper rock of the outcrop.*

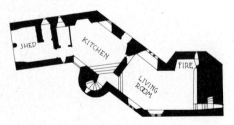

18 *Plan of lower levels, Stoneywell Cottage (1898–99), by Gimson. The house flows down the slope of the outcrop on which it is built.*

that ends in a steep slope to the sea. Looking back from the garden, the building seems to grow from the ground like an outcrop [15]. As in the 1895 model, the profile of the house is broken, rising irregularly to the peak of the central gable and big drum chimneys. Both the entrance and the garden fronts have features rooted in local tradition, but Prior merged them into designs of extreme originality.

In accord with Prior's organic theories, the building materials came from the land on which the house stood, or were produced locally. The walls are strangely textured by the free mixing of dressed stone with rubble. The same stone from the land is used in the terrace and garden walls, blending house with garden and garden with soil. The Barn was originally thatched and this made the feeling of closeness to nature even greater. But the local tiles that replaced the thatch, after a fire within a few years of building, do nothing to spoil the feeling of a house lovingly moulded by its designer and by the individual workmen engaged in its construction.

The Barn was the first of a series of similarly planned houses by Prior and by other Arts and Crafts architects. But before it was built Voysey had already picked up one idea from Prior's model cottage. This was the notion of placing the front door on the inner angle of an **L**-plan; Voysey used it well in a house designed in 1896 [24]. Other Free Style architects, too, were experimenting with lower and more intimate ceiling heights and with plans that would help to break down the boundaries formed between house and earth by formal quadrangular plans. Leonard Stokes designed a house in Ireland with 'a most interesting . . . skew plan' early in 1895,[17] and Charles Harrison Townsend's bending plan for Dickhurst in Surrey probably dates from 1896. So it seems that the possibilities of such experiments were being discussed among the Art Workers' Guild architects at this time.

Prior continued to develop the butterfly plan for the next few years. He showed another model, this time with sterner stone walls, at the Royal Academy in 1899; the plan was a full **X** in this version, with a fifth gable thrown out between two of the arms and topped by an odd cupola [16].[18] His largest work of this type was Home Place in Norfolk, designed in 1904, which will be described in chapter six. Meanwhile the idea was taken up by Edwin Lutyens, Baillie Scott and others.

There were other approaches to organic vernacular building besides Prior's. One of these is shown in an unexecuted but fully worked-out design of 1898 by Harrison Townsend for a house at Salcombe [20]. Here the plan was long and straight, but an organic effect was sought by using rugged stonework and battering at ground level and by a restrained use of curves throughout the exterior and indeed the interior of the house.[19] In Edwin Lutyens's Tigbourne Court of 1899 (one of the architect's peak years) an organic effect was also obtained through the texture of the stonework and by the use of a scheme which breaks up the block of the house into gradually ascending masses [19].

Perhaps the finest of all these attempts to blend a man-made structure with nature was achieved by Ernest Gimson, a great furniture and plaster designer, who was a strong influence in the Arts and Crafts movement. Gimson was an architect, but he built comparatively little. Nevertheless, one of the rare Gimson houses, Stoneywell Cottage in Leicestershire, achieves a closer harmony with its site than even Prior could manage [17].

Stoneywell Cottage is in strange countryside with occasional thrusting

19 Tigbourne Court, south of Witley, near Godalming, Surrey (1899), by Edwin Lutyens. Entrance front. The masses are as broken and organic as Prior's, while Lutyens's originality is exceptional.

20 Detail of unexecuted design of 1898 for Cliff Towers, Salcombe, Devon, by C. Harrison Townsend. The rounded forms expressed an organic feeling, similar to that of work by Prior and by the American, H. H. Richardson.

outcrops of rocks among rolling hills, and is remote and difficult to find. In visual terms, the design is anchored by a massive chimney which effectively projects an emerging outcrop of rock into the air. From this pivot, the house is built down the side of the outcrop, falling in three levels, the plan twisting with the shape of the site so that it ends up as an opened-up Z [*18*]. Gimson or, when he was away, his young assistant Detmar Blow worked constantly on the house during construction in 1898–99 and the result is a masterpiece of the rugged organic unity sought by this particular branch of Arts and Crafts architecture.

The other main branch of Arts and Crafts domestic building also sought a unity with nature, but in a very different way from the work of Prior and Lethaby. Here there was much of the refinement of the Aesthetic Movement and a new elegant simplicity. The chief exponent of this style from 1890 onwards was C. F. A. Voysey.

Voysey was from Yorkshire in northern England, of a family claiming the ancestry of the Duke of Wellington. He considered himself an artist-designer and was out of sympathy with the left-wing political idealism of Lethaby and many other Arts and Crafts men. His father was a Yorkshire clergyman expelled from the Church of England (for scorning belief in the existence of hell fire) and the founder of the Theistic Church. In his early twenties the young Voysey spent a year working for George Devey and became interested in English vernacular styles. He started his own practice in about 1882. No building commissions came his way at first, but at the suggestion of his friend Arthur Mackmurdo he tried his hand at wallpaper and textile design with great success. At last, in 1888, his first house was built, in a style which, although it was to mature, altered

little during his whole career.[20] His designs were published regularly in the progressive magazines *The British Architect* from 1889 and *The Studio* from 1893 onwards and their influence can be seen in the work of countless other architects.

The new simplicity practised by Voysey marked a tremendous aesthetic change, though his work was not in any way revolutionary in structure. Its first startling impact on his fellow architects came with the building in 1891 of a studio cottage at Bedford Park, the garden suburb in west London [*21*]. Most Voysey houses are emphatically horizontal, but here on a small site he built a simple white tower with bands of windows elegantly placed in the frontage and a contrasting low-pitched roof surrounded by delicate gutter-brackets that were to become an Arts and Crafts trade mark.

Voysey himself did not hesitate to hold forth in rolling phrases about his intention to replace the revived historical styles with his new simplicity. In 1892 he wrote:

The myriads of conflicting schools and catechisms fade away into insignificance and we begin to feel the invigorating sensation of being alone with Nature and our own intelligence . . . The fact is that we are overdecorated . . . Begin by casting out all the useless ornaments and remove the dust-catching flounces and furbelows . . . Eschew all imitations. Strive to produce an effect of repose and simplicity.[21]

During the following six years Voysey's practice flourished and he produced a notable series of medium-sized country

21 Studio cottage, 14 South Parade, Bedford Park, London (1891), by C. F. A. Voysey. Elegance and simple white forms with little reference to local building traditions were characteristic of Voysey's version of Arts and Crafts architecture.

22 *Perrycroft, Colwall, Malvern Hills, Hereford-shire (1893–94), by Voysey. Garden front. The first of his larger country houses, showing a masterly use of long horizontals and sited spectacularly high on a hillside. The chimney tops have unfortunately been replaced by standard pots.*

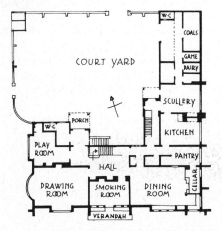

23 *Plan of 1893 for Perrycroft, by Voysey. An irregular L-plan of the same year as Lethaby's plan for The Hurst.*

houses which deserve attention. For, despite Voysey's occasional lapses into a coy sentimentality, these designs are among the finest contributions of the period to the attempt to develop a free architecture.

The characteristic horizontal Voysey design is rooted in the long vernacular houses of the Cotswolds. In many of these old buildings can be seen the long horizontals, the band over the ground-floor windows and the simple geometrical hipped roof that Voysey adapted into his personal vocabulary, adding such details as the ever-present buttresses. When he was building in an area with good building stone, the external walls would occasionally be of plain stonework. But in most of his houses, Voysey preferred to cover the basic brick with a rendering of roughcast, painted white to achieve the simplicity he sought, and capped with a slate roof. This choice of materials appears to have been a purely aesthetic preference that dated from 1890 when he moved into a Regency house of this type in London.

In his rejection of the ideal of using local materials and of adapting regional building traditions for each house, Voysey flew in the face of the theories of most of the Arts and Crafts men. Moreover, his house plans are less bold than those of some of his contemporaries. But in most other ways he was very much part of the movement; fitting his designs to their sites, preferring to draw every detail down to the furnishings himself and insisting on high standards of craftsmanship.

In 1892, the year after the Bedford Park house, Voysey built another small London studio in Hammersmith, whose horizontals anticipate the first of his great country houses, Perrycroft, designed for a Mr J. W. Wilson in 1893 [22].

The hillside site of Perrycroft is magnificent, hanging over a vast view along the Malvern Hills. Voysey here devised the first of several L-shaped plans he used for similar sites: the main rooms are in a range overlooking the view, with service rooms along the arm of the L at the rear and, in the angle, an entrance courtyard cut into the slope [23]. As he often did with his larger houses, Voysey designed a frontage on the garden or view side which is all horizontal simplicity punctuated by bold chimneys, but which is, at the same time, most subtly asymmetrical and varied in its detailing. On the entrance side of his houses, however, Voysey tended to allow himself a more fanciful and broken composition. At Perrycroft there is, on this entrance front, a tower with a charming spire, a bulging entrance porch and, on the upper floor, a continuous band window along the upper stairs and corridor connecting the bedrooms. Architectural historians have tended to present Voysey's virtues as being limited to elegance and cool rationalism, and indeed have chided him when he departed from this manner. In fact, he

24 Annesley Lodge, Platt's Lane, Hampstead, London (1896), by Voysey. Entrance front. A long horizontal L-plan with the front door at the inner angle, as in Prior's plan for The Barn of the same year. Voysey and Prior were next-door neighbours in St John's Wood at this time.

clearly delighted in contrasts of simplicity with surging curves.

In 1896 the long horizontals appeared in London in Annesley Lodge, the house that he built for his father in Hampstead [24]. In the same year he produced a fairly large house high on the Hog's Back in Surrey, called Greyfriars. As originally built, Greyfriars had perhaps the most visually impressive elevation of all Voysey's works. The plan was of necessity one long line along a contour of a steep hillside. Again, the entrance front is broken vertically into a number of sections, but it is the frontage onto the terrace overlooking the wide view that is most memorable. The design is rooted in a huge gable at one end, marking the high drawing-room inside [25]. One side of the gable sweeps low, almost to the

31

ground, the other drops to the roofline which then sweeps straight along the rest of the elevation. A sheltered winter garden nestles between two of the bold projecting rectangular bays that were to become another widely copied Voysey feature.

Unfortunately some of the effectiveness of this design was lost with an addition by another architect in 1913 that chopped off the dipping gable and added a wing protruding into the garden which flows behind the house and on along the same contour. These alterations make it impossible to see how Voysey originally handled the problem of integrating house and garden at Greyfriars, but his sensitivity to this concept can be seen in another house, Norney, built the following year near Shackleford in Surrey.

Norney has an almost flat site in broad and thickly wooded grounds. Again, Voysey played brilliantly with a variety of forms (unusually heavy ones in this case) on the entrance side, contrasting it with the serene simplicity of the garden front [26]. Here the house consists of two elegant gabled bays separated by two simple storeys of long banded windows. But the major achievement of Norney is the intense feeling of unity between house and garden.

The garden rises slightly towards the house in gentle layers, culminating in a shallow terrace made of the same stone as the window surrounds. From the foot of the walls, the sloping buttresses and luxuriant climbing plants take the eye and indeed the garden itself up the horizontals of the elevation to the slopes of the grey tiled roof. In this, as in a number of other Arts and Crafts buildings (especially those by Prior), the loving care poured into the achievement of unity with nature makes for an architectural experience of high order.

Voysey's standards were maintained to a remarkable extent in the houses he designed over the next few years, notably in the house called Broadleys overlooking Windermere (1898), which has a more mature version of the Perrycroft L-plan.

A number of other architects were influenced by Voysey's example of simplicity. As early as 1892, Charles Harrison Townsend (1851–1928), better known for his large Free Style public buildings during the following years, was commissioned to rebuild gradually a hamlet called Blackheath on the hills east of Guildford, in Surrey.[22] Townsend's church there will be discussed in chapter three, but he also built numerous cottages

25 *Original design of garden elevation, Greyfriars, near Puttenham on the Hog's Back, Guildford, Surrey (1896), by Voysey. A long linear plan on a* steep hillside. This fine frontage has been partly spoiled by an extension which cuts off the slope of the big gable.

26 Norney, near Shackleford, Surrey (1897), by Voysey. Garden front. The rising levels, with flower-beds and rambling plants up the walls, achieve the integration of house and garden which Voysey sought.

and the gem-like Congregational chapel that combines his own favourite rounded arch motif with the white roughcast and buttresses of Voysey. Townsend's domestic work is too little known; in the year that Voysey built Greyfriars (1896), a fireplace with seating designed by Townsend was acclaimed at the Arts and Crafts Exhibition. Again, simplicity is the keynote, but the design showed impressive strength and originality.[23]

Something of the same power, combined with austere elegance, is shown in a double house, the second of several houses in Cheyne Walk, Chelsea, designed by Charles Robert Ashbee (1863–1942). Ashbee was one of the most magnetic characters and wide-ranging craftsmen in the Arts and Crafts movement. He was the founder, in 1888, of the politically progressive and influential Guild and School of Handicraft in the poverty-stricken East End of London, producing and selling a wide range of high quality articles, many designed by himself. His first Cheyne Walk house, No. 37, was built for himself in 1894, a pretty design partly inspired by Norman Shaw. The second,

33

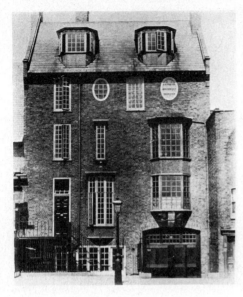

27 *Nos 72–73 Cheyne Walk, Chelsea, London (1897), by C. R. Ashbee. Destroyed in the Second World War. An individualistic late development of the asymmetrical frontage and of the double house pioneered by Godwin, MacLaren and others.*

Nos 72–73 Cheyne Walk, was done in 1897 and was startlingly different [27]. Both have been destroyed.[24]

The London double house occurs a number of times in Arts and Crafts architecture, perhaps originating in an earlier Edinburgh type of town house or in those designed by Godwin in Tite Street in 1878, and by MacLaren in Avonmore Road and Palace Court a decade later. The idea enabled architects to play ingeniously with two dwellings that shared the same level in some storeys, but not in others, and had to be expressed as one street façade. Ashbee's 1897 design brought off this effect brilliantly, retaining a severe simplicity of appearance, full of vertically emphasized features placed as carefully as in Godwin's

houses. This Cheyne Walk house has been quoted as an early example of the functional placing of the windows as dictated by the interior. The design of the elevation is, however, basically aesthetic rather than functional; for example, the two oval windows, the rectangular one between them and the two contrasting ones below might well express five different spaces within. In fact, they were on one side of a big studio with a raised gallery against that wall.

Ashbee's wilfulness in architecture is often appealing in itself and his work is refreshingly simple and elegant in taste, without any of the sentimentality sometimes shown by Voysey. A later couple of houses by Ashbee, Nos 38 and 39 Cheyne Walk (1899–1901), remain among the most

28 *Detail, No. 39 Cheyne Walk, Chelsea (1899), by Ashbee. One of a pair which are the only survivors of Ashbee's fascinating London houses.*

29 Hall and stairs, No. 39 Cheyne Walk (1899), by Ashbee. Frieze by F. C. Varley. Ashbee's best work had as much elegance as Voysey's, without the latter's occasional coyness.

interesting of the period in London [28–29]. They have long vertical windows and a curious gable that adjusts to buildings of a different height on either side.

During the late 1890s another architect was making a name for himself in Voysey's manner and in Voysey's own field, the medium-sized country house. This was M. H. Baillie Scott (1865–1945), who came to London from the Isle of Man at the end of the century.[25] One of his best early houses is White Lodge at Wantage, built in 1898–99 for the chaplain of a nearby convent [30]. Baillie Scott here took up the Greyfriars type of design, rooted in one great gable accent on the garden front, but translated it into something very much his own with the soaring verticals of the chimneys that give the elevation a springy lightness.

The interior of White Lodge [31] brings us to another of the differences between various leading Arts and Crafts architects. Ashbee and Voysey's fine houses of the 1890s (when the architects were allowed free rein) had a cool elegance in their interiors and furnishings that is reproduced on the exteriors, so that one is an integrated extension of the other. Baillie Scott, on the other hand, was strongly influenced in some of his interiors by the more complex Arts and Crafts decorative style that had

35

30 *White Lodge, St Mary's Convent, Denchworth Road, Wantage, Berkshire (1898–99), by M. H. Baillie Scott. Garden front. An individualistic version of Voysey's simplicity of form.*

31 *Drawing-room, White Lodge (1898–99), by Baillie Scott. Inventive and exotic, owing something to the Aesthetic Movement, in contrast with the cool simplicity of the exterior of the house.*

been evolved by Henry Wilson, Harrison Townsend, Edgar Wood and others during the same period, a development from the twining tendrils and flowers of Morris and of Mackmurdo, and even the textile and wallpaper designs by Voysey himself. Moreover, as will be seen in the next chapter, the publication in 1891 of William Lethaby's famous book *Architecture, Mysticism and Myth* had produced a wave of interest in the use of symbols from nature in the decoration of interiors. The tree, the rose and other motifs took the place of the sunflower of the Aesthetic Movement.[26] With Voysey, such motifs (especially his own favourite, the heart) were used only in detailing. In interiors by other architects symbols from nature are brought into the living-room. Thus at White Lodge, and elsewhere, Baillie Scott's decorative scheme is crowded with visual delights and originalities, which are in contrast with a chaste exterior.

To end this chapter, the third of Lethaby's four executed houses provides an instructive summing-up of the difference between his ideas of simplicity and those of Voysey's school. In 1898 Lethaby was commissioned to build Melsetter, a large house with a chapel and extensive outbuildings on Hoy Island in Orkney [*32*]. Here he used vernacular Scottish forms – quite unlike the treatment accorded to his houses in Hampshire and Warwickshire – consisting of strong shapes with rendered walls, as in MacLaren's houses in Scotland and Robert Lorimer's cottages at Colinton, Edinburgh, from 1893 onwards. At Melsetter a simplicity and building materials superficially similar to those employed by Voysey can be seen, but used with a power foreign to Voysey's taste. The roughcast rendering (called 'harling' in Scotland) covers walls of local rubble, and the reddish sandstone trimming was quarried on the island. The materials, the high vertical proportions of the house, and detailing such as the stepped gable link the building to its site and to tradition.

These then were the principles underlying the domestic free architecture of the Arts and Crafts movement in the 1890s:

simplicity, strength, and harmony with existing buildings and surrounding nature. Arts and Crafts architecture achieved a reputation for domestic building that made it celebrated among European and North American architects, to such an extent that Germany sent an architect cultural attaché called Hermann Muthesius (1861–1927) to London in the late 1890s to study the work.[27]

Thus by 1900 the Arts and Crafts architects had produced one resounding collective success: a new vitality and new standards for domestic work. Chapter three will deal with their attempts to produce a new architecture for public and other non-domestic buildings.

32 Melsetter House, Hoy Island, Orkney (1898–1902), by William Lethaby. The walls were roughcast because this was in the tradition of Scottish vernacular building, not for aesthetic reasons as in Voysey's houses.

3
The Free Style and Large Buildings

To start this chapter, it will be useful to clarify the meaning of the term 'Free Style'. Conscious attempts to create a new architectural style for large buildings in Britain during the late nineteenth century took many varied forms. A central influential line can be traced from work of the late 1880s which used historical features in quite a new way to buildings of the 1890s which transformed such ancient features into quite novel forms and then – as described in chapter seven of this book – into a simplified and bold monumental manner during the following decade. The line of succession in this central development might be described as Norman Shaw, Lethaby, Wilson, Townsend, Mackintosh, Ashbee and then Holden. Their buildings include some which use historical details, others which use none. Some major buildings using new and free forms were by eminent architects who did other work in one or more of the then fashionable historical styles, so the tale is by no means of one camp against another.

The need for a term to embrace the wide variety of attempts at an original style has long been felt by historians. The buildings concerned are usually clearly not Art Nouveau by any reasonable definition, nor are all of them the products of the Arts and Crafts movement. Late Victorian and Edwardian architects used a number of terms, including 'naturalistic style' and 'English vernacular'; but, most of all they talked of 'free design', of a 'free style' and of

'free' versions of particular historical styles. During the 1960s and 1970s British historians have therefore used increasingly the words Free Style for the varied work of this period which experimented with new architectural forms. It seems the most apt term to employ in this book, accepting the great differences between the experimental designs to which it is applied.

The notion of a new architectural style, free from historical precedent, seems to have grown up in the mid-1870s in England. Progressive architects had by then abandoned one Gothic ideal – that the Gothic was the only appropriate style for a Christian country – except in church building. The 'Queen Anne' style of the early 1870s, and a variety of other eclectic manners, still seemed too historically based to some architects. In 1875 Edward Godwin wrote: 'The day of architectural revivals may be setting – I for one sincerely hope it is.'[1] This chapter will trace the attempts to develop a new style up to 1900.

With the emergence of the Art Workers' Guild group of architects described in the previous chapter, a free domestic architecture did emerge during the 1890s. By 1892

33 New Quad buildings, Brasenose College, Oxford (1886–89, extended 1907–09), by T. G. Jackson. High Street frontage. An individualistic free adaptation of late English Gothic.

38

the President of the Architectural Association was saying in his presidential address: 'We have heard so much of late years about styles and the possibility of a new one being created, which is to become the style of the future.'[2] But the success of the Free Style movement in public and other large buildings was much more limited than in domestic architecture, for larger buildings naturally involved far more formidable problems.

A commission for a private house only required the architect to convince one, or perhaps two, clients that an adventurous design was desirable. Commissions for larger buildings involved councils, committees or boards of directors, as well as the assessors when a competition for the work was held. Domestic building normally involved the use of traditional materials which could be adapted to originality in design. But larger buildings demanded the incorporation of the new structural techniques and cost-saving building materials that came into use at the end of the century. Again, many Arts and Crafts ideas about relating a country house to its site – for instance by using strong horizontals, vernacular traditions and local materials, and by blending the garden and the building – were scarcely applicable to large buildings, especially those in cities with older works of varied periods and styles surrounding a site.

It must be remembered, too, that the majority of the architectural profession was unsympathetic or even hostile to the rejection of historically derived styles preached by those moving towards a Free Style. To a large extent the conservative forces dominated the Royal Institute of British Architects, while the progressive movement was centred in the Art Workers' Guild. Nor was the clash limited to questions of architectural style and

principles of design. The early 1890s saw a major conflict between those who wanted to make architecture a profession to rank with law or medicine and those who saw it as an art form with practical application. The campaign for 'professionalism' – with the resulting changes in architectural education urged by R. Phené Spiers, the teacher of architecture at the Royal Academy school, and others – was organized by the R.I.B.A., while the opposition was led by the A.W.G.

In 1892 the opposition to the R.I.B.A. expressed their arguments strongly in a book called *Architecture, a Profession or an Art?*, edited by Norman Shaw and T. G. Jackson. Many of the younger Arts and Crafts architects contributed essays to the book, each dealing with a particular aspect of the dispute. Shaw's essay was entitled 'That an Artist is not necessarily unpractical'. In it he wrote, 'The art of architecture is thus the co-ordination of the several crafts in the achievement of right or beautiful building.' Edward Prior wrote on 'The "Profession" and its Ghosts', J. T. Micklethwaite on 'Architecture and Construction' and Gerald Horsley on 'The Unity of Art'. William Lethaby's piece 'The Builder's Art and the Craftsman' summarized the argument of the whole book: 'Think of what architecture has done in and for the world! What it has done in the past it may do in time to come; but it is not the "professional" side that ever has, or ever could, give a human soul one ray of pleasure.'

In the end the R.I.B.A. won a professional structure and educational system, but the fight was a rallying-point for those involved in the movement towards new attitudes in design and helped to give a sense of identity to the young men who were looking for a new free architecture.

Ideas for a Free Style for large buildings had been tried out tentatively by a number of architects in the early 1880s, led by Norman Shaw and, briefly before his retirement and death, by Godwin. Philip Webb made one such attempt (though it involved the use of Classical details) in a building at Middlesbrough later in the decade. Then, when they set up in their own practices later in the decade, the members of the new generation of Art Workers' Guild architects started to experiment. Their Arts and Crafts principles discouraged them from ignoring tradition altogether, for one of their ideals was an architecture rooted in the English past, before the adoption of foreign styles began.

At first, the buildings to which they turned most frequently as an English traditional source for large-scale architecture were the great palaces and mansions of Elizabethan and Jacobean times, which predated the sophisticated foreign style of Palladio and the Italian Renaissance imported by Inigo Jones. Such Elizabethan and Jacobean sources were exemplified in the work of Robert Smythson and his contemporaries, in buildings such as Brereton House (1586), Hardwick Hall (1590–97), Charlton House (1607–12) and Hatfield House (1608–12). Their designs could be seen in the *Book of Drawings* left by John Thorpe (*c.* 1563–1655) and, more evocatively, in *The Mansions of England in the Olden Time* by Joseph Nash.[3] One of the best-known architects and writers of the Art Workers' Guild, Halsey Ricardo, expressed his generation's admiration for the Englishness of these late sixteenth-century buildings in 1897: 'Learning sits easy on them and, like the speech of their owners, the main fabric is English (and the English, too, of the Bible).'[4] It was of course understood that there should be no question of *copying* Elizabethan and Jacobean

34 *Front Quad buildings, Trinity College, Broad Street, Oxford (1883–87), by T. G. Jackson. Jackson's Jacobean manner was taken up by other architects as an attempt to develop a specifically English style for large buildings.*

buildings; they were to be merely a traditional source for a new Free Style. And it is precisely such a modernized version of Elizabethan design that can be seen in Ricardo's unsuccessful entry for the 1886 competition for the Aberystwyth College buildings.

A richer and heavier type of free Jacobean architecture was developed by Thomas Graham Jackson (1835–1924), Shaw's co-editor of *Architecture, a Profession*

41

35 *Crane Memorial Library, Quincy, Massachusetts, U.S.A. (designed 1880), by H. H. Richardson. Entrance front. This and other such buildings were illustrated in British journals as early as 1883. The American 'free Romanesque' manner influenced several adventurous British designers.*

inanimate, produce what are his ideals of beauty,' wrote Prior in 1889: '. . . the irregularities of Nature's growth, the outcome and the proof of life, the constant slight deviation from the ideal, in which is the genesis of beauty.'[5] And Lethaby wrote: 'What then, I want to ask, are the ultimate facts behind all architecture which has given it form? . . . on the side of style, nature.'[6]

When it came to expressing the rugged organic qualities of nature in building design, many of the young progressive architects were impressed and influenced by the work of the American H. H. Richardson. J. M. Robertson of Dundee (1844–1901) designed several houses in

or an Art? Jackson's largest concentration of buildings is at Oxford University where he worked for over thirty years. His first building there was the University Examination Schools (1876–82), whose elephantine and loosely Jacobean mass still dwarfs its section of the High Street. His many other Oxford buildings will not be listed here, but his development can be traced in such works as the strongly Jacobean Front Quad buildings of Trinity College (1883–87) [34], the fine New Quad of Brasenose College (1886–89 and later) [33] and later work of various types at Mansfield and Hertford Colleges. It was his Jacobean designs of the 1880s that influenced many buildings by Champneys, Hare and others.

A source of inspiration for a new style in architecture was nature itself, from which architects derived organic forms and shapes which suggested that a building was an outcrop from the ground. By the late 1880s both Edward Prior and William Lethaby were talking about this. 'Man can have no other source for his ideas of the good [than Nature]. So Nature's forces, animate and

36 *Observatory tower and new wing, Stirling High School, Scotland (1887–88), by James MacLaren. Craggy organic feeling in one of the rare large buildings by an Arts and Crafts architect. Sadly, MacLaren died in 1890.*

Richardson's early domestic manner in the early 1880s. Buildings by Richardson, and others working in his so-called American Romanesque style, were illustrated fairly frequently in British building magazines from 1883 onwards. In 1887 Charles Harrison Townsend, one of the Arts and Crafts architects, sent in two such American designs for publication in *The Builder*.[7] In 1888 and 1893 the students of the Architectural Association were taken on special expeditions to see Lululand, the house of 1886–94 at Bushey outside London which was Richardson's only building in England.[8]

The general objectives of this type of American architecture were later well set out by Frank Miles Day, President of the American Institute of Architects, in 1906. 'The first thing any architect must aim at is to keep in harmony with nature . . . it [the building] must appear, as it were, to grow from its site.'[9] Richardson's well-known Crane Memorial Library at Quincy, Massachusetts (designed in 1880), displays a free asymmetrical design, a ruggedly organic main accent around the door, a horizontality that flowed with the ground and a free use of large Elizabethan-type windows [35]; all of these features must have impressed younger British architects.

The first large building in Britain that took up Richardson's ideas was the observatory tower and new wing for Stirling High School in Scotland, built in 1887–88 by James MacLaren, a Scottish Arts and Crafts architect already mentioned in chapter two [36]. In visual terms, the tower of MacLaren's building supplies the strong vertical accent rooting the long horizontal of the new wing. But the tower itself has a Richardsonian feeling for irregular forms at the top, as if it were a rough outcrop reflecting the nearby great rock of Stirling Castle.

37 *New Scotland Yard police headquarters, Victoria Embankment, Westminster, London (1887–90), by Norman Shaw. The design incorporates elements of the Baroque and of Scottish Baronial into a strong free architectural manner of its own.*

It is worth noting that a fair amount of sculpture is integrated into MacLaren's rugged exterior, for this reflects one of the basic ideals of the Arts and Crafts architects who were members of the Art Workers' Guild. In 1889 MacLaren wrote: 'It is no doubt true that painters and sculptors are now more alive to the value of good architecture, and that architects themselves are also impressed with the necessity of taking into account painting and sculpture, and indeed all the allied arts, when conceiving their designs.'[10]

This reiterates the original objectives of the Art Workers' Guild which had been founded by a group of Norman Shaw's pupils (see chapter two). The largest of Shaw's own public buildings, the police

43

headquarters called New Scotland Yard on the Victoria Embankment in Westminster, was built in 1887–90 [37]. From some points of view it must be considered a *tour de force* of the early Free Style, for it picks up the cupola motif that can be seen in some slightly earlier designs and blends a variety of historical motifs into a powerfully original whole. Thomas Collcutt, himself an eclectic but sensitive architect, described the building in 1894 as 'in many respects the most notable erected during the last two hundred years'.[11] But at the same time it represents a passing transition in Shaw's development, for here is an early use – for him – of free Baroque motifs that were soon to lead him to the Classical Grand Manner splendours of Bryanston and Chesters.

The secret of understanding this transition lies precisely in the aims of the Art Workers' Guild to bring together the arts of sculpture, painting and architecture. The integration of sculpture into the exterior, and painting into the interior, of buildings seems to have led steadily towards a free Baroque revival.

The key building in the development of Arts and Crafts Baroque is one designed by John Belcher and A. Beresford Pite for the Institute of Chartered Accountants in 1888 [59]. It was probably Pite who deployed here many of the ideas of their fellow-members of the Art Workers' Guild. But to maximize the integration of sculpture and painting with the design, the two architects clothed the whole building in richly Baroque raiment inspired by Belcher's excitement at the Genoese Baroque which he had seen on a visit to Italy that year. The style seemed to Belcher to offer unparalleled opportunities for blending the arts, and for the exterior sculpture of the building he employed two of the finest sculptors of the day. What Belcher and Pite abandoned was the idea that a valid

architecture should have a vernacular or national root. It is ironic that the seeds of the destruction of the infant Free Style for larger buildings were sown here, for the Baroque style which Belcher and Pite used as a vehicle for an Arts and Crafts ideal became hugely popular and changed its character, as will be seen in later chapters.

The building was opened in 1893 and an 1894 editorial about it expresses the possibilities it raised neatly:

One of the most remarkable buildings of our time . . . remarkable not only for its purely architectural merits, but for the admirable way in which is incorporated the work of two of our most gifted sculptors, Mr. Hamo Thornycroft R. A. and Mr. Harry Bates A.R.A. . . . [An] influence tending to make Mr. Belcher's work what it is today, a part of the most original and advanced architectural art of this *fin de siècle*, [is] the influence of the Art Workers' Guild, an influence which no future historian of nineteenth century architecture can afford to ignore without being hopelessly at sea.[12]

It was this building that brought Belcher fame and high standing among progressive architects. This in turn gave him influence on much that was to follow in Britain, both within the Free Style movement and in the Baroque revival.

In February 1893 a young Scottish architect called Charles Rennie Mackintosh (1868–1928) gave a lecture to the Glasgow Institute of Architects in which he named Belcher, Shaw, Sedding and Stokes – as well as two notable Gothic architects, Bentley and Bodley – as those men who he felt were doing 'designs by living men for living men'. Mackintosh had joined the Glasgow firm of Honeyman and Keppie as draughtsman in 1889. By the time of his lecture, he had taken over a good deal of the firm's design work, and he was to become one of the inspired Free Style architects of the next two decades. His entry for the 1893 Soane Medallion competition (design for a railway station), the Glasgow Herald building of the same year (his first large design to be built) and his unsuccessful 1894 design for the Royal Insurance in Glasgow [*71*], can all be best explained as even freer developments of the free Baroque of Belcher and Pite, mixed with the other liberating influences of James MacLaren and of Sedding and Henry Wilson.

Henry (or Harry) Wilson (1864–1934) was a Liverpool man, educated at Kidderminster Art School and trained as an architect first in Maidenhead, then in London. He was a draughtsman in succession to John Oldrid Scott (second son of Sir George Gilbert Scott), John Belcher and John Dando Sedding. His appearance was unimpressive and perhaps even detrimental to his practice, but his talent as a designer was second to none in this period as architect, metalworker, sculptor and enamelworker. Wilson left John Belcher's office in 1888 after a year working there with the restless and inspiring Beresford Pite. At the following year's Royal Academy Exhibition, a design for a church at Maida Hill was shown under Belcher's name that must, on stylistic grounds, be judged the work of one or both of these two young men. It shows a church front that blends Gothic, late Romanesque and totally original motifs in a way that forestalls the most daring church architecture of the following decade.

Wilson joined Sedding as chief assistant in 1888, the year of the design of Holy Trinity Church in Sloane Street, Chelsea – the masterpiece of the early Arts and Crafts churches. It is notable that, before Wilson's arrival, Sedding's lovely work was already Arts and Crafts orientated in workmanship, but relatively restrained in its free treatment of Gothic styles. It may never be

38 *Holy Trinity Church, Sloane Street, Chelsea, London (1888–90), by J. D. Sedding and Henry Wilson. West frontage. Furnished by Wilson in the decade following Sedding's death in 1891. This elevation was a forerunner of many later secular and church designs.*

known how much Wilson contributed to the design of the building itself; he did, however, complete most of the furnishings, for Sedding died in 1891. But it seems that at least the west front, with its mounting cupola turrets and sweeping main window, is more typical of his powerful imagination than of Sedding [*38*].

45

39 First design of 1890 for the Public Library, Ladbroke Grove, London, by Henry Wilson. A design that influenced Mackintosh, Townsend and others. The library was built without the sculpture on the upper levels.

In 1890 Wilson himself, though still employed by Sedding, won a competition for the Public Library in Ladbroke Grove, London [39]. This was an extraordinary design that was undoubtedly to influence later Free Style work of the 1890s. The two main storeys were designed in a restrained manner based on Elizabethan architecture, with a powerful accent around the asymmetrically-placed doorway. At the upper levels Wilson let his imagination run riot, with cupolas, spires and sculpture that flowed and swooped around the roof. However, it seems that economy prevented much of this decoration from being carried out and the library was built in 1891 to the rather simplified design that can be seen today. The free asymmetrical planning and external composition of this building

illustrates an important point: many of the best Free Style buildings remained true to Gothic principles of 'fitness' for their purpose, even though they abandoned the detailing of the Gothic style. This entailed an empirical approach to planning and a rejection of the Classical tradition of starting from a clearly articulated and largely symmetrical plan.

In 1892 Wilson started work on St Peter's Church, Mount Park Road, Ealing (Sedding had left only notes about this commission). The building's structure is striking, with interior piers that emerge like fins between the west window lights through the roof and buttresses [40]. In about 1893 Wilson designed and built a tower for Sedding's earlier church of St Clement at Boscombe, on the outskirts of Bournemouth. And two years later he designed the mightiest of all his frontages, this time a west front and tower for St Andrew's at Boscombe [41]. The power, originality and vigour of detail in this unexecuted design are extraordinary.

Wilson himself was a poor businessman and failed to keep Sedding's extensive practice going. Gradually his great talents were directed away from architecture towards other crafts. But his architectural work of the early 1890s did not fail to influence fellow architects. Wilson did not join the Art Workers' Guild, the centre of the Arts and Crafts architects, until 1892, but his master Sedding had been one of the original members and Wilson himself was a friend of Lethaby (the two men were later to work together on a revolutionary design for the Liverpool Cathedral competition).

From 1885 onwards, Lethaby was collecting material for a book that was ultimately to be published in 1891 as *Architecture, Mysticism and Myth*.[13] This book became widely influential in the 1890s, and Lethaby certainly discussed the ideas in it with his friends during its six years of preparation. In the book Lethaby set out to trace 'the basis of certain ideas common in the architecture of many lands and religions, the purpose behind structure and form'. In ancient days, he argued, designers of buildings were aware of a deep reservoir 'of these symbols . . . from this common book of architecture, each took what he would, little or much, sometimes openly, sometimes with more or less translation . . .' Lethaby went on to explore in the body of the book the ways in which the cosmos was symbolized in buildings. 'It has ever been accepted as a physical axiom in China that heaven is round and earth is

41 *Design of 1895 for new west front for St Andrew's Church, Boscombe, Bournemouth, by Wilson. A powerful free design, not executed.*

40 *St Peter's Church, Mount Park Road, Ealing, London (designed 1892), by Wilson. West frontage. The motif of two monumental towers, with a great window of inventive detailing between them, was characteristic of Wilson.*

square' and 'when the world was a tree, every tree was in some sort its representation'. And so he continued with chapters on symbols representing the seven planets, the tree of life, the labyrinth and the sun, on pavements like the sea, ceilings like the starry sky and the egg that represents creation. But the relevance of the book in 1891 is summed up in Lethaby's introductory chapter:

if we would have architecture excite an interest, real and general, we must have a symbolism immediately comprehensible by the great majority of spectators. But this cannot be that of the past – terror, mystery, splendour. Planets may not circle nor thunder roll in the temple of the future. . . . What then will this art of the future be? The message will still be of nature and man, of order and beauty, but all will be sweetness, simplicity, freedom, confidence and light.[14]

47

42   *The Bishopsgate Institute, Bishopsgate, City of London (1892–94), by C. Harrison Townsend. The flowing tendrils and foliage of much Arts and Crafts decorative work here appear on the external walls of a building for the first time. The overall composition owes something to Wilson's slightly earlier designs.*

It is understandable that Lethaby's book puzzled many of its architect readers, for it was an attempt – often obscure and in some ways naïve – to give some badly needed profundity to current architectural thought. Lethaby himself later regretted the work and in 1928 wrote another version of these themes which was published as *Architecture, Nature and Magic*. But to those

48

in 1891 who were looking for a new Free Style it seemed to provide a basis for all the vague references of Arts and Crafts designers to nature as a source. Charles Rennie Mackintosh quoted the Lethaby book at length in his 1893 lecture and we can see its mysteries and ideas as one of the influences on Henry Wilson's tremendous designs and on the major buildings of Charles Harrison Townsend.

For it was in 1892 that symbols of nature were first integrated into the design of the exterior of an English public building by an Arts and Crafts architect in a manner developed from the earlier textiles and wallpapers of Morris, Mackmurdo and Voysey. This building was the Bishopsgate Institute, near Liverpool Street Station in the City of London, by Harrison Townsend [42]. Elsewhere in the world this appearance of the forms and symbols of nature had already occurred as early as 1888, for example in the work of Gaudí and Berenguer in Barcelona and in Louis Sullivan's Auditorium and Wainwright buildings in the U.S.A. But the development of the style in England seems to have been independent and was certainly quite different.

The designer of the Bishopsgate Institute was an Arts and Crafts zealot, though not from the inner circle of the movement. Charles Harrison Townsend (1851–1928) was born in Birkenhead, Cheshire, and came from a poor solicitor's family. He was articled to a Liverpool architect and moved to London in about 1880, joining the Art Workers' Guild in 1888. He was to build more large-scale Free Style buildings than any other Arts and Crafts architect. The design for the Institute won a competition in 1892 and the building which made his name was opened in 1894. It consists of a large library and public hall behind a narrow street frontage. In the highly original frontage can be seen a free adaptation of Elizabethan architecture, as well as the influence of H. H. Richardson and Henry Wilson. On the walls of the building is the tree of life symbol, sculpted with branches flowing over the surface, contrasting with other areas of plain masonry. Such a surface treatment of the motif might have seemed entirely beside the point to Lethaby himself, but that does not alter the likelihood that it was done under the influence of his writings.

The same tree motif is present to a greater or lesser extent in all of Townsend's non-domestic designs in the following decade. And in his next building he took up another of Lethaby's ideas on symbolism in architecture: 'Of all forms, the cube and the hemisphere are the most sacred ... To combine the two has been the builder's problem in all ages.'[15] Townsend's design was for a projected Whitechapel Art Gallery (which he later built on a rather smaller scale) exhibited at the Royal Academy in 1896 [43]. The drawing shows

44 *Townsend's revised design for the Whitechapel Art Gallery, Whitechapel, London, as built in 1899–1901. The two cupolas and Walter Crane's big mosaic were never executed owing to lack of funds.*

43 *Townsend's first design of 1896 for the Whitechapel Art Gallery, with a mosaic panel designed by Walter Crane. The underlying symbolism of the architecture is extremely complex.*

many references to Lethaby's book. First of all, there is a four-squareness at the centre of the elevation design (the plan has not survived), as in many Townsend buildings after 1892. The Bishopsgate Institute elevation was centred on a big square window, while the 1896 Whitechapel design has a symbolic central square concealed behind the slope of the battering of the towers. The towers themselves are clearly square in plan at ground level; they

49

cube with hemisphere, tree with stone, were expressed even more clearly in the tower of the Horniman Museum in south London which Townsend designed in the same year [45]. The museum was opened in 1901 and remains the most complete and satisfying public building in this particular development of the Free Style. Apart from the symbolic geometry and the tree of life carving of the tower, the street frontage is a rare union of the arts and the crafts, with fine metalwork in the detailing and a splendid mosaic panel by the painter Robert Anning Bell (another member of the Art Workers' Guild) blended into the composition. One notable fact about Townsend's public buildings should be mentioned here. The exteriors of these buildings are surging, organic, flamboyant and symbolic – as if displaying the buildings to the outside world. But once one has entered the buildings – in the case of the Horniman, via a sequence of varied spaces and turns almost Baroque in effect – the interiors are found (even allowing for financial limitations) to be unexpectedly simple, unobtrusive and functional; the clear spaces are cleverly planned and ingeniously constructed to obtain the best light and use of space on difficult sites. Ideas of harmonizing the expression and character of the outside of a building with the inside were clearly irrelevant to the designer of such buildings; to Townsend the functions of interior and exterior were quite different from each other.

45 The Horniman Museum, London Road, Forest Hill, Lewisham, south London (1896–1901), by Townsend. The most complete expression of the decorated type of Arts and Crafts Free Style in a large building. Mosaic by R. Anning Bell.

rise with rounded corners that merge gradually into four circular corner turrets and one larger one in the centre, all five capped by the cupolas that are symbols of the celestial hemisphere. Squares and semicircles play everywhere in the composition, often hidden in part or disguised as if to express 'the irregularities of Nature's growth' (in Prior's words) giving buildings the sort of organic character which also appealed to Townsend.

This first Whitechapel design was not built, but the magical combinations of square with circle (universe with Earth),

In 1899 Townsend revised the Whitechapel Art Gallery design [44], work began and the building was opened in the poor East End of London in 1901. Sadly, neither the topmost cupolas nor the fine mosaic, designed by Walter Crane, were ever executed and the gallery remains in an uncompleted state today. Nevertheless, the building provides one final example of

Townsend's very individualistic large-scale version of the Free Style, powerful and loaded with complex symbolism. He himself was conscious of this complexity and expressed his belief in it clearly in a paper called 'The Value of Precedent' in 1894: 'What does much of the work of the present day for which the artist claims originality show us? . . . the man of fashion . . . calls the result the "simplicity of originality". It is not. It is, instead . . . a negation that is poor substitute for invention . . .'[16]

By 1901, when Townsend's two major buildings were opened, his favourite vein of the Free Style – complicated and full of original decoration – was almost exhausted and was discredited by other Arts and Crafts architects such as Ashbee and Voysey. But the Townsend approach had other successful adherents. In London the firm of Treadwell and Martin designed a series of Free Style office buildings and public houses in the West End (Old Shades in Whitehall [*119*] and The Rising Sun in Tottenham Court Road are good examples) that are elegant and original. In his own eclectic but distinguished way, Norman Shaw showed a touch of the same manner in his design for the White Star Line shipping company in Liverpool, of 1897. In Glasgow, James Salmon the younger (1873–1924) built several Free Style office buildings of which the best known is No. 142 St Vincent Street, affectionately known as The Hatrack, of 1899. Bristol, Dundee, Norwich and other cities in Britain also have good examples of this type of building.

Many historians have been tempted to dub the more complex Free Style architecture as British Art Nouveau, but the only justification for this seems to lie in the occasional similarity of decorative detail. The true Art Nouveau architecture of France and Belgium had grown out of Viollet-le-Duc's structural theories, though it became an almost entirely aesthetic style, determined to reject history and considerations such as 'organic' contact with the site and the use of traditional building materials of the locality. In the sense that Gaudí's buildings in the Güell park in Barcelona, Guimard's huge Humbert de Romans auditorium in Paris (1897) and his Maison Coilliot at Lille (1898) were true Art Nouveau architecture[17] – with the curving tendrils and other mannerisms typical of the style forming an integral part of the buildings' structure – it must be said that none of the British Free Style buildings designed by the Art Workers' Guild members should be so described. The British architects' search was for an original modern architecture close to nature, true to the local traditions and even to local geology, or symbolizing the deep relationship of man to the universe.

Turning to the attempts of other Art Workers' Guild architects to develop a simpler style for larger buildings, the most remarkable early example (1885) is by one of the Guild's founders, Edward Prior. This is a strange terrace of houses, united in one design, that stands isolated on the quayside in the small village of West Bay in Dorset [*51*]. A vertical accent, rooting the frontage visually, is provided by an end house with two four-storey bay windows. From there the terrace runs off in long horizontals, shifting levels slightly with the ground beneath. Yet each unit forms a grid pattern of its own and the whole effect is one of restless tension. True to Prior's beliefs about the importance of using local materials, the stone and the tiles are Dorset produced, though from further away than he wished.

Prior's terrace was large, but it was nevertheless domestic work. It is only seven

46 *Central tower, All Saints' Convent, Shenley Road, near London Colney, Hertfordshire (1899–1903), by Leonard Stokes. Stokes was sympathetic to Arts and Crafts ideals, but kept to his own individualistic free manner, dominated by strong grid patterns.*

years later that such simplifying principles can be found being applied to a design for a big public building. This was Halsey Ricardo's competition entry of 1892 for the Oxford Town Hall [47]. Ricardo here took as his starting-point the 'more glass than wall' tradition of late Elizabethan mansions, proposing an extraordinary design in which the council rooms would apparently have been expressed on the exterior by huge areas of grid windows, while the offices were housed in a massive masonry 'castle' around this ceremonial section. It is an expressive and splendid design, but it was not mentioned by the competition assessor. Instead, Henry Hare's wild Jacobean dream palace was selected and built.

However, as a basis for a new Free Style, the Elizabethan grid did have some success later in the decade in a number of buildings influenced by T. G. Jackson's work. The tower of Leonard Stokes's big convent at London Colney in Hertfordshire (1899–1903) employed the grid impressively [46], while Henry Hare used it more sparingly in his unsuccessful entry for the Belfast City Hall competition (1897) and then adapted it in his design for the excellent Westminster College, Cam-

47 *Competition design of 1892 for Oxford Town Hall, by Halsey Ricardo. Not built. An extraordinary design by a leading figure in the Arts and Crafts movement.*

bridge (1899–1902), whose tower is worthy of comparison with one of Henry Wilson's earlier church designs [*48*].

Finally, the same grid supplied the framework for the only city building by Lethaby himself. This is the Eagle Insurance building in Colmore Row in the commercial heart of Birmingham [*49–50*]. Here Lethaby the functionalist meets Lethaby the symbolist. The square grid window at ground level (with a cube room inside) is echoed by the grid of the three upper storeys that form another overall square. But above them all float symbols of the sky

49 *Eagle Insurance Buildings, Colmore Row, Birmingham (1899–1900), by William Lethaby. The only large secular building by the Arts and Crafts leader. It combines his favourite symbolism with rational design and an austere aesthetic expression.*
50 *Plan of 1899, Eagle Insurance Buildings, by Lethaby.*

48 *Westminster College (Presbyterian), Queens' Road, Cambridge (1899–1902), by Henry Hare. Entrance front. The architect of the Jacobean Oxford Town Hall here used Elizabethan grid windows sparingly, with a sturdy tower whose originality is comparable with that of Henry Wilson's buildings.*

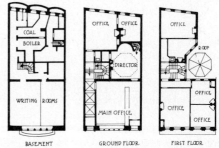

53

51 Pier Terrace, West Bay, near Bridport, Dorset (1885), by Edward Prior. An impressive early use of a flexible grid pattern by an Arts and Crafts architect.

(the wavy lines were a Byzantine symbol for clouds), the discs representing the sun, and the solar bird (the eagle of the firm's name) – all familiar to readers of Lethaby's book *Architecture, Mysticism and Myth*, though perhaps unexpected in a commercial setting. The harshness of the aesthetic scheme is in the tradition of Philip Webb, if any precedent is to be sought.

The final type of solution to the problem of finding a Free Style for public buildings

in the 1890s was again a simplifying one. The starting-point for this approach remains close to Voysey's style for domestic work. Perhaps the earliest example is the small Town Hall in Aberfeldy, Perthshire, built in 1889–90 by the Scottish Arts and Crafts architect James MacLaren. Here the clean lines, sweeping gables, white roughcast (a Scottish vernacular feature, as well as an English one) and rustic turret common in Voysey's work a little later can be seen, but with touches such as the round stonework arches that could only be by MacLaren. Voysey and MacLaren were both members of the Art Workers' Guild and may have discussed such designs. So

54

intense and varied was MacLaren's architectural practice during the last two years before his death from tuberculosis in 1890, that his pioneering influence seems to be felt everywhere. But it should not be concluded that all these ideas were MacLaren's alone, for the importance of the cross-fertilization of ideas between members at the Art Workers' Guild must not be forgotten.

Certainly there appear to be strong links between the Aberfeldy Town Hall and Harrison Townsend's village church of *c.* 1892 at Blackheath near Guildford.[18] Yet the Aberfeldy design does not appear to have been published at the time so Townsend was either working on his own (except perhaps with the help of some inspiration from Voysey) or else he had been shown MacLaren's drawings. Whatever the background, the church is a charming and appropriate Free Style solution to the problem of its particular function.

Two other approaches to a simple architecture for public buildings are worth examining here. The first is a project of about 1894 for some swimming baths at West Bay, Dorset, by Edward Prior [*52*], the second a competition design of 1898 by Charles Rennie Mackintosh for a concert hall for the 1901 Glasgow Exhibition [*53*]. Both show a willingness to experiment with new forms that were to come into use decades later, but neither was built.

A notable apartment building, rather in the manner of Voysey, was built by H. Thackeray Turner in Guildford in 1894. Voysey's own first non-domestic building was not at all novel in structure, though it is visually striking all the same. This public house, the Wentworth Arms at Elmesthorpe in Leicestershire, was designed in 1895 and, unusually for Voysey, leaves the local building material – brick – uncovered

52 Design of c. 1894 for swimming baths at West Bay, Dorset, by Edward Prior. Not built. An adventurous design, seeming to look far ahead to the possibilities of concrete structure.

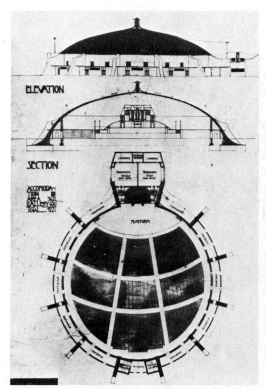

53 Design of 1898 by Charles Rennie Mackintosh for a concert hall for the Glasgow International Exhibition, to be held three years later. Not built. Another design which seems to look forward to many much later buildings.

55

by roughcast. But these two buildings are essentially blown-up house architecture, as was John W. Simpson's Roedean School of 1898.

In the same year as the design of the Voysey pub (1895), a competition was held for a large charitable building in Bloomsbury, London. Many of the Arts and Crafts architects submitted designs,[19] probably because Norman Shaw was the assessor and may have put it around that he hoped for adventurous ideas. And indeed the winning entry, by the young architects Dunbar Smith and Cecil Brewer, produced a building that showed how Voysey's simple manner could be developed to meet the challenge of larger buildings. This building, originally called the Passmore Edwards Settlement, is now known as Mary Ward House, Tavistock Place [55]. When it was opened in February 1898 the architectural magazines gave it a nervously complimentary welcome. 'The originality of

55 *Mary Ward House, Tavistock Place, Bloomsbury, London (1895–98), by Dunbar Smith and Cecil Brewer. The frontage of brickwork and plaster is visually rooted in the organic forms of the stone entrance porch. The result of a competition assessed by Norman Shaw, this design set a general style for numerous buildings by the L.C.C. Architect's Department.*

54 *Wesleyan School, Long Street, Middleton, Manchester (1899–1902), by Edgar Wood. The delicate composition and white walls of the school contrast with Wood's severe brickwork church which fills the third side of the courtyard.*

the design is a little aggressive at first sight. But the originality is at least refreshing.'[20] Smith and Brewer's street frontage stems from a massive, even organic, stone doorway topped by two stone eggs (the symbols of creation suggested in Lethaby's book). From this rough protruding doorway, the brick composition spreads between two gentle towers, rising to a smooth white plaster storey under the projecting eaves. It was an approach taken up strongly by the architects of the London County Council in their housing estates after 1900.

The combination of stone, brick and plaster was also taken up by the Manchester Arts and Crafts architect Edgar Wood (1860–1935). Wood was an extraordinary and isolated figure, the Bohemian son of a wealthy cotton industrialist. He was born and brought up in Middleton, five miles west of the centre of Manchester, where he chiefly practised, and many of his buildings remain there today. During the 1890s most of his work was domestic, but in 1899 he designed a complex of a Methodist church and schools in Middleton. The church is austere, of brick that has been harshly treated in the following 75 years by the acids of an industrial atmosphere. The schools introduce a clean and gentle touch of white roughcast, contrasting with high brick buttresses and a delicately designed pattern of windows [54].

The final building to be examined in this chapter is perhaps the greatest of all. This is the Glasgow School of Art at Garnethill in Glasgow. The design by Charles Rennie Mackintosh (under the name of his firm Honeyman and Keppie) won a limited competition in 1896 [56] and the first part, in Renfrew Street, was opened in 1899. The design of the street frontage is based on a rocky organic composition around the main entrance, spreading out to three bays on one side, four on the other, in huge studio windows [58]. The idea for the organic entrance section, proclaiming the main door and the Director's office and studio above, was doubtless derived from Smith and Brewer's Mary Ward House design of the previous year,[21] but in Mackintosh's hands the idea is transformed and blended into the stone body of the building.

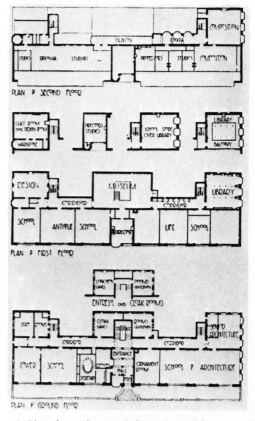

56 Plan of 1896 for ground, first and second floors, Glasgow School of Art, Renfrew Street, Glasgow (built 1897–99), by Charles Rennie Mackintosh. The library wing was not started until about 1907, when it was built to enlarged and very different designs by Mackintosh.

Mackintosh occupies a very special position in the history of Free Style architecture. An intense admirer of the Arts and Crafts architects, he was rejected by them on the one occasion of his participation in the Arts and Crafts Exhibition of 1896. Yet his Glasgow School of Art, with

57

57 Main staircase, Glasgow School of Art (1896–99), by Mackintosh. Voysey's interiors were probably an inspiration for the architect, but Mackintosh transformed such sources into his own personal Free Style.

its great library building added in 1907, took the Free Style soaring to heights it never quite reached elsewhere. To walk through the passages and studios of the art school, with young students moving everywhere among the characteristic Mackintosh spaces and detailing [57], is more evocative of the ideals of Lethaby, Prior and their fellows than a visit to any other large building of the period. It is the Free Style's masterpiece as well as Mackintosh's.

By the end of the century the Free Style of the Arts and Crafts architects could claim some considerable achievements in large buildings as well as many fine houses. But the prospects for a widely used Free Style, that would become a new national style, remained remote. The pioneer architects were too individualistic, and their efforts too varied, to find general acceptance by run-of-the-mill architects and the public.

58

This difficulty was expressed neatly in a paper of 1902 by Harrison Townsend and in the comment on it by Hermann Muthesius,[22] the German architect and writer who spent many years studying contemporary 'free' English architecture (the books Muthesius published at the beginning of the century initiated a comparable Arts and Crafts movement in Germany, which in turn had much influence on the Bauhaus in the 1920s). In 1902 Townsend said: 'It is in placing individualism, fully equipped by education, before stylism that one sees the possibility of architecture becoming once more a speaking tongue, by the means of which man's wants and ideals of today shall be clothed in the outward shape those wants and ideals ask, and not in the worn-out trappings of the past.' Muthesius commented sympathetically on Townsend's paper, while putting his finger on the heart of the problem of developing a Free Style. He described the Whitechapel Art Gallery as 'one of the finest buildings of decidedly modern character . . . an original architect can dispense with rules and precepts . . . but in the hands of lesser men originality can develop into mere absurdity.'

The Free Style offered no such rules and precepts to lesser architects, no accepted standards of what was good, to reassure prospective clients. And in 1900 there was an easier nationalist alternative to turn to: the revival of the English Baroque style of Wren, Vanbrugh and Hawksmoor. This revival will be examined in chapter four.

58 Main doorway, Glasgow School of Art (1896–99), by Mackintosh. The big grid windows range on either side of the organic stone entrance bay, four studios on one side and three on the other.

4
Public Buildings and the Baroque Revival

THE VICTORIAN Gothic revival never succeeded in killing the popularity of the grandiose Classical manner for public buildings in Britain. Throughout Queen Victoria's reign, town halls and public schools continued to be built in a number of Classical styles long after the death in 1863 of C. R. Cockerell, the greatest Victorian Classicist. Leeds Town Hall (1853–58) by Cuthbert Brodrick, the Wren-influenced Wellington College (1856–59) by John Shaw, Leicester Town Hall (1874–76) by F. J. Hames, Portsmouth Guild Hall (1886–90) by William Hill, Greenock Town Hall (designed 1881) by H. and D. Barclay, and numerous National Provincial Banks by John Gibson are examples of its varieties in Britain. In Scotland Alexander 'Greek' Thomson led a Neo-Classical school that dominated city buildings until the 1880s, and in 1883–88 the heavy Baroque Glasgow Municipal Chambers – Glasgow's City Hall – were built by William Young (later to design the War Office in London) after a competition in which several French-influenced Beaux-Arts designs were rejected.

Such buildings were despised by progressive architects as tasteless, old-fashioned and irrelevant. The large-scale Classical Beaux-Arts manner of France with its disciplined planning was foreign, and thus repugnant to British nationalism. What must be considered here, therefore, is the revival among 'serious' architects of esteem for the Baroque (or English

Renaissance, as it was called at the time) and its adoption in the Edwardian period as a truly national style for Great Britain and her Empire.

The seminal building of the revival was probably Kinmel Park, designed by W. Eden Nesfield in 1866. But, ironically, the new reputation of Baroque architecture stems in more than one way from Arts and Crafts architects. Arthur Mackmurdo's title page of his 1883 book *Wren's City Churches* is so well known as a forerunner of Art Nouveau decoration that the contents of the book itself are often overlooked. But here the inventively Classical churches of Sir Christopher Wren are being praised by one of the young Arts and Crafts pioneers! Moreover, the first London architect to take up the Wren manner successfully was a pupil of Norman Shaw called John McKean Brydon (1840–1901) in his winning competition entry of 1885 for the Chelsea Vestry Hall (now known as the Town Hall) [60]. Brydon was one of the architects in the Baroque revival, although he has been largely ignored by architectural historians.

59 Institute of Chartered Accountants, Great Swan Alley, off Moorgate, City of London (1888–93), by John Belcher and Beresford Pite. A building of crucial importance in the Baroque revival, combining Genoa-inspired detailing with Arts and Crafts ideals. The free inventiveness of its use of Classical features started a vogue for the Baroque among many 'progressive' architects.

60 Chelsea Vestry Hall (now called Town Hall), Chelsea Manor Gardens, off King's Road, Chelsea, London (1885–87), by John Brydon. South front. Brydon, a Scot, proclaimed the English style of Inigo Jones and Wren 'as distinct from, and in some respects superior to, even the Italian Renaissance' and urged architects to 'bring forth fruit worthy of the high ideal'. This Town Hall was extended onto the King's Road by the architect's friend Leonard Stokes in 1904–08, after Brydon's death.

John Brydon was, like Shaw and many other good architects of his time, a London-Scot. He was born in Dunfermline, studied in Liverpool and Italy, and worked for David Bryce in Edinburgh before moving to Campbell Douglas in Glasgow in 1863. Then in 1867 Brydon moved to London, to Nesfield's office and on to Norman Shaw's. His own first major building was St Peter's Hospital, Henrietta Street, Covent Garden (1883–84), built in a dullish Queen Anne style, complete with sunflower panels. He was very active in the Architectural Association and a close friend of Leonard Stokes, but, significantly, he never joined the Art Workers' Guild, the centre of Arts and Crafts architecture.

Brydon's Chelsea Vestry Hall (built in 1885–87 and later extended by Stokes onto the King's Road[1]) is a restrained and attractive adaptation of the English Classical style of about 1710. A temple portico with coupled Ionic columns and luxuriant but stiff stone carving expresses the presence of the hall itself. This is flanked by two wings, each with three Venetian windows, brick with stone dressing and rather tentative block surrounds of the Gibbs type. It is all very English and all very different from the Victorian Classical varieties that had come before it.

It is not known whether Brydon was at first alone in his campaign for the revival of English Baroque architecture. For example, was it a coincidence that the Imperial Institute competition design of 1887 by the eminent Scottish architect, Sir R. Rowand Anderson, was strongly reminiscent of Wren? But there is evidence that Brydon knew exactly what he wanted. In February 1889 he delivered a lecture at the Architectural Association in London on 'The English Renaissance' which shows that he was strongly aware of current desire for a national British style (see chapter one). According to the editor of the *Architectural Association Notes*, 'The men up for the March examination looked upon it, coming at this particular time, as manna sent from Heaven.'[2]

In his lecture[3] Brydon outlined the story of Italian Renaissance architecture, leading up to Michelangelo and Palladio, then turned to Inigo Jones. According to Brydon, Jones's Whitehall Palace plans 'lay the foundation of that peculiarly English phase of the style which it never afterwards lost ...' Brydon then turned to Sir Christopher Wren, of whom he said that 'in capacity for work and facility of accomplishment, he was an English Michelangelo'. After comparing St Paul's Cathedral

favourably with Les Invalides (its contemporary), he described Wren's work at Hampton Court Palace: 'the garden front has a stately picturesqueness about it which is thoroughly English'.

Towards the end of his lecture Brydon declared his preferences even more openly.

With the death of Wren may be said to have closed the early English Renaissance, which had lasted about 100 years. It had now become fairly established as the national style – the vernacular of the country. With the advent of Vanbrugh and Hawksmoor and Gibbs begins the later Renaissance . . . characterised by great vigour and picturesqueness, and by a freedom from restraint and an honesty of purpose not always to be found in later Classic.

Finally he recommended the style as the 'nearest to us in time and similitude of requirements, a great mine of artistic wealth'.

Already other architects were starting to take notice of this quiet version of the English Baroque as a possible basis for the new national style that was so widely demanded by an increasingly prosperous and imperialistic-minded public. Brydon's

61 Bryanston, near Blandford Forum, Dorset (1889–94), by Norman Shaw. Garden front. In his designs of 1889 for two large country houses, this and Chesters, Shaw moved into his last stylistic phase, a free Baroque with strong Neo-Wren overtones.

62 No. 170 Queen's Gate, Kensington, London (1887–88), by Shaw. Brydon had worked in Shaw's office in the 1870s. This town mansion marks a striking change in Shaw's work to a Dutch-influenced Wren style.

63

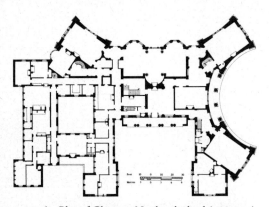

63 Plan of Chesters, Northumberland (1889–91), by Shaw. The curving three-quarters X-plan Baroque mansion was added to an old smaller house.

own master, the eminent Norman Shaw, adopted it as early as 1887 in the town mansion he built at No. 170 Queen's Gate, Kensington, in a manner that reflects the Dutch influence on Wren's own work [62]. Two years later, Shaw went much further with the domestic Baroque style in two big country houses. The first was Bryanston in Dorset (1889–94), an immense central block of brick, dressed with stone and of considerable originality, with two extensive wings that sweep back to form a three-sided entrance courtyard [61]. It was in 1889 that Lethaby left Shaw's employment and, with Lethaby's Avon Tyrell of 1891 in mind, it is interesting to notice how Shaw carried on the banded stone and brick of the house at Bryanston into the terrace and garden walls.

The other Shaw Baroque country house of this time was a large addition to a fairly small house at Chesters, near the Roman Wall in Northumberland (1889–91). Here the Baroque is much more extreme, curving in plan like three-quarters of an X,

64

as if it were derived as much from the Roman Baroque of Borromini or da Cortona as from anything English [63].

The source of this wilder Mediterranean influence on Shaw's work was possibly (for he openly admired it) the key building of a short period which brought together the Arts and Crafts movement and the Baroque style. This was the Institute of Chartered Accountants in the City of London [59], won in competition by John Belcher in 1888 and widely illustrated in the architectural magazines of the time. The progressive weekly *The British Architect* described the design in January 1889, as 'of more than ordinary excellence . . . novelty of treatment and variety of detail . . . in how satisfactory and dignified a manner the whole scheme has been worked out by Mr. Belcher.'[4] The significance of this building for the Free Style architects has already been outlined in chapter three. But Belcher's real importance lies in his Baroque work, so this is a suitable point to examine his background.

John Belcher (1841–1913), who took the chair at the first meeting of the Art Workers' Guild, was the son of a prosperous City of London architect of the same name. He studied for a time in Paris, then returned to London and soon took over all the design work in his father's office. He worked his way through successive phases of French Classical, Burges-type Gothic, Shaw-type Queen Anne and (after young Beresford Pite became his chief assistant in 1885) free Elizabethan.[5] In 1888 Belcher was forty-seven years old. Pite was twenty years younger; he came from a family of architects and was involved early in several progressive movements. Pite was a creative powder-keg, ready to explode at the fire of any new idea, and the two men won the competition for the Chartered Accountants building with the extraordinarily intense Baroque design which was completed in 1893 and largely survives today.[6]

The exterior of the Institute of Chartered Accountants integrates the sculpture of Hamo Thornycroft and Harry Bates – both members of the Art Workers' Guild – into the architecture, and breaks up the generally Classical treatment with features such as the cupola turret at the break of levels on the Great Swan Alley front and the sculpted oriel at the corner. The interior is ingeniously planned and plays strange tricks with the scale of the rooms and doorways [64], while the staircase that threads its way up the building changes its appearance and width at every level.

The Institute of Chartered Accountants is a unique building and, like everything in which Beresford Pite had a hand, fits into no rational pattern. In spirit, it is as exotic and imaginative as the wildest Baroque of Hawksmoor and Vanbrugh [65]. In no other way can it be considered a prototype for the particularly *English* Baroque style (Belcher's immediate inspiration was Genoa), yet it was the forerunner of a succession of Baroque buildings by Arts and Crafts architects during the following decade.

Before tracing that line of development, however, it is necessary to return to John Brydon and his quieter and more English version of the Baroque. In March 1891 Brydon won a further competition for the Chelsea Polytechnic with a Gibbs-like design, thick with block surrounds. In the same year he visited the Georgian city of Bath for the first time to prepare himself for the competition for the major extensions to the Guildhall, of 1766–75, in the High Street. There were 15 entries for the competition, but Brydon won the first premium with a design that is sensitive to Thomas Baldwin's old building, yet

64   The library, Institute of Chartered Accountants (1888–93), by John Belcher and Beresford Pite.

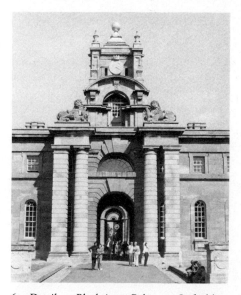

65   Detail,   Blenheim   Palace,   Oxfordshire (1705–25), by Vanbrugh and Hawksmoor. A typical example of the specifically English Baroque of the early eighteenth century. The Englishness and freedom from strict Classical rules of this style were important to many architects who were looking for a new national style in the 1890s.

65

66 *Extension of 1891–95 by John Brydon to the Guildhall (1766–75, by Thomas Baldwin), High Street, Bath. From this design onwards, most of Brydon's buildings were in a full English Baroque.*

67 *Council chamber interior, the Guildhall, Bath (1891–95), by Brydon.*

uncompromisingly 1890s in detail [66]. Brydon's work was completed in 1895 and left only the shell of Baldwin's Guildhall. The figure of Justice and the dome behind Baldwin's pediment are Brydon's as are the wings and the Baroque cupolas worthy of Hawksmoor on either side.[7] The sculptured bands behind the columns by G. A. Lawson are derived from Belcher and Pite. Inside, Brydon added ceremonial rooms of great sumptuousness, including a council chamber with a marvel of a plaster ceiling [67].

In 1894 Brydon was commissioned to design the Classical buildings to surround the newly discovered Roman Baths and he went on to extend this work to the new concert room beside the neighbouring pump room. In 1896 he was again commissioned to add a museum and art gallery to his north wing of the Guildhall to celebrate Queen Victoria's Jubilee. He did this with a strongly Baroque dome recessed in the corner design [68]. This completed his important work at Bath; the city centre today owes a great deal of its attraction to him.

In 1898 Brydon was appointed architect to the immense new Government Buildings, on the corner of Parliament Square and Parliament Street in London. He completed the plans but died before the building was above ground level. It was finished by a less talented man and will be considered in chapter ten. But Brydon's early campaign for specifically English Classicism was triumphant. The Arts and Crafts movement had failed to produce a public architecture that satisfied British national pride. And so it was English Baroque that vied with the giant Classical buildings of contemporary France and America.

Early in the 1890s the fashion for the Baroque was spreading. In 1891 a competition was held for the main part of the Victoria and Albert Museum in Kensington. Here, as so often, Alfred Waterhouse was the assessor; in this role his influence during the 1890s was immense. The competition was won by Aston Webb and Ingress Bell, whose heavy eclectic building – with some brilliant spatial effects inside – was ultimately completed in 1909. But it was the unaccepted design by John Belcher (with Beresford Pite still his chief assistant) that attracted the attention of architects [69]. A typical comment of the time read:

Mr. Belcher has come nearer to a 'young lion's' idea of a large public building than any of the other competitors. There is a dignity about his design that satisfies, and the broad and simple way the whole is handled caused this morning more than one growl of satisfaction. . . . it is a fine design, the finest in the competition. The drawings too . . . are exceedingly good and, if we mistake not, we can trace the hand of our old friend Mr. Beresford Pite.[8]

The Belcher and Pite project showed a long Baroque frontage to the Cromwell

68 *Municipal Art Gallery and Museum, Grand Parade and Bridge Street, Bath (1896–97), by Brydon. The last of Brydon's series of municipal buildings at Bath.*

69 *Sketch of competition design of 1891 for the Victoria and Albert Museum, London, by John Belcher. Not built, but the design was much praised and was a major influence on the Baroque revival.*

Road, punctuated by four strong cupola turrets and with a central entrance in a colonnade that curved back deeply into the building. Behind this range was a higher one topped by two almost Michelangel-esque domes, and further back still a tall Baroque tower mounted to a five-stage top, richly sculpted. As in the Chartered Accountants building, there is little that is specifically English about the type of Baroque architecture employed; it was the sheer originality of invention within that general manner that attracted young architects.

All the same, nationalism was an important factor. In 1893 Reginald Blomfield – who had been associated with Lethaby for a time, but was to become an influential figure at all stages of Edwardian Classicism – was writing of 'the great architectural age of Wren and Gibbs'.[9] Blomfield's own country house designs of the 1890s – for example, Wittington in Buckinghamshire of 1898 – are very much in the Wren English manner. Another very successful architect was making his first essays in free Baroque in the early 1890s. This was Edward Mountford (1855–1908), a Worcestershire man who worked his way through a number of minor architectural firms before starting an extensive practice based on competition successes during the 1880s.[10] Until his Sheffield Town Hall of 1890 he worked in an eclectic manner of the type widely used at the time. He was a hearty, jovial man, keener on cricket than anything else. His Battersea Town Hall on Lavender Hill, south London (1892–93), shows him moving towards a free Wren-like Baroque, although some of the detail – especially of the interior – retains a Jacobean Renaissance character.

Like Brydon, but unlike Belcher, Mountford never joined the Art Workers' Guild, though he was very active in the affairs of the Architectural Association. This is quite significant, for it is symptomatic of two different approaches to the Baroque revival. The Arts and Crafts architects of the Art Workers' Guild were interested in the potential of the Baroque for its originality and for the sake of the integration of architecture with the decorative arts. It was this group who contributed most of the 1892 book *Architecture, a Profession or an Art?*, edited by Norman Shaw,[11] which argued the case against the enforced registration of architects – a bitter controversy at the time – that was proposed by the Royal Institute of British Architects. The Architectural Association, on the other hand, became a centre for those who saw typically English Baroque as the new national style that would express the high tide of British imperial and commercial power. In February 1899 the editor of *The British Architect* wrote: 'in this country we now and then get a little impatient and a good deal curious to know when and how the long-talked-of new national style is to develop.'[12] Most eminent architects belonged to one camp or the other, though Leonard Stokes and Beresford Pite each had a foot in both camps.[13]

It must be emphasized here that, largely for reasons of nationalism, the Beaux-Arts Classical architecture so well established in France had little or no influence on British architectural design until after the end of the century. Through the work of R. Phené Spiers, from 1870 onwards, efforts were made to introduce something of the French system of organized architectural education to England.[14] But the English revival of Classicism in its Baroque forms in the period 1890–1905 owed nothing to contemporary French building design, except perhaps a desire to emulate its grandeur.

70 *Detail, Athenaeum Theatre, 179 Buchanan Street, Glasgow (1891), by John J. Burnet and John A. Campbell. Both architects were Beaux-Arts trained, but this building marked the start of their movement towards the notable Baroque and Free Style buildings which they designed separately during the Edwardian period.*

In Glasgow, the leading designer was now J. J. (later Sir John) Burnet (1857–1938), the inheritor of his father's prospering firm. From 1886 to 1897 John Archibald Campbell (1859–1909) was Burnet's partner, and in 1891 the two men (both trained by Pascal at the Ecole des Beaux-Arts) produced a strikingly original Baroque design for the Athenaeum Theatre in Buchanan Street [70]. Burnet moved as easily as Norman Shaw from style to style, showing great mastery in all, so this building is perhaps less surprising a by-

product of the Institute of Chartered Accountants than are the still freer Baroque designs by Charles Rennie Mackintosh for the Glasgow Herald (1893, with Scottish Baronial touches) and the Royal Insurance (1894, but not built) [71]. Mackintosh is known from his 1893 lecture to have admired the architect of the Chartered Accountants building, and he doubtless saw in it the same possibilities for a free integration of the arts in building as had some of the English Arts and Crafts architects.

71 *Competition design of 1894 for the Royal Insurance building, Buchanan Street, Glasgow, by Charles Rennie Mackintosh. Not built. This drawing and the Glasgow Herald building of the previous year seem to reflect Mackintosh's hope that Belcher and Pite's type of Baroque would produce a new style for the future.*

In London, Aston Webb and Ingress Bell used a quiet version of the Arts and Crafts type of Baroque for the Royal United Services Institute (1893–95) which they built beside Inigo Jones's Banqueting House in Whitehall [72]. In 1896 the competition for the Royal Insurance building in Liverpool was won by a local architect, J. Francis Doyle, with a freely inventive Baroque design integrating much sculpture in the façades (Norman Shaw, the assessor, improved the design before construction).

Among the entries passed over for this Liverpool building was a fine one by Belcher and Pite [226]. But in the following year Belcher had one of his great successes. This was the winning entry in the 1897 competition for Colchester Town Hall, again assessed by Norman Shaw. Belcher was working by himself on this occasion, for Pite had set up his own practice and had also entered the competition.[15] The Colchester building will be described in chapter ten [174].

One of the other entries for the Colchester competition deserves attention. This was designed by the talented Henry Hare, and was of extraordinary power and massiveness, employing Arts and Crafts Baroque motifs with a strange violence [73]. In many ways the Colchester competition and the Diamond Jubilee year 1897 were turning-points in the Baroque revival. Belcher's building was free in approach, but showed him moving towards an English Baroque of the Vanbrugh type that was to dominate his big buildings for the next seven years. More generally, the year saw the start of many High Baroque buildings that were to be completed during Edward VII's reign and remain linked with the King's name.

To end this chapter, an account is needed of the later development of the particular type of Baroque inspired by Arts and Crafts ideals of integrating the arts of sculpture and painting within architecture.

Beresford Pite, one of the most idiosyncratic and fascinating architects of the period, became increasingly interested in the work of Michelangelo during the 1890s. In 1898 *The Architectural Review* published a long study of Michelangelo's architecture by Pite, in which he recommended the great Italian to architects as a

72 Royal United Services Institute, Whitehall, London (1893–95), by Aston Webb and Ingress Bell. A restrained essay in the newly fashionable free Baroque which harmonized successfully with Inigo Jones's neighbouring Banqueting House.

70

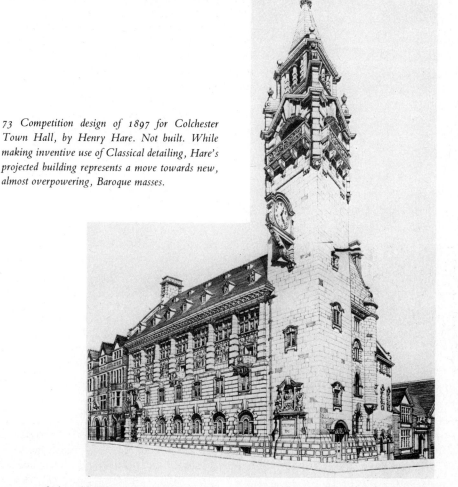

73 Competition design of 1897 for Colchester Town Hall, by Henry Hare. Not built. While making inventive use of Classical detailing, Hare's projected building represents a move towards new, almost overpowering, Baroque masses.

source of ideas.[16] 'The jaded designer will refresh himself with the vigour and originality of the whole.'

This inspiration is evident in much of Pite's own work. In 1896, while still employed by Belcher, he designed three buildings in Marylebone under his own name.[17] The best-known and most attractive of these is the shop and offices at No. 82 Mortimer Street, where two powerful Michelangelesque figures sit on one pediment and hold up another [75]. In 1899 Pite built a larger free Baroque office building at No. 37 Harley Street, Marylebone [74]. This is a remarkable example of the balanced asymmetrical street frontage in the line of those by Godwin, MacLaren and Ashbee, but with Baroque sculpture integrated into the design.

As late as 1898 – after building the Glasgow School of Art – Charles Rennie Mackintosh was still experimenting with

J. B. Everard and S. Perkins Pick and built in 1900–03, combining some excellent sculpture with the architectural features and using an awkward site cleverly.

Finally, two buildings by architects who were both founders of the Art Workers' Guild should be mentioned. The first is St Paul's Girls' School in Hammersmith, London, designed by Gerald Horsley and built in 1900–04 in a pleasing manner closer to Shaw's Bryanston and the growing Neo-Georgian fashion than to real Arts and Crafts Baroque. The school has the type of barrel-vaulted hall that was to become an Edwardian feature for such large rooms, but which has no ancestors in the early eighteenth-century English Baroque of Hawksmoor, Wren and Vanbrugh [77].

74 No. 37 Harley Street, Marylebone, London (1899), by Beresford Pite. Baroque detailing in a very original asymmetrical free composition.

an Arts and Crafts approach to the Baroque in an unaccepted design for the National Bank in Glasgow. And Thomas Collcutt gave up the eclectic manner usually associated with his name for one of the best examples of the Belcher and Pite style, the Lloyd's Shipping Register building in the City of London (1900–03). In other cities, too, good examples can be found by lesser known architects. One of the most charming is the National Westminster Bank in the little street called St Martin's, in Leicester. The building was designed by

75 No. 82 Mortimer Street, Marylebone, London (1896), by Pite. Designed while the architect was still John Belcher's chief assistant. Pite looked to Michelangelo for much of his inspiration.

72

76 *Detail, Humphry Museum and Medical Schools (now Zoology Building), Downing Street, Cambridge (1900–04), by Edward Prior. The great Arts and Crafts architect was apparently briefed to design a Classical exterior, and did so with typical originality.*

The other building is the only venture of the great Free Style architect Edward Prior into the Baroque: the Medical Schools and Humphry Memorial Museum in Cambridge (now the Zoology Building), built in 1900–04. It appears that the client specifically required the external use of a Classical manner[18] so unusual to Prior, but the latter used what local materials he could – following his personal principles in the matter – and produced one of the most intriguing pieces of Arts and Crafts Baroque. The part of the building designed for teaching is a long simple block of steel and concrete floor construction, its elevation punctuated by three pedimented bays brought slightly forward. The stonework is striated horizontally in the

manner of Vanbrugh's Blenheim Palace. At one end, the museum projects at a diagonal angle from the rest in a florid but subtly detailed octagon [76]. In the interior, Prior discarded most of the Classical trimmings and produced rooms of an originality typical of their architect. The building marks a suitable conclusion for an account of a style that attempted to create a new living architecture out of a harmonious combination of the arts within the framework of the Baroque.

77 *Interior of the great hall, St Paul's Girls' School, Brook Green, Hammersmith, London (c. 1900–04), by Gerald Horsley, one of the founders of the Art Workers' Guild. Large barrel-vaulted halls became a hallmark of the Baroque revival, without precedent in English architecture of the early eighteenth century.*

73

5
Church Architecture – Late Gothic and Byzantine

IN SECULAR architecture – whether for domestic, business or public buildings – the prevailing trends during this period included the Baroque revival, the various eclectic manners of the late Victorian period and the attempts at a new Free Style by some of the Art Workers' Guild architects. In church architecture the picture in Britain at the end of the nineteenth century was very different. It is true that Arts and Crafts designers carried out a number of churches in a variety of free styles, as illustrated in other chapters. But ecclesiastical architecture was still dominated by the Gothic style, with all its rich range to choose from, which was favoured by Church authorities long after the High Victorian achievements of Butterfield, Burges, Street and the older George Gilbert Scott. Only the Byzantine revival of the 1890s and 1900s challenged the Goths seriously; Edwardian Baroque, symbol of political and commercial power, was almost totally rejected for church work.

By the 1880s the first generation of great men of the Gothic revival had been followed by a successful second wave; John Loughborough Pearson and George Frederick Bodley were born at about the same time as Burges and Street, but their pre-eminence came later. Of the rather younger men, James Brooks, William White, John Dando Sedding, John Francis Bentley and the younger George Gilbert Scott were among the most notable. But all these men died before the end of Edward

74

VII's reign and left the field to a younger generation still, whose work will dominate the later part of this chapter.

John Francis Bentley (1839–1902) is of particular interest in this period of church architecture, for after he had built a number of splendid Gothic churches, his Westminster Cathedral led the way in the Byzantine revival. Bentley was born and educated in Yorkshire, trained as an engineer and builder, and then learned architecture from Henry Clutton in London. In 1862 he was converted to Roman Catholicism and went on to develop a successful practice in Catholic churches. Perhaps the finest of Bentley's Gothic works is the Church of the Holy Rood at Watford near London (1883–90), with its great span of nave and its richly decorated chancel and high altar [79]. It has been described by the historian H. S. Goodhart-Rendel as 'the most lovely church the nineteenth century gave to England'.[1]

Meanwhile, in Scotland, church architecture exhibited a complex picture, with different religious sects adopting their own favourite styles. The early Victorian Gothic revival never gained any grip on

78 Entrance front and campanile, Westminster Roman Catholic Cathedral, Victoria Street, London (1895–1903, the interior decorated gradually later), by John Francis Bentley. Bentley's soaring free version of the Byzantine style was mixed with many fashionable motifs of the time.

79 *High altar, Church of the Holy Rood, Market Street, Watford, Hertfordshire (1883–90), by John Francis Bentley.*

Scottish building as a whole, for its high period in England coincided with a major Greek Classical revival in the northern part of Britain, dominated by William Henry Playfair (1789–1857) in Edinburgh and the great Alexander Thomson (1817–75) in Glasgow. Only in the 1860s and later did the Scottish Church authorities take up the Gothic style, which led to a good number of churches by William Leiper, J. J. Burnet and J. A. Campbell, F. T. Pilkington (especially the Barclay Church, Edinburgh, of 1861–62) and others. One of the most impressive of all these designs is the

76

Barony Church in Castle Street, Glasgow, designed by Burnet and Campbell in 1886 [*80*]. A lofty exterior echoes the High early English Gothic style of the interior, with soaring stone arches and elongated lancet windows on a vast scale. Burnet also built a notable series of long, low Gothic churches with stumpy towers.

The Barony Church is no light-hearted exercise in Gothic, but a grave essay in the enclosure of space by stone. Yet it does combine this gravity with a vertical elegance that became a feature of English Gothic at the end of the century. The development of the work of J. L. Pearson (1817–97) shows a gradual increase of a lighter elegance that illustrates this aspect of

80 *Interior, the Barony Church, Castle Street, Glasgow (1886), by John Burnet and J. A. Campbell. A sternly impressive work in the early English Gothic style. In Scotland, Victorian Gothic was rarely used even for churches until late in the century.*

building of breathtaking elegance and ingenuity in its flow of space from one level and enclosure to another [*82*].

The last example of this late Gothic elegance and lightness to be mentioned here is a rarely visited masterpiece in that centre of the arts and museum world around the Albert Hall in London. This is the marvellous Holy Trinity Church in Prince Consort Road, Kensington (1902–04), by another leading Gothic revivalist, George Frederick Bodley (1827–1907), in which a

81 Interior, Truro Cathedral, Cornwall (1880–1910), by John Loughborough Pearson. Light and lofty forms became more frequent in the later work of the Victorian Gothic masters.

82 Staircase of the Rylands Memorial Library, Deansgate, Manchester (1890–99), by Basil Champneys. Gothic was rarely used in secular buildings by this date. Champneys achieved brilliant spatial effects in the interior.

late Victorian church architecture.[2] Pearson was a leading figure in the Gothic revival as early as 1850. His great church of St Augustine at Kilburn in north London (1870–80) is a good example of his almost overwhelming manner at that time. Ten years later, his design for Truro Cathedral in Cornwall (1880–1910) is in a lighter, soaring style [*81*], as is his other cathedral, at Brisbane in Australia (opened 1901). To leave the purely religious field for a moment, the Rylands Memorial Library in Manchester (1890–99), by Basil Champneys, is an unexpectedly late Gothic secular

77

83 Interior, Holy Trinity Church, Prince Consort Road, Kensington, London (1902–04, completed later), by George Frederick Bodley. Gothic architecture reached a peak of airiness and slender elegance in this late work by one of the great Victorian church architects.

84 Interior, Bothenhampton Church, near Bridport, Dorset (1887), by Edward Prior. In this early Arts and Crafts Gothic church the nave is dominated by arches that spring low from the massive walls.

forest of slender piers float up through a brightly daylighted space to the delicately vaulted roof [83]. Bodley was a former pupil of Sir George Gilbert Scott, who would have been astonished to see this development.

While the older men were producing a new type of light and airy church at the end of the century, the leaders of the next generation were experimenting with very different Gothic forms. Norman Shaw himself was scarcely younger than Bodley. But in the 1880s his office was full of talented pupils and many of them seem to have had a hand in Shaw's All Saints' Church at Leek in Staffordshire (1885–87). This was the period immediately after the founding of the Art Workers' Guild and at least two of the Guild's founders, Lethaby and Horsley, are known to have contributed to the church as members of Shaw's staff. At Leek the forms which Shaw used are strong and broad, both inside and outside, with a wide nave, shallow but powerful pointed stone arches and a flood of daylight from big windows at both ends. The intricate stone tracery of these windows is of considerable originality; indeed the whole church uses the Gothic style in a very new anti-scholarly way.

Two years after the design of Shaw's church at Leek, another of his pupils, Edward Prior (also a founder of the Art Workers' Guild), built a very small church at Bothenhampton, near Bridport in Dorset, which is a bold step towards a free Gothic-based Arts and Crafts style for churches [84]. The exterior is simple and scarcely noticeable. By contrast the interior is one of great intensity. There are no aisles, but stone arches thrust up from almost floor level in the massive walls, joining overhead to form a powerful rib-cage for the nave. This space ends at a solid stone wall, pierced only by a high arch that opens into the much smaller chancel. This narrowing of space towards the altar is echoed by the rising levels of the floor at the east end of the building, and by increasing darkness relieved by a trefoil and three lancet windows. Prior himself designed the stained glass and Lethaby the altar frontal in this small masterpiece of church architecture.

The same desire to develop the Gothic church into something original can be seen in the last works of John Dando Sedding (1838–91). Sedding was born in Somerset and most of his early work is in the west of England. He set up practice in London in 1875 and in October 1890 he gave a paper to the Architectural Association in which he declared: 'If you are to succeed in architectural design along modern lines it will only be by being enthusiastic about the handicrafts – by knowing how to design interesting stonework, woodwork, ironwork, embroidery and other of the sub-industries of architecture.'[3] William Morris was the inspiration of such an approach and it is for promoting and putting this ideal into practice, rather than for stylistic innovation, that Sedding is most important.

Sedding built several London churches towards the end of his life, but the finest of them (indeed the finest church of the Arts and Crafts movement in London) is Holy Trinity in Sloane Street, Chelsea (1888–90, gradually furnished later). The west front of the church, whose design appears to be more typical of Sedding's assistant Henry Wilson, has already been described in chapter three. Here the interior will be considered, for it is the best example of Sedding's own ideals expressed in a building [*85*].

The nave and chancel of Holy Trinity form a stone-vaulted hall of great breadth and spaciousness, with two aisles. It is a

85 Interior, Holy Trinity Church, Sloane Street, Chelsea, London (1888–90), by J. D. Sedding and Henry Wilson. The masterpiece of Arts and Crafts Gothic in London, furnished by Wilson, Gimson and others during the 1890s.

simple space, given mystery by the low arcades of the surrounding chapels and other smaller enclosures. And it is given a feeling of glory by the immense windows, filled with eloquent tracery, at both ends. In its mixture of various types of Gothic, Holy Trinity is anti-scholastic. As hinted in the quotation from his Architectural Association paper given above, Sedding saw the Arts and Crafts movement more as a way of increasing the quality of craftsmanship than

86 Tower, St Agatha's Church, Stratford Road, Sparkbrook, Birmingham (1899–1901), by W. H. Bidlake. One of the fine works by the leading Arts and Crafts architect in Birmingham.

as a path towards an original architecture. The painter Christopher Whall perhaps pin-pointed this in a story he told of a visit to Holy Trinity with Sedding. 'I looked at it in silence trying to take it in. He cocked his head on one side and said: "Well? Well, is it too naughty? I hope it's not too naughty?" I said: "I don't see your point in mixing the styles. It's using *style* all the same." '[4]

Whall's remark has some justification, but the point was apparently secondary in

Sedding's mind. Holy Trinity was intended to be a triumphant demonstration of the union of the arts and crafts in God's name and in the decade following Sedding's death in 1891 Henry Wilson largely succeeded in making it just that. Wilson himself designed some fine metalwork screens and the heart-shaped pendant lights, Ernest Gimson also did some of the metalwork, while Edward Burne-Jones and other notable painters designed the windows. The church was never quite completed, for the disks over the nave arches were meant to be sculpted and the ceiling vaults painted. All the same, it is a treasure-house of its period.

Wilson went on to design some architectural schemes of powerful originality after Sedding's death, but it was left to others to develop Arts and Crafts Gothic further after the mid-1890s. Basil Champneys, the architect of the Rylands Memorial Library illustrated earlier, stated in 1901, 'I am a strong advocate of Gothic for Anglican churches',[5] but his Gothic style was remarkably free by the end of the century. St Luke's Church in Kidderpore Avenue, Hampstead (1898), shows strong Arts and Crafts influence, with chunky forms and flowing detail.

In Birmingham, a vigorous outpost of the Arts and Crafts movement, W. H. Bidlake produced a series of fine free Gothic churches. Perhaps the best of these is St Agatha's, Sparkbrook (1899–1901), whose tower shows much originality and perhaps the influence of Wilson [86]. This development of Gothic work was to lead to a series of remarkable churches in the Arts and Crafts Free Style by Lethaby, Prior, Townsend, Randall Wells and others at the start of the new century, but these will be considered in chapter eight.

The other important development in English church architecture in the 1890s was the revival of the Byzantine style, the round-arched and multi-domed architecture of early Christianity. The revival had started earlier. R. Rowand Anderson built St Sophia's Roman Catholic Church at Galston, Ayrshire, as early as 1886. The cathedral at Marseilles was already in hand, William Morris had lectured on Byzantine art in 1879 and Lethaby published a book on Santa Sophia in 1894. But the popularity of the style in England seems to have stemmed largely from one major building: the Roman Catholic Cathedral in Westminster.

The Catholic Church had been planning to build a London cathedral for some time. Finally, a site off Victoria Street in Westminster was bought and in 1895 Cardinal Vaughan appointed John Francis Bentley to be the architect. Bentley's church of 1883 at Watford has already been described and, as a well-known convert to the faith, he had designed and built a good number of other Roman Catholic churches, using the Gothic style. After his appointment, he visited Italy with Cardinal Vaughan in search of inspiration. Then,

when the decision was taken to use the Byzantine manner as the earliest Christian style, Bentley went on by himself to see other examples of such architecture in south-east Europe. Upon his return to England he started the design of the cathedral at Westminster and the building, without interior decoration, was opened in 1903.

The design Bentley produced was no copy of what he had seen abroad. To start with, both the cost factor and the London atmosphere made the use of much marble on the exterior inadvisable. Bentley chose to use red brick banded with stone and a general manner that seems to show some influence of Collcutt and of Norman Shaw's slightly earlier New Scotland Yard. Bentley's detailing was free Byzantine with many fashionable 1890s *motifs* [78], while Shaw's was an eclectic Baroque and Baronial.

The plan of Westminster Cathedral [87] is based on a long nave made up of a succession of broad domes of bare brick over square bays, creating huge cool spaces whose lower levels have over the years been

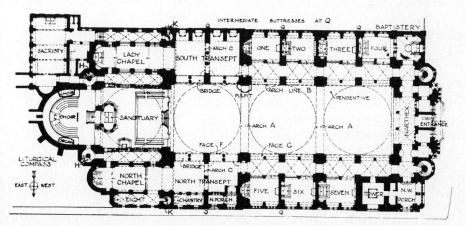

87 Plan of 1895, Westminster Roman Catholic Cathedral, by John Francis Bentley.

88 Detail, Christ Church, Brixton Road, South London (1897–1903), by Beresford Pite. The idea for using the Byzantine style may have been inspired by Bentley, but its use by Pite is more chaste and wholly personal.

cased with much marble and other decoration. The entrance front too is impressive, piling layer upon layer of masses above the doorway with a rising series of buttressed cupolas that lead the eye up to the towering campanile.

By the end of the 1890s other leading architects had followed Bentley's lead. There are examples of Byzantine work by leading members of the Art Workers' Guild, including Beresford Pite, Sidney Barnsley and Henry Wilson. Robert Weir Schultz published a good article on 'Byzantine Art' in the very first volume of The Architectural Review (1896–97). Pite's

Christ Church in Brixton Road, south London, was the architect's launching commission when he left John Belcher's employment to set up by himself in 1897, though it was built only in 1902–03 [88]. This church has the strong serenity associated with Byzantine work. Unfortunately another architect added a buzzing and gawky central tower to the road frontage in 1908 which now gives the entrance side an ungainly appearance. But the side elevations and interior are intact and it is perhaps the best of Pite's many striking works. It is worth noting the Byzantine semicircular arched windows with two pillars inside their span – widely used in all sorts of building during the years up to 1914 – that made an early appearance in this church.

Henry Wilson's extensive Byzantine furnishings of 1897–1908 for the austerely distinguished Gothic church of St Bartholomew, Brighton, are another of the tours de force of the Byzantine revival [90]. The scheme comprises a baldacchino and high altar, pulpit, Lady altar and font with much marble and marvellously inventive metalwork designed by Wilson.[6]

In 1900 the Byzantine revival stepped out of the boundaries of church architecture into university building with the designs by Sir Aston Webb and Ingress Bell for the University of Birmingham. The large range of buildings, dominated by a high campanile and a massive multi-domed great hall, was opened in 1909. At the other extreme of scale, the Campbell Mausoleum in St Mary's Cemetery at Kensal Green, London (1904), by C. H. B. Quennell, is a small work, characteristic of the revival in England [89].

The development of the English Byzantine style will not be traced further here, but it should be noted that the Roman Catholic Church took up the example of

Bentley and Cardinal Vaughan at Westminster Cathedral with particular enthusiasm, perhaps to point up the contrast with the Gothic associated with the Church of England. Byzantine style Roman Catholic churches went on being built throughout England up to the Second World War and beyond.

In 1903, the year that Bentley's Westminster Cathedral was opened, a competition was held for another great building, the Church of England Cathedral in Liverpool. Two years earlier, a proposal by those organizing the competition that it should be limited to Gothic designs had brought bitter protests from many leaders of the architectural profession. *The Architectural Review* had published pages of comment by leading architects.[7] 'Architecture should be something living, and not a

90 Baldacchino and altar (1899–1900), St Bartholomew's Church, Brighton, Sussex, by Henry Wilson. Part of the glorious Byzantine furnishings which Wilson carried out in this Victorian Gothic church between 1897 and 1908.

89 The Campbell Mausoleum, St Mary's Cemetery, Kensal Green, London (1904), by C. H. B. Quennell. A typical small-scale work of the Byzantine revival.

dead imitation of past work,' wrote John Belcher. 'Why talk of a style? Do they not know that genius will provide . . .?' asked J. J. Burnet. Norman Shaw rejected the whole idea of a competition and suggested that the Westminster Cathedral precedent be followed: 'Having, after much consideration . . . selected their man, let them put the designing of the cathedral unreservedly in his hands.' Arts and Crafts

83

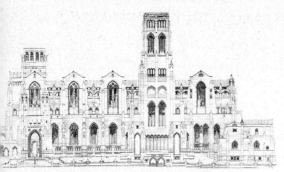

91 *Elevation of the winning design, Liverpool Anglican Cathedral competition (1903), by Giles Gilbert Scott.*

architects such as Prior, Ricardo and Townsend followed the general line taken in Voysey's comment, 'Any restriction as to style, no matter which, is equivalent to demanding affectation and crushing all sincerity.' Most devastating of all, the grand old man of the Arts and Crafts movement, Philip Webb, doubted whether the judges would select anything reasonable anyway, 'even if they understood the meaning of the word "Gothic" '.

The competition went ahead, however, with slightly widened restrictions on style. Beresford Pite submitted a tremendous Byzantine design (Bentley was dead and had never entered competitions anyway), Mackintosh a soaring free Gothic entry, Wilson and Lethaby a joint project with adventurous concrete vaulting and a very original conical tower. Some of these projects will be described and illustrated in chapter eight. But the design selected by the assessor, the ageing Goth, George Frederick Bodley, was done by a twenty-two year old grandson of Sir Gilbert Scott, Giles Gilbert Scott (1880–1960), who was still doing his training with Temple Moore. The organizers were embarrassed when the extreme inexperience of the winner became known;

they appointed Bodley to act as joint architect with him and work started in 1904. In fact Bodley died in 1907 and Scott carried on by himself with a commission that lasted the rest of his life, but brought him many others as well as a knighthood in its wake.

Giles Gilbert Scott's winning design for the Liverpool Anglican Cathedral was a restrained essay in free middle-period English Gothic [91]. It is based on a straightforward Roman cross plan, with a high tower over the main crossing and extra crossings at the western end (containing baptistry and entrance porch) and towards the east (for chapter house and choir vestry). As the years passed he revised the plans (in 1910 he produced what was virtually a completely new design [92]) and the cathedral – as almost completed at the time of writing – is now a far more powerful mass than Scott originally proposed and of considerably greater individuality in the interior [93].

92 *Sketch of Liverpool Cathedral as redesigned by Scott in 1910 after Bodley's death. Largely completed by the time of Scott's death in 1960, the design went through many revisions. The central tower, as completed, is proportionately taller than shown in this sketch.*

93 Lady Chapel interior (1903–11), Liverpool Cathedral, by Scott with Bodley.

This gradual movement towards the expression of strong volumes in church exteriors is typical of Scott's other churches and it is a characteristic, too, of his teacher Temple Moore (1856–1920). Moore was one of the best of the Edwardian Gothic architects. He had worked for many years with Giles Gilbert Scott's talented father (George Gilbert Scott the younger) before starting his own practice. One can follow Temple Moore's development with fascination through such church designs as St Mark's at Mansfield (1897), St Cuthbert's at Middlesbrough (1900) [94] and St Wilfrid's at Harrogate (1905). There is always a feeling of powerful geometrical volumes in the exteriors, but the expression matures into stronger and stronger forms. And the interiors mature too, as shown in that of St Wilfrid's which is a masterpiece of purity of line combined with spatial complexity [95].

There were many other good church architects practising at this time and W. D.

95 Interior, St Wilfrid's Church, Duchy Road, Harrogate, Yorkshire (1905–14), by Moore. In contrast with the strong masses of the exteriors, Moore's church interiors are often delicate and intricate essays in the enclosure of space.

94 St Cuthbert's Church, Newport Road, Middlesbrough, Yorkshire (1900–02), by Temple Moore. Moore was a master of solid geometry as expressed in the powerful forms of his church exteriors.

Caröe (1857–1938) in particular, who showed as much originality and almost as much power as Temple Moore and Scott, should be mentioned. J. Ninian Comper (1864–1960), whose work had altogether different qualities, was an Aberdeen Scot, articled to Bodley and Garner. He did a vast amount of church restoration or addition work and built a considerable number of new churches too. Two of his many Edwardian churches are crucial to the development of his own very personal manner, which he called 'Unity by Inclusion'.

During his early practice Comper was an enthusiastic supporter of the English Use movement, a campaign within the Church of England to return to its own original ritual as set out in the rubric of the 1549 Prayer Book. His church of St Cyprian, Clarence Gate near Regent's Park, London (1901–03), is a light elegant church designed for the utmost ritual simplicity [*96*]. Comper himself said that it 'neither seeks nor avoids originality' but sets out 'only to fulfil the ideal of the English Parish Church ... in the last manner of English architecture' (that is, the Perpendicular Gothic style).[8]

By 1906, however, Comper had started to formulate his Unity by Inclusion principle in his big church of St Mary's, Wellingborough (1906–30) [*97*]. The Perpendicular English Gothic is enriched here by features and details from the Italian Renaissance and English *Gothick*, while Comper's own favourite gold columns, decorated with motifs such as dragons, which he was to use repeatedly, appear here for the first of many times. It is a style that appears mannered to many people and could be disastrous when employed by less talented designers. Yet Comper himself made its enchantment work more often than not.[9]

Caröe, Giles Gilbert Scott and others continued to build their own versions of Gothic churches right up until the Second World War and even later, so the Gothic revival did not die in the Edwardian period. The Roman Catholic Church continued to build churches in the Byzantine style for just as long. The Arts and Crafts Free Style achieved a series of major, if small-scale, church masterpieces during the Edwardian years, as will be seen in chapter eight.

96 Interior, St Cyprian's Church, Clarence Gate, London (1901–03), by Ninian Comper. At this date Comper's church interiors were not far from the contemporary work by his master, Bodley.

97 Interior, St Mary's Church, Knox Road, Wellingborough, Northamptonshire (1906 – c. 1930), by Comper. A good example of the architect's theory of 'Unity by Inclusion', combining elements of various styles in a light, almost gay, overall manner with much gleaming decoration.

6
Free Design and the Edwardian House

THE EXPLOSIVE outburst of new ideas and expression in English domestic architecture during the 1890s was an exceptional phenomenon. During the next decade these ideas were developed and broadened, though without the same intensity of invention. Perhaps it was this slackening of inspiration that allowed Arts and Crafts architecture to grow the Neo-Georgian style almost as an offshoot. For it was Arts and Crafts architects such as Ernest Newton and Mervyn Macartney who led the way towards the Neo-Georgian style – in some ways the quieter domestic counterpart of the Baroque revival in larger buildings – which will be described in chapter twelve. But the reign of Edward VII also saw developments of extraordinary significance for town planning – the garden city and the garden suburb – as well as the construction of blocks of flats built to higher standards and on a massive scale for the working classes.

Few of the immense country mansions on the scale of the Georgian and Victorian days were built after the end of the century. One of the largest was William Lethaby's Melsetter of 1898–1902, and even that was modest compared with the High Victorian palaces of wealthy peers and tycoons. The 1900s were, however, notable for the number of fairly small country houses that were built for middle-class clients. Lethaby's last house, High Coxlease (1900–01), is typical in size, though exceptional for its Arts and Crafts strength and for the mysterious

symbolism expressed in its walls [99].

Among other work, the turn of the century saw a climax in the development of Edwin Lutyens (1869–1944), the young Arts and Crafts architect who built many Free Style houses (the majority of them in Surrey) and then went on to become the most famous Grand Manner architect in the decade before the Second World War. Lutyens's own background was a curious one. Eleventh child of a soldier who had turned painter, he was often ill as a boy and had little education of any sort except one year in the office of the architect Sir Ernest George. But he had talent and wit, and he married a member of the aristocracy who brought him valuable contacts. Lutyens's Tigbourne Court of 1899 has been described in chapter two as one excellent example among his many notable houses of this time. By 1901 Lutyens's practice was spreading far beyond Surrey. Deanery Gardens in the village of Sonning, on the Thames in Berkshire, was built for the owner of *Country Life* magazine (the design of whose office building in Covent Garden brought Lutyens to London and to use the Grand Manner for the first time two years later). As with so many of the best Lutyens

98 Deanery Gardens, Thames Street, Sonning, Berkshire (1901), by Edwin Lutyens. Detail of garden front. One of the architect's most lovely works of this period, in an inventive Arts and Crafts style with Elizabethan roots.

99 High Coxlease, south of Lyndhurst, Hampshire (1900–01), by William Lethaby. Garden front. The last house by the most important theorist of Arts and Crafts architecture. The garden frontage expresses a composition of advancing and retreating volumes. The house was originally whitewashed and the central Venetian window was added later.

100 Happisburgh House, Happisburgh, northern Norfolk (1900), by Detmar Blow. Entrance front. An X-plan house by a disciple of Prior and Gimson.

houses, Deanery Gardens has roots in the Elizabethan country house. The huge mullioned grid window and the chimneys of the house show these typical Arts and Crafts traditional elements, but the design is developed freely from there into a work of

real originality [98]. The house is remarkable, too, for the soft warmth of its brickwork and the pleasing scale and lighting of the interiors.

Marshcourt at Stockbridge in Hampshire was also built by Lutyens in 1901 and is again an individual design growing from traditional roots [101]. This series of Lutyens houses built between 1896 and 1903 reaches a level of achievement equal to that of the best contemporary domestic architecture by Voysey, Mackintosh and Baillie Scott. One of the last of the great sequence, Papillon Hall in Leicestershire (1903), is of special interest as it shows Lutyens experimenting with the butterfly plan.

The butterfly plan is a term later given to the variations on the X-plan which were first developed in 1895 by Edward Prior. Prior's designs of the 1890s, and particularly his 1897 house The Barn, have already been analysed in chapter two. Many other Arts and Crafts architects followed and extended Prior's basic idea, which was that a broken and non-rectangular plan of this type would make a house blend more closely with its site. Prior himself combined this with an irregular, mounting skyline, but few other architects followed him in this respect.

After The Barn, Prior did not actually build another of these houses with experimental plans for seven years, but in 1900 his young disciple Detmar Blow designed and built Happisburgh House overlooking the remote north coast of Norfolk [100]. The plan is an X with an elongated central section containing the main living-room (now used as a dining-room for the country club it has become). This is flint country and Blow adapted the traditional patterns on the outside walls, crowning them with a roof of local thatching. True to Prior's theories relating to the use of organic materials, 'the house is built entirely of beach shingle and flints, bonded with bricks; the roof covered with reeds grown on the estate; with the exception of some woods and glass, nothing was imported. It was built by the men of the district, assisted by a foreman and other leading men who work with the architect. . . . The floors are of fire-resisting concrete.'[1] It is Blow's most interesting and startling house, although, rather curiously, when visited it lacks the particular atmosphere of loving care that is felt in the very best Arts and Crafts houses.

Lutyens's experiment with the butterfly plan at Papillon Hall (the name was a typically Lutyens joke about the shape of the plan) is a happy version of Prior's ideas, as was the house called How Green at Hever in Kent, designed by R. Weir Schultz in 1905.[2] The master, Prior himself, started to design his most ambitious house in 1903 and it was completed in 1905. This is Home Place (originally called Kelling Place, now a nursing home), just east of Holt, in northern Norfolk [*102*]. The house is built on a half-**X** plan that flows out into the

101 Marshcourt, near Stockbridge, Hampshire (1901), by Edwin Lutyens. Another of Lutyens's marvellous houses built between 1896 and 1903, before he turned from a free vernacular approach to the brilliant Classicism of his middle years.

102 Home Place (originally Kelling Place), near Holt, northern Norfolk (1903–05), by Edward Prior. Garden front. The last and largest of the 'butterfly-plan' houses by this extremist practitioner of Arts and Crafts theories.

103 Dining-room, Home Place (1903–05), by Prior. A contemporary photograph, showing Prior's simple and traditional taste in domestic interiors.

garden. Black-and-white photographs cannot do justice to this Arts and Crafts masterpiece. In reality the rather restless forms and flint patterning are made harmonious by the careful selection of colours; local brown stone dressings and Norfolk tiles with paler brown flints and pebbles from the grounds are used to face the walls, the whole blending into an overall glowing honey-colour. The work was superintended for Prior by Randall Wells and Detmar Blow, using their own key craftsmen and local labour. House and garden walls were built of mass concrete, pebble faced, and the floors were concrete reinforced with iron chain! Like Lethaby's Brockhampton church, Home Place demonstrates how interested some of the

Arts and Crafts architects were in early experiments with the use of concrete. Contemporary photographs show rather austere interiors [*103*]; Prior had little interest in decorative novelty, preferring to use old sturdy furniture or new work of strong simplicity in the manner of Gimson.

The entrance frontage of Home Place is made up of a series of vertically emphasized bays, a free design of bold patterns based on the local tradition of flintwork. This strange composition, with its pebbled texture, tall gables and spiralling chimneys, is one of the high achievements of the Arts and Crafts movement. The garden frontage too, blended with its garden by walls of the same materials and mounting to the peaks of the central roofs and curling chimney pots, is the fiercest expression among all his buildings of Prior's phenomenal and often contradictory genius. His few later houses are intriguing but quieter, though his last two churches –

described in chapter eight – show that his creative powers were by no means exhausted.

Prior's experimental plans found many followers, but the approach was too complex for widespread adaptation. In contrast, a house built for his own use by another Arts and Crafts master became a prototype for thousands of semi-detached suburban houses built throughout England and even North America during the following three decades.

This was The Orchard, a simple and charming house built in 1900–01 by C. F. A. Voysey for his own use, in Shire Lane at Chorley Wood in Hertfordshire [104]. Voysey's imaginative sweep, so much in evidence in his designs of the 1890s for quite large country houses, had little success during the Edwardian decade itself. His commissions tended to be small and most of his houses of this period – the 1905 design for a house at Woodford makes the point – show a mature use of his personal style, rather than a flow of new ideas. The Orchard has a plan of no great interest except for its straightforwardness. The interiors and furnishings were of a typical simplified delicacy [105]. The well-known frontage (barely asymmetrical) has Voysey's favourite white roughcast and mullioned band windows, with a gable at each end across the hipped roof. It was the elevation formed by these two gables, separated by a lower horizontal centre, that provided a ready model for the semi-detached house to be adapted by other architects and later by countless speculative builders.

In 1905 Hugh Baillie Scott developed the Voysey design into twin houses for an exhibition of cheap cottages at Letchworth to publicize the initial stages of the first Garden City [106]. Baillie Scott's design is of even more interest, however, for its plan,

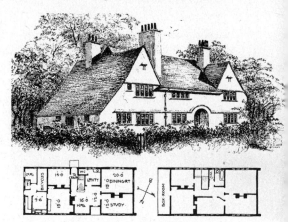

104 *The Orchard, Shire Lane, Chorley Wood, Hertfordshire (1900–01), designed by C. F. A. Voysey for himself. Entrance front and plan. A typically delicate composition, only just asymmetrical, which provided a model for numerous later suburban semi-detached houses.*

105 *Interior, The Orchard (1900–01), by Voysey. A classic example of a Voysey interior.*

106 Twin cottages, Letchworth Garden City, Hertfordshire (1905), by M. H. Baillie Scott. Entrance front. Voysey-inspired, but the open planning of the modest interiors was of significance for the future. The touch of half-timbering between the two gables became more evident in Baillie Scott's other houses which were forerunners of the popular timbered houses of the 1920s.

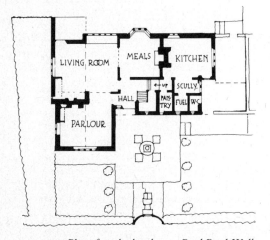

107 Plan of a suburban house, Reed Pond Walk, Gidea Park, Essex (1910–11), by Baillie Scott. The flow of space between living-room, dining area and parlour is typical of Baillie Scott's imaginative work in house planning.

94

which showed an extraordinarily open flow of space in the ground floor.

Charm and individualism, together with experimental open plans, were Baillie Scott's particular contribution to domestic architecture. His house for a Swiss client in Zurich (c. 1903) and Bill House at Selsey-on-Sea in Sussex (1906–07) show his picturesque originality, while the half-timbered viewing tower of Bill House is prophetic of the countless black-and-white timbered house frontages built all over England in the 1920s and later. In the designs for his houses, Baillie Scott worked away steadily at opening up the flow of space within the planning. After the Letchworth cottages mentioned above, he took the idea further in such designs as his unbuilt corner house for Hampstead Garden Suburb (1907) and his suburban house at Gidea Park (1910) [107]. The plans show dining areas and parlours as spaces that flow without doors out of the main living-rooms.

In about 1905, Charles Robert Ashbee put up a strange little building called The Five Bells at Iver Heath in Buckinghamshire. Here Ashbee, most unusually, adapted Voysey's design of The Orchard in a completely symmetrical form that might be mistaken for council housing of the sort built on the edge of so many English villages up to the 1960s.

By this time, much of Ashbee's most striking architecture – the Cheyne Walk houses in particular – was already built. He continued to do much vernacular building (barely distinguishable today from much older cottages) around Chipping Campden, where he had moved his Guild and School of Handicraft in 1902. But most of his Edwardian work was in the design of silverware and other crafts until he became involved in town planning at the end of the decade.

108 The Hill House, Helensburgh, Dunbarton-shire (1902–04), by Charles Rennie Mackintosh. Garden front. The first house of Mackintosh's free manner, with the outer angle of the L-plan opened up and a Baronial-type tower inserted.

Ernest Gimson, too, had turned away from architecture to the furnishing and decoration of houses. His furniture of this period is of unrivalled integrity and excellence, while his decorative plaster-work has a lyrical beauty. Halsey Ricardo, a close friend of Gimson, also designed much fine plasterwork. But Ricardo's most notable designs were for many of the famous tiles produced by William de Morgan.

To return to the houses themselves, there were too many of high quality built by Arts and Crafts architects during the first decade of the century to allow them to be illustrated here. But in passing, particular note must be made of Westbrook at Godalming (1900–03) by H. Thackeray Turner, Garth House at Edgbaston in Birmingham (1901) by W. H. Bidlake, the diapered Sandhouse at Witley in Surrey (1901–03) by F. W. Troup, Minsted near Midhurst (c. 1903) by Mervyn Macartney and Redlands in Four Oaks near Birmingham (1904) by Bateman and Bateman, who admired Lethaby. All are linked by the strength and quiet individuality of design that was becoming typical of the Arts and Crafts houses after the bolder adventures of the 1890s.

In Scotland, on the other hand, Charles Rennie Mackintosh built his finest and most inventive house during the early part of the decade. As its name suggests, the Hill House (1902–04) is on the slopes above Helens-burgh, a seaside town twenty miles north-west of Glasgow. To make the most of the sea view, Mackintosh provided a long plan roughly in the shape of an L, with passages on the landward side. But he left open the outer angle of the L, using this recess as a visual pivot of the design, which he

95

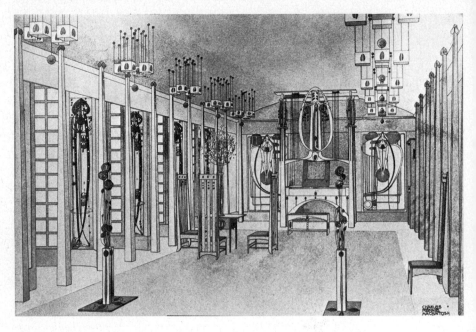

109 Competition design of 1901 for the music room of the 'Haus eines Kunstfreundes', Darmstadt, by Mackintosh. Not built. The decorative style developed by Mackintosh, and by his friend George Walton, here achieves a high level of almost abstract beauty.

composed of strong vertical forms developed from traditional Scottish features [108]. The interiors and the furniture are among the finest produced by Mackintosh's intense genius [110].

Mention must be made here of another house design by Mackintosh, but one that remained unbuilt. This was his entry for the 'Haus eines Kunstfreundes' competition of 1901 in Darmstadt [109]. Baillie Scott gained the top prize, with one of his imaginative ground-plans, but Mackintosh's elevations and interiors – which won second place – were brilliantly original and later influenced Josef

96

Hoffmann's famous Palais Stoclet in Brussels (1905–11). Mackintosh's design for the music room is an extraordinary development of the type of decoration done by his friend George Walton in interiors such as the billiard room of The Leys at Elstree, also of 1901.

The material chosen by Mackintosh for the outside of the Hill House was roughcast (or 'harling'), a traditional Scottish rendering. Roughcast was an English traditional material, too, and was widely used by those of the Arts and Crafts architects who were influenced by Voysey. Harrison Townsend was one of these, though he had often opposed Voysey's ideas during the 1890s. The house Townsend built for himself at Blackheath near Guildford – where he had designed most of the village – in about 1907 is one of his few really interesting works after Great Warley church (see chapter eight). The house is called Cobbins and the evident Voysey influence is transformed into a striking design by long eaves that dip from the gables almost to the ground.

A much more progressive originality of structure is shown in two Arts and Crafts houses built shortly after Cobbins. In 1907 the Manchester architect Edgar Wood built a house in Hertfordshire that was entirely flat-roofed, in reinforced concrete. This house, Dalny Reed near Royston, was followed a year later by another which brought the approach to maturity.

Edgar Wood's Upmeads reflects the contemporary move towards rectangular design and decoration that can be seen in works of the same period by Mackintosh and Holden [*111*]. But here the form employed is a logical expression of the structure of the building, for the flat concrete roof removes the need for gables or sloping tiles and gives the architect new freedom in interior planning. As early as 1910 the house was illustrated in the book *Small Country Houses of Today*[3] with a comment by the editor, Lawrence Weaver, that 'Upmeads cannot fail, by its logical qualities and . . . originality, to rivet the attention of everyone and the admiration of not a few.'

These and other designs by Wood and his partner Sellers are exceptionally early expressions of new structural techniques in the external appearance of small or medium-sized houses. As for really large country houses, few were built during the Edwardian period and fewer still made any attempt at free design. The two major exceptions were those by Leonard Stokes and by Edwin Lutyens.

Stokes's Minterne House, at Minterne Magna in Dorset, was built in 1904–06. The original Tudor house of the Digby family had been destroyed and Stokes built a huge free design, with many Tudor echoes incorporated, on the original foundations.

110 *Drawing-room alcove, the Hill House (1902–04), by Mackintosh.*

111 *Upmeads, Newport Road, Stafford (1908), by Edgar Wood. Garden front. Wood's revolutionary houses of this time, with their flat concrete roofs, reflect the move towards rectangular forms which appears in the contemporary work of Holden, Mackintosh and others.*

97

112 Castle Drogo, Drewsteignton, Dartmoor, Devon (1910–30), by Edwin Lutyens. Entrance front. An Edwardian dream expressed in a fortified castle, now the property of the National Trust.

The climax of the composition is the powerful stumpy tower at the end overlooking the pretty valley, down which flow some of the finest gardens in the country.

The big Lutyens house of the time has less Arts and Crafts feeling but more sheer panache. Castle Drogo was designed in 1910 as a building three times the size it eventually reached when work ended in 1930. It stands on a hilltop at Drewsteignton on Dartmoor, a fantasy of a medieval castle in real stone [112]. Nor does the fantasy fade inside the castle, for some of the games with spaces and solids and levels in the main rooms and masonry stairways are among Lutyens's most scintillating performances.

More frequently, however, the rich men of the time altered or added to existing great houses. In 1903–06 Robert Lorimer (something of a Scottish Lutyens, in that he

went on from an Arts and Crafts youth to fame as a Grand Manner architect) added a major new wing to the large house called Hallyburton, at Coupar Angus in Scotland. Lorimer kept much of the traditional Baronial style of the old house while fining down its decoration in a harmonious extension. The design was of good quality but Lorimer was not breaking new ground; the tradition of blending extensions with old Scottish houses went back into the nineteenth century.

While these houses were being built for the wealthier classes, impressive progress was being made in suburbs for city workers and in housing for the working classes. Although this book does not deal with town planning, a brief account of developments in that field is necessary when considering large-scale housing of the time. There are several mid-Victorian examples of big housing estates around mills or factories; Saltair near Leeds, designed in 1850 and built during the next two decades, is the best known. London's garden suburb of Bedford Park, with houses designed by Edward Godwin in

1876 and then by Norman Shaw and others from 1877 onwards, brought to life a new ideal of small houses among green trees and gardens for middle-class city workers. The soap magnate Lever sought to provide such conditions for poorer factory workers in his Port Sunlight town on the Mersey estuary, started in 1888. Quaker conscientiousness achieved even better results with the semi-detached houses of the Bournville model village built in 1895–1904 for the workers in the famous Cadbury chocolate factory at King's Heath, Birmingham, to designs by the architect Alexander Harvey [*113*].

113 Cottages at Bournville village, King's Heath, near Birmingham (1895–1904), by Alexander Harvey. Model housing for the workers of the Cadbury chocolate factory.

The movement came to a head with a book published in 1898 by Ebenezer Howard, at first entitled *Tomorrow*, but subsequently republished with acclaim in 1902 as *Garden Cities of Tomorrow*. Howard proposed new cities of about a thousand acres (three-quarters of a mile across), planned with much care and providing optimum living conditions for their inhabitants, to be built in agricultural country. The basic plan was circular, with a park at the centre, then rings of houses and an outer fringe for commerce and industry. In 1903 Howard helped to form a company that quickly started the first Garden City, at Letchworth in Hertfordshire, less than forty miles from London. The planners and chief architects were Barry Parker and Raymond Unwin, appointed after a competition which Lethaby too entered. Parker and Unwin came to this job with the experience of a garden suburb at New Earswick in Yorkshire, already planned in 1902, and their original rough plan for the competition was modified very little [*114*]. Letchworth Garden City held an exhibition in 1905 of prototype low-cost houses [*106*], but the town grew only slowly over the years. Unwin and Parker went on to bring a similar approach to Hampstead Garden Suburb, planned in

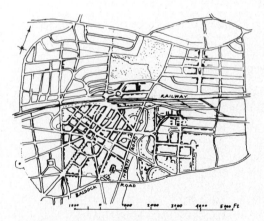

114 Map of the centre of Letchworth Garden City, Hertfordshire, planned in 1903 by Barry Parker and Raymond Unwin (this part built in 1904–16). The rough sketch map submitted by the designers for the competition was executed with only minimal alterations.

99

1906, where the architect of the central buildings was Edwin Lutyens. The most notable advance at Hampstead, however, was the pleasant high-density multiple housing by Baillie Scott and others. Baillie Scott's Nos 6–10 Meadway (1908) and Waterlow Court (1908–09) [116] are examples of remarkably enlightened and humanitarian architecture.[4]

Meanwhile, the reorganization of local government in the 1880s brought new impetus to large-scale housing within existing cities. In particular, the 1888 Housing of the Working Classes Act gave

the recently created London County Council responsibilities and powers to carry out a massive programme of slum clearance and rehousing. Thomas Blashill, the former architect to the Metropolitan Board of Works, was appointed L.C.C. Architect and recruited a talented group of young architects under him to design the individual housing projects. Owen Fleming was outstanding among the staff; he was an active member of the Architectural Association,[5] and deeply influenced by the Socialist ideals of William Morris and Philip Webb. Other notable members of the L.C.C. staff included Halcrow Verstage, Matthew Dawson, Minton Taylor, Winmill, Hiorns and Canning – again they were in touch with Philip Webb through the meetings of the Society for the Protection of Ancient Buildings – who also shared progressive political ideals and

115 Millbank Estate, behind the Tate Gallery, London, by the L.C.C. Architect's Department. The housing block shown here, Millais House, was one of the first two built in 1899–1900, but the whole large estate was completed by 1902.

visited municipal housing schemes in Europe to gather ideas.

In 1893 Fleming was appointed head of the L.C.C. Architect's new Housing Division and in the same year work began on the first big slum clearance and housing project.[6] This was the Boundary Street Estate in Shoreditch, replacing The Jago, an infamous East End slum. Fleming's overall plan provided a central garden, with roads radiating out from it. After establishing general guidelines, he left the design of most of the buildings to individual architects under him on the L.C.C. staff. The blocks of flats are generally five storeys high, of brick and terracotta, and show the influence of Philip Webb. The first stage was built in 1893–95.

In November 1896 the London County Council approved the outline plan of what was to become the most famous of its early housing projects, the Millbank Estate behind the Tate Gallery in Westminster. In 1897 the Council decided on an architectural competition for a specimen block of flats, to be assessed by the esteemed architect W. D. Caröe. The result was finally announced in January 1899, the winners being Spalding and Cross. Their design was built as Hogarth House, the central block of the whole estate, in 1899–1900. But meanwhile, the Architect's Department had been instructed to design all the other blocks and these were prepared at various stages by Fleming's staff between 1897 and 1899 [115]. The first building was started in 1899 and the final block was completed in August 1902.[7]

The plan of the Millbank Estate radiates from a rectangular public garden and consists of five-storey blocks of flats, as in the earlier Shoreditch estate. The architecture is again reminiscent of Philip Webb: good quality brickwork of a traditional structure, the patterns of windows express-

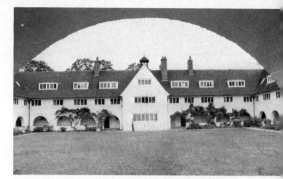

116 Internal courtyard, Waterlow Court, Heath Close, off Hampstead Way, Hampstead Garden Suburb, London (1908–09), by M. H. Baillie Scott. Of all Baillie Scott's imaginative multiple housing schemes for the suburb, this was the only one built.

ing the interiors, broad gables above. It is friendly architecture for its large scale, and the streets within the estate are well planted with trees.

Old Thomas Blashill finally retired in 1899, expressing doubts about the cost of building housing to the high standards recently set by the L.C.C.[8] It was only after his retirement that the real L.C.C. drive for slum clearance and rehousing got under way. His successor as L.C.C. Architect, W. E. Riley, was not really an architect but a brilliant construction organizer of Admiralty dockyards and direct labour housing schemes. In his twenty-one years in the L.C.C. office, Riley's administration achieved a vast amount of housing of good quality, as well as numerous schools, fire stations and hostels for the poor. Nevertheless, it was the consistent design standards and free general style of the almost unknown young architects working under Riley that has set its stamp on so many parts of London and which influenced early council housing in many other British cities.

7
Large Buildings and the Edwardian Free Style

THE EXPERIMENTS with different approaches to a free architecture for large buildings in England during the 1890s – Wilson's and Townsend's freely decorated and symbolist designs as well as the strong simplicity of other architects – have been outlined in chapter three. The more decorated type of Free Style started to die out at the beginning of the twentieth century and quickly became unfashionable among the Arts and Crafts architects.

The reasons for this were partly economic – sculpture and mosaics cost money, after all – but also reflected a strong reaction against the Art Nouveau of the European continent. The desire for originality in architecture had attracted the new decorative style in some architectural detailing in Britain but, from about the year 1900, the more *avant-garde* British designers started to react sharply against the sinuous flowing lines that had been typical of much adventurous work on both sides of the English Channel.

Two characteristic examples of this switch in taste date from 1900[1]: the attack by the eminent Arts and Crafts designer Lewis F. Day on the 'pronounced disease' of Art Nouveau, and the protest by a group of architects (including Edward Prior) against the acceptance of some Art Nouveau furniture by the Victoria and Albert Museum.

In 1901 *The Architectural Review* pilloried the Art Nouveau furniture exhibited at the Museum and sounded the alarm for architects: 'Architecture itself is attacked by the disease and in Germany and Austria queer goitred styles have sprung up in which some "decorative" feature has swallowed constructive significance and beauty.'[2] In 1904 the progressive magazine *The British Architect* published a criticism of Belgian Art Nouveau describing it as a 'wild, purposeless and foolish debauch in design' though admitting that it had 'inventiveness and energy'.[3] A new aesthetic puritanism had settled on the Arts and Crafts designers. The pure lines of Ashbee and the honest simplicity of Gimson had won the day for a few years, though they too were soon to lose ground to the Neo-Georgian revivalists.

The hopes for a new honest English architecture, based on tradition but free of all copyism, were preached by W. Howard Seth-Smith (1852–1928) in his inaugural address as President of the Architectural Association in London in 1900, when he advised the Association's students to find a middle path, ignoring those traditionalists who 'appear to regard draughtsmanship and design as the be-all and end-all' as well as 'the non-traditional school insisting that we should divest our minds of the forms of past work and invent our own'. Seth-Smith

117 Detail, Boulting and Sons offices and adjacent buildings, Riding House Street, Marylebone, London (1903), by H. Fuller Clark. One of the most original examples of the Edwardian Free Style.

118 *Entrance to the Royal Arcade, Castle Street, Norwich (c. 1900), by G. J. Skipper. Most of Skipper's numerous buildings in Norwich are Classical, but here he used coloured tiles and his own version of Arts and Crafts motifs.*

ings and public houses by Treadwell and Martin, for example in Bond Street and Whitehall [119], and other buildings by Niven and Wigglesworth dating from this time.

Other London buildings deserve special note for their inventive Free Style. In 1903 the stove manufacturers T. J. Boulting and Sons erected a corner site office building in Riding House Street, Marylebone, to designs by H. Fuller Clark that break up the frontages with a richly varied series of projecting vertical bays [117]. And in the following year the most splendid of Leonard Stokes's many telephone exchange buildings was built in Gerrard Street near Leicester Square [121]. The

suggested that 'as a matter of experience it will be found that the full truth lies somewhere between these extremes'.[4]

After the end of the century the strongly decorated forms of the Free Style were more common in commercial buildings seeking to advertise their own presence than in other large buildings in England. The brightly tiled entrance to the Royal Arcade in Castle Street, Norwich (c. 1900), by George Skipper [118], the ceramic splendours of Everard's factory in Bristol (1900) by Henry Williams and the curvaceous office building at No. 3 Soho Square, London (1903), by R. J. Worley [120] show the influence of Harrison Townsend's free design of the 1890s and are good examples of its occasional commercial use. There are also a number of remarkably original London office build-

119 *Left, the Old Shades public house (1898), right, Whitehall House offices (1904), Whitehall, Westminster: both by Treadwell and Martin. The long slender piers of Treadwell and Martin's style can be seen on the elevations of many London office buildings of the time.*

rounded arches on the ground floor and the complex grid pattern above, favourite features in Stokes designs, were here treated with a richness of relief that made the building a Free Style masterpiece. Alas, it is now destroyed.

Other buildings of the time showed less distinction and hardly any self-discipline. The Methodist Central Hall in Renshaw Street, Liverpool (1904–05), was designed by Bradshaw and Gass as a weird pile of a building that jumbles fashionable details, such as the sinuous decoration of the central windows, with Baroque cupolas that mount up to a high dome.

The same period saw a number of public libraries designed in a highly decorated Free Style. One of the best of these is the library in Garrick Street, Wolverhampton (1900–02), by Henry Hare, a talented designer in most of the styles of this

120 Office building, No. 3 Soho Square, London (1903), by R. J. Worley. A freely inventive design with Arts and Crafts decorative plasterwork.

121 Telephone Exchange, Gerrard Street, Soho, London (1904), by Leonard Stokes. Demolished 1935. In Stokes's ambitious design the grid pattern of the upper levels was successfully blended with some *Classical decorative touches and with the architect's favourite ground-floor rounded arches.*

122 Public Library, Garrick Street, Wolverhampton, Staffordshire (1900–02), by Henry Hare. Freedom of design with eclectic detailing integrated into an overall composition of much charm.

time [*122*]. In Wolverhampton he created a series of fine light reading-rooms, cleanly planned on a difficult corner site. The details are eclectic, including Jacobean and Baroque features as well as others of originality or fashionable at the time such as the cupolas with disc-topped pinnacles. But a comparison with the Liverpool Methodist building points up the excellence with which Hare assembled these elements into one of the most attractive Edwardian public buildings. Something of the same sureness in handling fairly extremist design may be seen in Caversham Public Library near Reading (1907) and in libraries in many parts of Britain put up at the start of the century.

The flamboyant forms of such buildings were of course far from acceptable to young progressives and to the Arts and Crafts idealists by this time. Clearly they were not

satisfied with what had been built up to the start of Edward VII's reign. Halsey Ricardo, an embattled Arts and Crafts man, expressed this dissatisfaction in his review of 1901 of *Die Englische Baukunst*, the influential German book by Hermann Muthesius that described the new English buildings of the 1890s. 'Mr. Muthesius', wrote Ricardo, 'congratulates us on our national architecture. He takes the house as the most essential sign of the [architectural] times. We would prefer to be judged by our schools, hospitals, asylums and public buildings.'[5]

Two little-known designs for other public libraries provide a clue to the hopes of the Free Style movement and a contrast with the two examples of libraries already given. The first stands in the High Street of Gosport, near Portsmouth in Hampshire [*123*]. The architect was Alfred Cross and the library dates from 1901–02. Here the design pivots on a corner entrance tower of brick and hung tiles that seems to have its roots in MacLaren's organic work a dozen years earlier. But from the tower spread two wings of a Voysey-like simplicity in their white roughcast upper levels and curling gutter brackets. The building is a notable achievement in the restrained line of Smith and Brewer's Mary Ward House.[6]

The other public library design gives us a hint of what Voysey, one of the masters of domestic Arts and Crafts architecture, might have achieved if he had done more large scale work. In 1902–03 Voysey had already built the Sanderson Wallpaper Factory at Chiswick on the outskirts of London, one of the most interesting early rational buildings, which will be dealt with more fully in chapter nine [*153*]. In 1905 he unsuccessfully entered a competition for the Carnegie Public Library in Limerick, Ireland [*124*]. His design was intended to be built of stone, its walls punctuated by elegant buttress pillars. The main accent was a grid oriel over the doorway, but a touch of gaiety was added to the elevations by the use of round arches over all the other windows and by the small curved peaks along the roofline between the buttresses.

Voysey did another non-domestic design that year and this was built. It was for a public house called the White Horse Inn at Stetchworth near Newmarket, a fine relaxed rhythmical composition punctuated by a courtyard gateway. This building, however, is essentially an enlargement of the architect's domestic style and it is no surprise to find that it has now been converted into a private house.

The influence of Voysey's famous simplicity and white walls can be seen in public buildings by other architects of the time, including some designed by the young Turks of the L.C.C. Architect's Department. The section in charge of the design of fire stations was headed by Charles Winmill, an inheritor of the ideas of William Morris and Philip Webb. Only

123 Public Library, High Street and Walpole Road, Gosport, Portsmouth, Hampshire (1901–02), by Alfred Cross. The wings show the simplicity of Voysey, while the tower achieves an organic effect.

124 Design of 1905 for proposed Carnegie Public Library, Limerick, Ireland, by C. F. A. Voysey. One of the great domestic architect's few designs for a public building, giving a hint of what he might have achieved in such work.

125 *Fire Station, West End Lane, Hampstead, London (1901), by the L.C.C. Architect's Department (Fire Section architect, Charles Winmill). A successful adaptation of Voysey's domestic manner to a public building.*

complicated, but even stronger in its brick massing, is the buttressed factory built for Messrs Willens and Robinson in North Wales in 1901 by H. Bulkeley Creswell, a leading member of the Architectural Association in London [126].

This rather austere trend of the Free Style has many of its roots in the rare London work of Philip Webb and in his last great country house, Standen in Sussex (1891–94) [3]. Many of the young L.C.C. architects had frequent contact with Webb (and with Lethaby and Morris) at meetings of the Society for the Protection of Ancient Buildings and at the informal discussions about architecture over the meals after the meetings. But if Webb and Lethaby were the inspirers of this strong Free Style of architecture, the manner soon became closely associated with the name of the young Charles Holden: 'the man who had

one of the many L.C.C. fire stations of the period – that at Eton Avenue, Hampstead, of 1914 – is known for certain to be designed by Winmill himself, but there were clearly some talented architects under him. The fire station at West End Lane in Hampstead is dated 1901 and is a charming variation on Voysey's manner, with its white roughcast, band windows, grid bay windows at ground level, hipped roof and a curious capped tower for hose drying [125].

Another of these London fire stations, in the Euston Road (1901–02), brings us to a more severe version of the Edwardian Free Style [127]. Here the plan is clearly expressed on the exterior in bold free forms, within the framework of a traditional structure. Strong brick verticals, trimmed with stone, are varied by a complex pattern of projecting bay and oriel windows and an unexpected connecting balcony. Less

126 *Willens and Robinson factory, Queensferry, North Wales (1901), by H. Bulkeley Creswell. The impressive buttressed brickwork of this functional building brought favourable comment from the building press of the time.*

108

127 Fire Station, Euston Road, London (1901–02), by the L.C.C. Architect's Department. The influence of Philip Webb can be seen in this type of free design by the Department.

the greatest influence over all of us', according to H. S. Goodhart-Rendel.[7]

Charles Holden (1875–1960), born six years after Edwin Lutyens, was a Lancashireman educated in Manchester. After training in Bolton, he came to London and spent a year working for the great Arts and Crafts designer and architect, C. R. Ashbee, in 1898. Holden was obviously influenced by Ashbee's genius, but his own

originality and the inspiration of Henry Wilson can be seen two years earlier in the chunky Arts and Crafts design for a market hall, which won the Soane Medallion in 1896.[8]

After working for Ashbee, Holden became assistant to H. Percy Adams, who had an established practice in hospital architecture. Adams had no particular feeling for design and as early as 1900 Holden was responsible for the plans for the big Belgrave Hospital for Children near Kennington Oval in London (completed 1903), though these were published under Adams's name. There is a quality of total conviction about the powerful free massing

109

of the hospital that left no doubt about the arrival of a major new talent [128]. Holden's taste for chunky massiveness can be seen in a series of bold Neo-Mannerist office buildings in London which will be described in chapter thirteen. Of Holden's more obviously free architecture, the next building was the King Edward VII Sanatorium near Midhurst in Sussex (1903–06).

Holden's sanatorium is the culminating masterpiece of that particular branch of the Edwardian Free Style which adapted vernacular domestic forms to larger buildings [129]. The plan is centred on a large **H** of three-storey main buildings, spreading long, low wings out into the surrounding gardens. Apart from occasional stone chequering, the walls pick up the local Sussex style of brick and hung tiles, using a mixture of red and grey bricks to avoid the 'glaring red so usual in new work'.[9] But the vigorous originality of the compositions which Holden created from such a vernacular starting-point are startlingly strong without becoming overpowering. The chapel is a small *tour de force*: an **L**-plan, with the altar at the angle under a stumpy tower, and each arm a nave (for men and women respectively, as required by the clients). Both naves had open arcades on one side; the architect explained that it was part of his brief to allow the circulation of fresh air to avoid tubercular infection! The whole complex is a highly successful piece of free design that surely impressed the older Arts and Crafts architects such as Lethaby and Prior, though Holden did not have their idealistic extremism. For example, Prior would have used only local building materials whereas Holden used brick from Bracknell in Berkshire and from Luton in Bedfordshire for this building in Sussex.

Next, in 1905, Holden won the competition for the Central Reference Library in a key position beside the Cathedral in Bristol. This design was to have a great influence on work by other architects (including perhaps the Voysey library design already mentioned, which was done a few months after Holden's designs were published). The road frontage is long and typical of Holden in its bold chunky forms, while the grid windows separated by heavy buttresses piling up towards the roofline express Holden's

128 *Belgrave Hospital for Children, Clapham Road, Kennington Oval, London (1900–03), by Charles Holden when aged twenty-five (as chief assistant to H. Percy Adams). Entrance front. Holden's powerful early designs show his admiration for Henry Wilson and traces of his year working for C. R. Ashbee.*

129 Detail, King Edward VII Sanatorium, Easebourne Hill, near Midhurst, Sussex (1903–06), by Holden. The architect's favourite piling up of strong masses was carried out, in this case, in warm domestic building materials.

130 Bristol Central Library, Deanery Road, Bristol (1905–07), by Holden. Garden frontage. The architect-historian Goodhart-Rendel described Holden as 'the man who had greatest influence over all of us'. This building certainly contributed to Mackintosh's library at the Glasgow School of Art and to designs by others, including Voysey and Edgar Wood.

usual feeling for solid masses. The frontage on the other side of the building is even more remarkable, with soaring buttresses and piers emphasizing its verticality, and the one great curve of the staircase echoed by three blank arches in the middle section [130]. The planning of the building is relatively straightforward with book stacks on the ground floor, offices, and a high reading-room with freely Classical detailing under a daylit tunnel vault. Of the interiors, the green and blue tiled entrance hall is the most striking. The intense, bold quality of the exterior is lastingly

131 Royal Infirmary buildings, Marlborough Hill, Bristol (c. 1906–12), by Holden. The sparse Classical details are incidental to the strong freedom of the overall design.

III

impressive,[10] though it contains the seeds of Holden's life-long resistance to the functionalist expression of new building techniques.

Perhaps Holden's best London building is Rhodesia House at No. 429 Strand, built as the offices of the British Medical Association in 1907–08 [228]. Here Holden's favourite quasi-Classical buttresses pile up in tier upon tier, punctuated by the weather-worn sculpture by Epstein that shocked contemporary taste when it was unveiled. In Bristol again, Holden's dramatic designs of c. 1906 for the Bristol Royal Infirmary were built and completed in June 1912, but are now difficult to appreciate because of a series of additions by later architects [131]. Once more, the simplified masses are relieved by a few Classical details, but the design as a whole has no connection with any historical or contemporary form of Classicism.

What were the origins of Holden's powerful development of the Free Style? The influence of Philip Webb and Lethaby has already been mentioned and from the evidence of Holden's earliest designs it is hard to doubt that a major factor was his own personal aesthetic sense. In a later article[11] the distinguished architect-teacher Sir Charles Reilly told of a gadget which Holden used to design the volumes of his buildings; this consisted of thick bundles of rods, each rod square in section, strapped together so that Holden could draw groups of rods up to different heights to obtain the precise variation he wanted of the piled-up three dimensional compositions so typical of his work. Such a method was well suited to the chunky effect he clearly liked.

But there were other influences at play from England, from Europe and from North America. Perhaps the most obvious of these is the four-squareness of the designs from this period by Ernest Gimson, who was both an architect and the finest of the English Arts and Crafts furniture designers. Gimson's furniture never lost its strong use of solids even when his followers of the 1890s surrendered to Georgian good taste and revivalism in the next decade. And in contrast to the flowing plans and forms of his early architectural work, his occasional later houses are austere to the point of severity in their plain, solid shapes.

Even more important in Holden's work was the feeling for monumental scale shown in the 1890s building of Henry Wilson, who, Holden said, was the chief conscious influence on him at the time.[12] In North America, the sheer solid volumes of buildings such as Louis Sullivan's Wainwright Building in St Louis (1890) and Guaranty Building in Buffalo (1895) must have impressed Holden, although he preferred to break up their monolithic forms into powerful piled-up masses.

Holden's most obvious precedent for such compositions was the famous Secession exhibition hall for the group of anti-academic artists in Vienna, built in 1898 by the architect Joseph Olbrich. The hemispherical dome of the Secession building was made up of a mass of Art Nouveau metal foliage, but its overall form is geometrical and the chunky Stripped-Classical shapes which build up to the dome are close to Holden in feeling. This new affinity for cuboid masses can be seen in other countries at around the same time, for instance in Frank Lloyd Wright's Larkin Building at Buffalo (1904) and Unity Temple at Oak Park, Illinois (1906), and even in the tower of Josef Hoffman's Palais Stoclet in Brussels (1905). And as in some of Holden's buildings, these architects played irreverently with Classical details in their free approach to design.

If, as seems possible, the work of Charles Rennie Mackintosh had any influence on this manner in general and on Holden in particular, it must have been via Vienna. For Mackintosh's only showing to the progressive English architects (at the Arts and Crafts Exhibition in 1896) was dismissed by them as decorative Art Nouveau; on the other hand his complete room exhibited at the 1899 Secessionist Exhibition in Vienna was a triumph and his work remained influential in Austria.

To return to England and the Edwardian Free Style, one major building of the time shows something of Holden's concern with large, simple, but broken masses. This was the University College of North Wales at Bangor, designed in 1905–06 by Henry Hare and opened in July 1911 [*132*]. As in all Hare's buildings (and many by Holden), historicist detail was used for decoration, in contrast to the freedom of the general massing.

Other architects were groping for a way to express a brick cladding on the new and economical steel frames for large buildings. An early example is Beresford Pite's Ames House of 1904, a low-budget hostel for the Young Women's Christian Association in Mortimer Street, London. Pite relieved the plainness of the structure by vertical projecting accents, and by patterns and overlapping layers of the brick surface. The same play with layers of brickwork under blank arches can be seen on the elevations of Pite's All Souls' School in Foley Street (1906–08), not far from Ames House, in St Marylebone. The layering of the brick surfaces may also be seen in much work of the time by the L.C.C. Architect's Department, and in the contemporary big housing schemes and the immense Hostels for Single Working Men, such as Bruce House, of 1907, in Drury Lane, Covent Garden. But here there is further variety added in the areas of white plaster on ground and top floors, once again following the tradition

132 *University College of North Wales, Bangor (1905–11), by Henry Hare. The architect stripped away most of his usual historical detailing in these splendid buildings.*

set by Smith and Brewer's Mary Ward House of 1895, described in chapter three.

Another interesting L.C.C. Architect's Department building of the time, but more of a showpiece, is the Central School of Arts and Crafts, built in Southampton Row, Holborn, in 1907–09. Lethaby was the Principal of the Central School and himself prepared the specification for its new building. But the design was chiefly the work of one of the L.C.C.'s bright young men, A. Halcrow Verstage. It was decided that the importance of the School merited stone elevations, and in these Verstage can be seen feeling his way towards a new expression of the building's structure. Round and segmental arches echo each other across the frontage, deeply cut on the ground floor and at the corner, in shallow relief across the rest of the façades. Here and there are strange details and decorative features redolent of Lethaby's symbolism: the egg symbol of creation, squares, and circles within squares. It is a fascinating design, but its restlessness prevents it from amounting to a really satisfying whole.

A similar restless exploration can be seen in the stone frontages of Beresford Pite's extraordinary scherzo in the Neo-Greek style in Euston Square, London: the London, Edinburgh and Glasgow Assurance Company's building of 1907 and 1912. In contrast, the Free Style of the Middlesex Guildhall of 1906–13 by James Gibson in Parliament Square, Westminster, is a brilliant fantasia of free Gothic striving to blend with the neighbouring Abbey and Parliament; nothing like as experimental as the two buildings just described, but a far more assured and convincing performance.

Edwardian progress towards a rational style for the new structural techniques of steel and reinforced concrete will be traced in chapter nine. But for those writing at the time, the idea of expressing the structure of a building in the architecture of its exterior was by no means the chief reason for seeking a new architectural style. In 1907 the New Year editorial of the magazine *The British Architect* commented, 'we are in a state of unrest and transition such as is surely inevitable after the long sleep of copyism', and went on to mourn the current fashion for the Georgian style as another delay in finding 'something which may express a little better our more genuine national characteristics'.[13] This was fair enough comment for such English work, Holden apart, but in Scotland impressive things were happening.

Four Scottish architects of great talent produced their finest Free Style works in Glasgow between 1902 and 1910. John A. Campbell (formerly John Burnet's partner) followed his original and romantic office block at No. 157 Hope Street (1902) with the more severe Northern Insurance building in St Vincent Street (1908–09), whose unexpectedly rationalist rear elevation will be described in chapter nine [*164*].

Burnet himself produced a number of buildings in Glasgow at the turn of the century which were close to the High Edwardian Baroque current in England. It was not until several years after his 1896 visit to America (where he visited his friend McKim and conceivably Louis Sullivan in Chicago) that he began to experiment with the new structural techniques for large buildings. Burnet's Civil Service and Professional Supply building in George Street, Edinburgh (1903–07), with its eccentric composition of Classical features,

133 McGeoch's store, No. 28 West Campbell Street, Glasgow (1905–10), by John Burnet. Demolished 1971. One of the greatest achievements of Edwardian architecture. The originality and strength of the design make the decoration almost irrelevant.

is a most curious first fruit of this development, while R. W. Forsyth's department store in nearby Prince's Street (1906–10) is splendidly strong, if still thickly enriched with Classical detailing.

Burnet's finest building of this period was in Glasgow: McGeoch's huge iron-mongery store at No. 28 West Campbell Street (1905–10, demolished 1971) [*133*]. McGeoch's was built with loadbearing walls that encased a framework of iron columns and steel joists, with reinforced concrete floors. Again, there was some Classical detailing on the exterior, but this was insignificant compared to the free expression of soaring, massive power in the frontages. McGeoch's store was an architectural masterpiece of its period, a totally convincing attempt by Burnet to express the structure of a building in an exterior which reflected pride in the building's commercial function.

Even more original and inspired were Charles Rennie Mackintosh's two large buildings of this decade. The first was Scotland Street School in Kingston, Glasgow (1904–06), another case of a building where Mackintosh turned his low-cost budget into a design virtue [*134*]. The building is of reddish Dumfriesshire stone and is carefully planned to the scale of the children who still use it. It has a strong rectangular form relieved by the marvellous curtains of glass in the round staircase towers and by the cascade of horizontal windows beside the towers. It was an influential design on Scottish schools built during the following decade.[14]

Mackintosh's second and greatest build-ing must be considered in conjunction with the work of the fourth Glasgow architect who reached his peak during these years. This was the younger James Salmon, in partnership with John Gaff Gillespie. Salmon's finest building, Lion Chambers in

134 Detail, Scotland Street School, Kingston, Glasgow (1904–06), by Charles Rennie Mackintosh. Inventive and humane in scale, the school is a good example of Mackintosh's talent for design on a low budget.

Hope Street, Glasgow (1905–06), is comparable with Mackintosh's con-temporary designs in its vertical emphasis and in its individuality [*156*]. Despite the obvious similarities between these works, it is impossible to gauge the extent to which either designer may have influenced the other, though the two men are known to have been friends. Salmon's Lion Cham-

135 *Library wing (1905–09), Glasgow School of Art, Renfrew Street, Glasgow, by Mackintosh. The outcome of many revisions to the original design, the building transcends most work of the period.*

McGeoch building, Holden's Central Reference Library and with Mackintosh's last important building to make 1905 a year of notable advances in free design.

For it was also in 1905 that Mackintosh started to revise his original design for the library wing that would complete his Glasgow School of Art, planned nine years earlier. The revision went through several stages and the building was done in 1907–09. It is Mackintosh's masterpiece and the supreme work of the Free Style in Britain.

The dimensions of the interior of the library itself followed the original plans of a decade before. But now Mackintosh developed that interior into a small functional library of timber construction that is at the same time a breathtaking experience in abstract spatial design – boldly imaginative and harmoniously complex [136]. The rest of the new wing was redesigned, too, with extra stairs, more studios at the top and other additions that entailed quite different elevations. This exterior of 1905–09, with its great vertical sheets of glass and the contrast of window patterns with bold plain wall surfaces, has a soaring quality of remarkable originality and beauty [135]. The influence on Mackintosh of Holden's 1905 design for the rear elevations of Bristol Central Library is clearly to be seen – Mackintosh never ceased to move forward, using ideas from other architects when they seemed of value and importance to him – but the library wing of the Glasgow School of Art transcends such other sources of inspiration and must be rated a work of architecture on the highest plane.

bers is an office building for lawyers, with richly varied elevations consisting of a skin of glass and roughcast concrete hung on a steel framework around twenty-one slender, tapering columns. In 1908 Salmon recommended this type of exterior as combining a functional use of building techniques with a style which still retained a visual link with old Scottish castles.[15] Lion Chambers is a major achievement of the Free Style, ranking with Burnet's

136 *Interior of library (1905–09), Glasgow School of Art, by Mackintosh. The finest interior of all the great Scottish architect's work.*

8
The Edwardian Arts and Crafts Churches

THE PREVIOUS chapters have described the development of Edwardian Free Style design in non-domestic secular buildings. But perhaps the most intense architectural achievements of the beginning of the century in England were the churches built by the Arts and Crafts architects. Most of them are small and far from the major cities, so they are comparatively little known.

The Arts and Crafts church tradition stems from the work of the group around Norman Shaw and from that of John Sedding in the 1880s, outlined in chapter five. Sedding's ideas were developed by some younger architects, notably by Edward Prior in his marvellous little church of 1887 at Bothenhampton in Dorset and in the churches built by Sedding's own pupil, Henry Wilson, in the following decade. These buildings were designed in a manner that suggested a new style which retained Gothic roots.

Of Sedding's importance, Henry Wilson wrote in 1898: 'It is not what he accomplished that we must admire, but the triumphs he suggested . . . because he was so full of unused activities, his influence was so dynamic, his personality affected so many.'[1] The direct Sedding message was mostly concerned with the need for harmonious team-work of highly accomplished artists and craftsmen, including the architect, rather than with architectural forms or structure.

Some of the 'triumphs he suggested' were realized by Wilson – who inherited

the Sedding practice, but soon let it shrink – in his church designs of the 1890s, reinforced by his own wayward genius and by the ideas of Lethaby. Apart from the churches mentioned in chapter three, Wilson's St Mark's Church at Brithdir in Merionethshire (1895–97) and Lethaby's haunting little chapel for Melsetter House on Hoy island in the Orkneys (1898–1902) should be noted.

Lethaby's own last and greatest building was the first of a series of Edwardian Arts and Crafts churches. This is the church of All Saints, deep in the Herefordshire countryside at Brockhampton, near Ross-on-Wye [138]. It was commissioned about 1900 by Alice Foster, an American lady who owned a big house nearby, in memory of her parents and it was built in 1901–02. Lethaby did not use a contractor, but hired the craftsmen and labourers himself.

Brockhampton church has an extraordinary atmosphere of almost primeval sacredness about it, more reminiscent of Glastonbury or Avebury's prehistoric earthworks than of a purely Christian place of worship. The site is rich in trees and the building itself is an endlessly subtle mixture of high craftsmanship, structural innovation and Lethaby's own symbolic forms. The plan is a simple chancel and nave, separated by a square under the

137 Interior with font, All Saints', Brockhampton (1901–02), by William Lethaby, showing the contrasts of texture in stonework and carving.

138 *All Saints' Church, Brockhampton, near Ross-on-Wye, Herefordshire (1901–02), by William Lethaby. A work of complex symbolism of form and decoration, employing experimental concrete vaulting under the local vernacular thatched roof.*

139 *Interior, All Saints', Brockhampton (1901–02), by Lethaby. Above the stone arches, the roof is vaulted in mass concrete. Lethaby's 'tree of light' chandelier at the crossing has been replaced.*

tower, with brief transepts. True to Arts and Crafts principles of originality growing from local building tradition, the design has clear roots in the typical thatched Herefordshire medieval church. Much of the masonry is intentionally rough-textured, but with details of the most exquisite design and craftsmanship [137]. Under the thatch, which provides efficient insulation, the roof and wall structure is of mass concrete vaulting with stone arches springing from low walls; a pioneering use of concrete that produces a unique interior [139]. But there are deeper secrets hidden in the building that come from the ancient and universal architectural symbolism which Lethaby had retold in his 1891 book *Architecture, Mysticism and Myth*.[2]

It has been seen in chapter three how in this book Lethaby had demonstrated the sacred significance of shapes such as the cube and the pyramid found in holy buildings of most cultures – ancient and more modern,

Oriental and European. The cube and the pyramid both appear in the bell-tower entrance to Brockhampton church in the form of a tiled pyramid over a wooden bell-stage cube, over a stone entrance-porch cube. The crossing tower formed another cube above the arch springs in the original drawings, but Lethaby's assistant architect, Randall Wells (who worked full time on site between Lethaby's own visits), altered the proportions for structural reasons during the building. Godfrey Rubens, the biographer of Lethaby, has pointed out that many of the window shapes and tracery in the church are developed from old astrological patterns which 'represent the microcosmos and are similar to the Buddhist "world pattern" '. At the east end the windows make use of more specifically Christian symbolism, including the triple lancet of the Trinity and the star which has sometimes been used as the symbol of Christ and birth.[3] Numerous other symbols are blended into the design.

While working as Lethaby's assistant, Randall Wells was commissioned to design and build another church at Kempley in north-west Gloucestershire, a few miles away from Brockhampton [*140*]. Wells's design is not charged with Lethaby's mysterious symbolism, but it is a mainstream Arts and Crafts work. The motif of the exterior lies in the particular acute angles of the roofs and gables above the nave, the parallel but lower vestry and office range and the tower. These sharply angled solids play with each other as abstract forms and the same angle is echoed in the diagonal grid of the large west window, in the arches of the other pointed windows and in the interior of the church. Here the walls are so low that one seems to be inside a room of a completely triangular section, crossed by great decorated beams. Randall Wells was as purist as Prior in his

140 Church of St Edward the Confessor, Kempley, north-west Gloucestershire (*1903*), by Randall Wells. The architect, a disciple of Lethaby and his assistant at Brockhampton, made the play with angles the overall theme of this design.

141 Competition design of *1903* for Liverpool Anglican Cathedral, by William Lethaby, Henry Wilson and others. Not built. A highly original free development from Byzantine sources by an Arts and Crafts movement design group. The experimental concrete vaulting is as inventive as the detailing and the monumental tower.

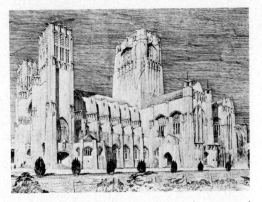

142 Competition design of 1903 for Liverpool Anglican Cathedral, by Charles Rennie Mackintosh. Not built. A soaring essay in a free version of the Gothic style.

selection of materials, using Forest of Dean stone and local timber. He employed only local labour and, although the furnishings were by Ernest Gimson and the lectern by Ernest Barnsley (both leading Arts and Crafts designers), the metalwork was by the Kempley blacksmith and the external sculpture was carved by the village carpenter from a design by Wells.

Kempley church was built in 1903 and in the same year two extraordinary Arts and Crafts Free Style designs were entered for the Liverpool Cathedral competition. Neither was premiated. One of these was by two of the foremost figures of the Arts and Crafts movement, Henry Wilson and Lethaby himself, leading a design group that also included R. Weir Schultz, Stirling Lee and F. W. Troup [141]. This was one of the most astonishingly novel designs to come from the Arts and Crafts movement, heavy with Lethaby's symbols and pioneering an undulating concrete vaulted roof over walls whose window tracery was of extreme originality. High over the

cathedral itself, the design shows a great sloping tower with all of Henry Wilson's feeling for splendour of scale.

Another notable but unpremiated entry for the competition was by Charles Rennie Mackintosh, full of soaring inspiration, though closer to the traditional Gothic than Lethaby and Wilson's design [142]. Mackintosh built only one church, at Queen's Cross in Glasgow (1897–99). The church is a personal development from Wilson's work of the early 1890s with an interior that contains some fine furnishings but is a rather disappointing space in general. The sheer inventiveness of the outside, however, is worthy of the Scottish master.

At the time of the Liverpool Cathedral competition, Charles Harrison Townsend was building the finest of his Arts and Crafts churches. This is the church of St Mary the Virgin, down the hill from the village of Great Warley in Essex. It was built in 1902–04 and, like Lethaby's church, was a memorial. The church is small and both plan and exterior are fairly simple. The plan involves a nave and an open-screened side chapel that adds spatial complexity to the interior. The outside is of a Voysey-like roughcast, with favourite Townsend motifs such as the long sweeping eaves, buttresses and a horizontal row of small rectangular windows. But inside is one of the most intensive examples of an Arts and Crafts decorated interior [143]. The simple pointed barrel roof is punctuated by silvery arches of dense floral decoration. Everywhere there is a glimmer of inset mother-of-pearl. A silvered relief of vines, with heavy bunches of grapes, spreads over the surface of the apse. Richest of all, the screens between nave and chapel as well as nave and chancel consist of rows of trees of bronze, pewter and walnut, bearing flowers and fruits and angels among their intricate foliage. The metalwork was by Sir William

Reynolds-Stephens, though the motifs in the design are so typical of earlier decorative work by Townsend that the two men must surely have worked on the initial designs together.

Yet another offshoot of Arts and Crafts originality, this time in the north of England, is to be seen at Edgar Wood's Christian Science Church in Daisy Bank Road, Victoria Park, in the southern suburbs of Manchester (1903–08). The plan is a basilica, with two arms at one end (containing halls and offices) placed at a diagonal angle to make up a **Y**. The entrance front composition of high gable windows in the form of a crucifix, round arch and overlapping turret has a fresh manner matched by the designs for the interior [*144*].[4] The problems Wood met in

144 *Christian Science Church, Daisy Bank Road, Victoria Park, south Manchester (1903–08), by Edgar Wood. Entrance front. In building this individualistic Arts and Crafts church, Wood saw the restrictions which traditional structure imposes on free design and decided to develop the use of concrete.*

143 *Interior, St Mary the Virgin, near Great Warley, Essex (1902–04), by Charles Harrison Townsend. The marvellous screens and other metalwork were executed by William Reynolds-Stephens.*

building these new forms by traditional structural methods led him to his later experiments with concrete.

The next of the Edwardian Arts and Crafts churches is further north still. It is one of Edward Prior's most brilliant buildings and must rank with Brockhampton church as the highest achievement of the movement in ecclesiastical architecture. This is the large St Andrew's Church at Roker, a suburb of Sunderland in County Durham [*145*]. It was built in 1904–07. The brief was that the church should seat 700 people and that its tower should be a coastal landmark for ships. Prior's response was a

145 *Tower and east end, St Andrew's Church, Roker, near Sunderland, County Durham (1904–07), by Edward Prior. Prior's supreme achievement in church architecture.*

147 *St Jude's Church, Hampstead Garden Suburb, London (1909–13), by Edwin Lutyens. The design integrates detailing of various styles into a vigorous overall composition.*

146 *Interior, St Andrew's Church, Roker (1904–07), by Prior. Prior used great stone ribs which bring the masonry of the outside walls directly into the interior.*

massive castle-like form whose interior is formed by tremendous rib arches, carried through from the external walls built of Durham stone [146]. It is a splendid space of moving, austere grandeur and there is an impression that the roof overhead is the ribbed inside of a ship's hull – symbolic of the church's position near the sea, though perhaps unintentionally so. The furnishings, especially the organ-case, are among Ernest Gimson's finest grid woodwork designs.

Prior's success as a designer-architect is an example of the conflict between theory and practice frequently found in Arts and Crafts architects, as well as in the whole movement committed to individual craftsmanship in an age of machine production. Thus in 1901 Prior wrote, 'The function of the designing architect is passing – has passed away', and in 1905 he exhorted Birmingham students to pioneer a revolutionary approach in their proposed cathedral. 'If built by them as architect-masons and architect-carpenters, if sculptured by them as craft sculptors, if decorated by them as craft painters, smiths, glaziers and tilemakers – the cathedral would be, as were the ancient cathedrals, a growth from the art life of today.'[5] Yet it would have to be a rare group of designer-craftsmen who could produce anything of the organic vigour of Prior's own best buildings.

A map of the Arts and Crafts churches would show them widely spread over most of Britain, from Lethaby's chapel in the Orkney Islands, to Sedding's and Wilson's churches in Cornwall and Wales, and to Townsend's in Essex and Surrey. Some of the finest examples are in northern England, designed by Wood and Prior, and the Midlands produced its own Arts and Crafts churches in Birmingham. The most notable of the Birmingham church architects was W. H. Bidlake, whose earlier work has already been mentioned. In the Edwardian period he built Bishop Latimer Church at Handsworth, a Birmingham suburb, in 1904.

London, the capital, has far less to show. The most original church of the decade is St Jude's in Hampstead Garden Suburb, designed in 1909 by Edwin Lutyens (the chief architect of the suburb's public buildings) [147]. Lutyens had been a true and distinguished member of the Arts and Crafts movement during the 1890s, but by this time he had cast aside its ideals. St Jude's is a tremendous design with roofs that sweep low, a powerful tower and spire, and a fine interior. But no Arts and Crafts

148 Interior, St Peter's Roman Catholic Church, Falcon Avenue, Edinburgh (1906–07), by Robert Lorimer. Like Lutyens, Lorimer turned from Arts and Crafts domestic architecture to an inventiveness of his own (as seen in this church) in styles ranging from the Classical to Scottish Baronial.

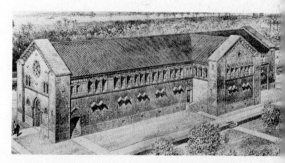

149 All Saints' Cathedral, Khartoum, Sudan (designed 1909), by R. Weir Schultz. The architect was an ardent Arts and Crafts practitioner, close to Lethaby.

150 *St Osmund's Church, Parkstone, Poole,
Dorset (1913–16), by Edward Prior. Entrance front.
The design used a free Byzantine style, for Prior's
work was added to a chancel already built in that
manner in 1904–05 by another architect. The striking
west frontage mixes red, yellow and brown bricks,
handmade locally. In this, his last important building,
Prior's usual strong originality can be seen.*

151 *First design of 1913 for Namirembe Anglican
Cathedral, Kampala, Uganda, by Beresford Pite.
The cathedral was completed with slight alterations in
1918, but the tall tower was never built.*

principles are involved and the composition is an inspired combination of
different historical styles. It is equally
difficult to categorize another brilliant
church by a former follower of the Arts and
Crafts movement: St Peter's Roman
Catholic Church, Falcon Avenue, Edinburgh (1906–07), by Robert Lorimer [148].
The design, especially the high white arches
of the interior, have few historical references. Yet the use of the term 'Arts and
Crafts' seems inappropriate.

The Arts and Crafts architects had no
opportunity to build a cathedral in Britain,
but they did gain commissions for two
cathedrals abroad. In 1909 Robert Weir
Schultz, one of the Lethaby and Wilson
design group for the Liverpool Cathedral
competition, was commissioned to build
the cathedral for Khartoum in the Sudan.
Weir Schultz produced a low and massive
design of thick masonry to overcome the
heat, with open arcades of small sharp-
pointed windows high in the walls [149].

Then Beresford Pite did a highly
ambitious and original design for the
Namirembe Anglican Cathedral in Kampala, Uganda [151]. Pite's scheme was for a
long narrow cathedral with triple transepts
and with domes at the crossings and on the
complex western tower. It was built in a
reduced and modified form in 1913–18.
Pite dealt with the problem of heat by using
small windows in large recessed blank
arcades with pointed tops. Higher up, these
change to round arches to blend better with
the brightly tiled dome. The western tower
was never built.

The hints of Byzantine style in the
Kampala cathedral design were far more
strongly expressed in Edward Prior's last
major work, St Osmund's Church at
Parkstone in Poole, Dorset. The first stage
of this work had been built, in 1904–05, by
another architect in a cool version of the

fashionable Byzantine style. But most of the church is by Prior, built in 1913–16. He followed the general style but developed it, and the western frontage is his final blazing *tour de force* of church architecture [150]. A bold shallow arch, typical of the architect, cuts over the door between the two multi-shafted towers. Above the arch and a balustrade, Prior has placed a glorious wheel window. The façade is topped by a gable above a blank arcade whose deep voids are echoed in those of the strong Byzantine cupolas on each tower. The wheel window is an inspired touch, but above all it is the organic texture and smouldering mixed colours of the brick-work that give the frontage its special fascination.

Henry Wilson worked for Prior on some of the fittings for St Osmund's, as was common practice among the architects of the Art Workers' Guild. Lethaby, Prior, Wilson, Ricardo and Gimson were a

particularly close inner group who often sub-commissioned furnishings or decoration from each other when given charge of a building project.

Wilson did hardly any buildings after the end of the nineteenth century, though his interiors for St Bartholomew's, Brighton, were partly executed after 1900 (see chapter five). After a period as editor of *The Architectural Review* from 1896 until 1901, he turned more and more to metalwork, his other great love, and to teaching. His last great work, however, must conclude this chapter. For although the splendid bronze Elphinstone Tomb in King's College at the University of Aberdeen is a sculptured monument, rather than a building, it shows much of Wilson's architectural sense of scale [152]. Wilson received the commission in 1912 and worked on it for two years. In 1914 he went to Venice to do the bronze casting, but the First World War overtook his work and the great pieces of bronze had to be hidden. The monument finally reached Aberdeen thirteen years after it had been commissioned and was erected in 1926.

152 The Elphinstone Tomb, King's College, University of Aberdeen (designed 1912–14, completed 1926), by Henry Wilson.

9
Towards Rationalism – Offices and Factories

By THE END of the Edwardian period, most of the images now associated with Edward VII's reign were out of date. The elaborate, gorgeous clothes, the sunny country house-parties and the sheer prosperity of the rich in the first years of the century have left a nostalgia for a serene golden age. But for the Edwardian working classes life was far from a golden age and they were no longer ready to accept their poverty. When the King died in 1910 the Parliament Act introduced by Asquith, the Liberal Prime Minister, was in the middle of its stormy passage – it was passed in the end, depriving the House of Lords of the right to veto government bills. Then Lloyd George's momentous National Insurance Act started the slow progress towards a social security and pensions system to prevent abject poverty. The great coal-miners' strike of 1911 showed that the Syndicalist theories of direct action on pay disputes could secure social change. So progress towards political power for the working classes was beginning. On the other hand, the Kaiser's belligerent visit to London in the same year of 1911 foreshadowed the millions of deaths in the great war that started three years later.

Social changes also had a direct bearing on architecture and building. New ideas for housing and schools began to spread. It was in 1910 that the women's suffrage movement adopted a policy of violent demonstrations in favour of women's right to the vote. It is notable that no woman architect has been mentioned in this book

dealing with a period of British architecture which reached well into the twentieth century. There had been a move to admit women to the Architectural Association as early as 1893, but it was rejected by 78 votes to 37 at a special general meeting.[1] Things changed gradually and by 1908 the Arts and Crafts architect R. Weir Schultz could tell a Caxton Hall conference on 'Employment for Women' that 'Recently two women who were articled to an eminent architect went in for and passed the very stiff examination of the RIBA and were admitted members of that body. One of these ladies carried off in 1905, from among 14 competitors, the silver medal of the Institute.'[2] He went on to say that the Architectural Association still did not admit women architectural students, but that the Royal College of Art, King's College and University College in London did so.

Progress towards 'rationalism' in architecture – which architectural historians have traditionally defined as the expression of a modern steel or concrete structure on the exterior of a building, rather than hiding the structure under Classical detailing – was, however, slow. As early as

153 Sanderson Wallpaper Factory (now Alliance Assurance offices), Barley Mow Passage, beside Turnham Green, Chiswick, London (1902–03), by C. F. A. Voysey. An exceptional achievement, combining rationalism with much delicate charm.

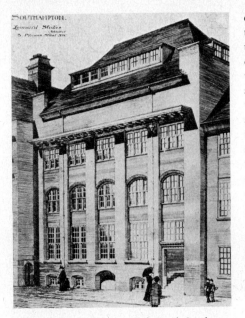

154 *Telephone Exchange, Ogle Road, Southampton (1900), by Leonard Stokes. Everything above the second floor windows has now been rebuilt. In Stokes's building Classical features almost disappeared in an elevation which expressed structure and, to some degree, function.*

express steel or concrete structures felt that their training was quite inadequate for the task. Thus Lethaby gave up architectural design after his experiments with concrete vault structure between 1900 and 1903. 'It is absurd', he wrote in 1912, '. . . that the writer [Lethaby himself] should have been allowed to study cathedrals from Kirkwall to Rome and from Quimper to Constantinople; it would be far better to have the equivalent knowledge of steel and concrete construction.'[5] Yet Lethaby's own sole design for an office building, the Eagle Insurance in Birmingham (1899–1900), used grid windows that showed the way for the future as well as conveying the architect's symbolist ideas [49]. And it was other Arts and Crafts architects who made most of the moves towards rational expression that followed.

1901, *The British Architect* magazine noted 'important new developments in construction and materials during the latter part of the century. . . . Architects have now a practically unlimited range of materials to choose from . . .'[3] Yet in 1907 a young architect claimed that much of the profession 'exhibits absolute unpreparedness for anything in the nature of change. We ought to study the influence of iron just as we study the influence of Garden Cities. It is an economical force in the country . . .'[4]

One of the problems was that many of the thoughtful architects who would have been likely to devise an architecture to

155 *Design of 1900 for a printing works, Cornwall Street, Birmingham, by Bateman and Bateman. Probably not built. The designers, a Birmingham firm, were admirers of Lethaby.*

130

Three notable designs in this respect date from 1900.[6] Leonard Stokes's Southampton Telephone Exchange creates a grid around high brick piers that run up three storeys, the severity broken by one level of round-topped windows and a decorated cornice [154]. Brewill and Bailey's design for the Ram Hotel in Nottingham is a four-storey grid with flat projecting windows, though it is dressed up with much Jacobean detail and a broad gable above. More remarkable is the Jones and Son printing works by the progressive Birmingham architects, Bateman and Bateman [155]. This design was exhibited at the Royal Academy in 1900, but it was an exception to the general standard which drew an editorial (presumably by Henry Wilson) complaining that 'The flavour is mostly that of the past . . . When are we to have the really fine public building of straightforward and dignified composition, built structurally with honest materials . . . ?'[7]

The next English exercise in rationalism came from an unexpected designer, Voysey. The Sanderson Wallpaper Factory was built in 1902–03 in Barley Mow Passage, off Turnham Green in Chiswick, a western suburb of London [153]. It is very little known, though it is perhaps Voysey's best building after 1900 and an extraordinary combination of structural expression with visual pleasure. The elegance of the high piers from which the structure is slung, the slightly wavy horizontals with which Voysey brings lightness to the structural grid and the sensitively functional use of the white glazed brickwork are quite exceptional. The factory is Voysey's only large non-domestic building and is fortunately well treated by the insurance company that now owns it.

Neither Voysey nor his many followers went further with the new style achieved in the Sanderson factory and it was some years

156 *Lion Chambers, Nos 170–172 Hope Street, Glasgow (1905–06), by James Salmon with John Gaff Gillespie. A skin of roughcast concrete panels and glass on a steel framework. Salmon advocated the use of these materials, with a few traditional Scottish features, as a style which integrated functionalism with vernacular tradition.*

before the next landmarks were reached. The grid structure of steel frame buildings was sometimes reflected in the newly rectangular designs of Edwardian Free Style architects. But the important difference is precisely that fine compositions such as Holden's library in Bristol (1905–07) and Mackintosh's library wing of the Glasgow School of Art (1905–09) use the grid pattern for reasons of style, rather

157 Rear elevation, Civil Service and Professional Supply building, George Street, Edinburgh (1903–07), by John Burnet. An early functional grid elevation.

frame of the building. And he added a few features that linked his work to traditional Scottish architecture. In its more complex way, Salmon's attempt to devise an architecture that would express a modern structure is as successful as Voysey's.

Burnet's Civil Service and Professional Supply building in Edinburgh dates from 1903–07 [157]. The striking rear elevation drawings are dated January 1904, very early for such unpretentious work. Nevertheless, the elevation is essentially back-street architecture; the front of the building is in Burnet's very personal free Baroque manner of the time.

There was no move in Britain to use and express metal in buildings with the sheer French gaiety of La Samaritaine department store in Paris (1906–07) [158]. Here the

158 La Samaritaine department store, rue de la Monnaie, Paris (1906–07), by Frantz Jourdain. French architects were quick to develop a decorative style, largely of metal, suited to steel frame buildings.

than as an expression of an internal frame. In fact, both these buildings are constructed basically of load-bearing stone.

Other buildings in Scotland, however, did express a steel frame structure on their elevations. Of these the most impressive is James Salmon's Lion Chambers in Hope Street, Glasgow (1905–06), already described in chapter seven [156]. Salmon set out intentionally to vary the relief and the window pattern of the thin rendered cement skin which he hung on the internal architect, Frantz Jourdain, used a steel frame ingeniously in plan, and expressed it outside by big plate windows between wildly decorated metal-covered uprights and horizontals. Contemporary British steel buildings were far more sober.

The use of steel frames spread rapidly in Britain during the first decade of the new century. The other new structural material, reinforced concrete, followed very shortly after. Again the Arts and Crafts architects were among the first to experiment with concrete as a building material, but without the steel reinforcement that could give it the necessary strength when used horizontally. Lethaby's vaulting at Brockhampton church (1901–02) and Prior's walls at Home Place (1903–05) were of mass concrete, unreinforced. Neither took their experiments any further except on the drawing-board.

By 1906 one English textbook on reinforced concrete was in its third edition.[8] The same year saw the first notable British architectural design that used and expressed the material. This was the Dronsfield Brothers office building in King Street, Oldham – an industrial town north-east of Manchester [159]. The architect was Henry Sellers (1861–1954) who had recently gone into partnership with Edgar Wood, the most important Arts and Crafts architect in northern England. The Dronsfield building (1906–07) is entirely roofed in reinforced concrete, a fact well expressed by the chunky flat-topped volumes. Sellers may have digested some influence of Holden[9] in these volumes and of Mackintosh in the front elevation, but the general architectural expression is very novel. The functional approach is maintained in the materials, too. Oldham had the heavy atmospheric pollution typical of industrial towns, and so the exterior is of largely self-washing materials. The main material is

159 *Dronsfield Brothers office building, King Street, Oldham, north-east of Manchester (1906–07), by J. Henry Sellers in partnership with Edgar Wood. The first building using the flat reinforced concrete roofs experimented with by this partnership.*

pale green glazed brickwork, with polished granite for the lower storey and the dressings. The green and grey colouring is a considerable surprise among the more usual neutrals of industrial Lancashire.

Edgar Wood's concrete roofed houses of 1907 and 1908 have already been mentioned in chapter six, but in 1908–10 Wood and Sellers together built their two largest works using the same technique. Elm Street School and Durnford Street School are both in Wood's home town of Middleton, on the north-eastern edge of Manchester. Both are very free and original designs, warm and friendly in scale and in the combination of brick and stone they employ [160]. In both, the reinforced concrete roofs are used to obtain maximum flexibility of planning. Again the influence of Holden can be seen in detailing such as the piled-up buttresses of the towers. Otherwise, it is only the round-topped windows of Elm Street that prevent the schools from being mistaken for much later buildings.

The Wood and Sellers buildings moved forward a long way in their use of reinforced concrete, but they still employed much load-bearing brick in their walls. In 1909 the magazine *The British Architect* organized a competition for a shop and office building whose frame was to be constructed entirely from ferro-concrete. Two of the entries are of particular interest for they seek an architectural expression suitable for a new type of structure.[10] The clearest articulation of the construction is in one of the two Voysey entries [162]. Above the shop, four vertical white bands dominate a simple grid rising three storeys. Three higher levels include flat cantilevered oriel windows, the sole projections from the plane surface of the front. Only at the very top did Voysey feel it necessary to escape from the grid pattern with a big curling gable.

The other particularly intriguing entry was by J. Gaff Gillespie, the partner of

161 *Competition design of 1909 for a shop and offices of ferro-concrete, by J. Gaff Gillespie (the partner of James Salmon). Not built. The forms and some of the decoration seem to look forward to the 1920s.*

162 *Competition design of 1909 for a shop and offices of ferro-concrete, by C. F. A. Voysey. Not built. The gable brings the only light relief to an imaginative but severely functional design.*

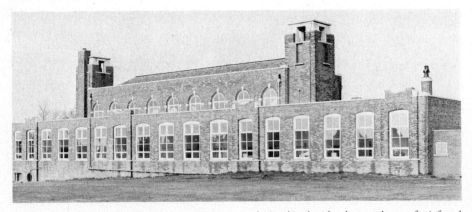

160 *Elm Street School, Elm Street, Middleton, north-east of Manchester (1908–10), by Edgar Wood and J. Henry Sellers. A sensitive feeling for* scale, combined with a large-scale use of reinforced concrete roofs. The detail of the towers is reminiscent of Holden.

*163 Factory for Birmingham Small Arms Ltd,
Armoury Road, Birmingham (1914). No architect.
Three parallel blocks, each 600 feet long and 60 feet
wide, designed and built by the Trussed Concrete
Steel Co. Ltd for the production of weapons for the
First World War.*

Glasgow's James Salmon [*161*]. Gillespie's design emphasized the solid volumes of the concrete, in contrast to Voysey's expression of a concrete grid frame. As far as decoration is concerned, Gillespie certainly escaped from Voysey's touches of Classical detail and his design seems a precursor of the Art Deco style of the 1920s.

These unexecuted concrete designs came as close to a concrete architecture as anything achieved in Britain before the 1914–18 war. The notable reinforced-concrete framed factory for the Birmingham Small Arms company, which was built in Armoury Road at Small Heath, Birmingham, in 1914, was designed by the Trussed Concrete Steel Co. Ltd and involved no architect [*163*]. In 1913 Lethaby made some prophetic comments about the material. 'It must be admitted that, notwithstanding its virtues, concrete has certain special defects. Such, for instance, are poor surface and colour, and the tendency to crack . . . It is a plastic material and is unfitted to take sharp edges and delicate forms . . . concrete structures call for quite a different type of design than ordinary works of stone and bricks. Big rounded forms seem suggested by this plastic material.'[11] In 1913 such thoughts must have been well beyond the vision of most of his listeners, though it is ironic to look at some 1890s rounded designs by Prior (for West Bay) and by Mackintosh (for the Glasgow Exhibition) and to consider how suitable reinforced concrete would have been for these unexecuted buildings [*52*, *53*].

The use of steel frame structures, however, did produce some major buildings before 1914 which clearly expressed their interior frame construction on their elevations. Continuing Salmon and Burnet's development of steel design in Scotland, John A. Campbell (Burnet's former partner) produced two important buildings in Glasgow shortly before his death in 1909. These were the Edinburgh Life Assurance at No. 124 St Vincent Street (1904–06), and the Northern Insurance at Nos 84–94 St Vincent Street (1908–09). Both have prestige main frontages (the

164 Rear elevation, Northern Insurance building, No. 84–94 St Vincent Street, Glasgow (1908–09), by John A. Campbell. The frontage is directly expressive of the steel frame structure.

136

Northern Insurance has three impressively towering vertical accents), built of load-bearing masonry above the ground floor. These main street elevations are free of historicism, but have no startling visual qualities. It is in the rear elevations that Campbell found an exciting expression of the steel frame. In the Northern Insurance building the surface is textured by a series of projecting vertical bays straight up to the topmost storey, which is a clean horizontal interrupted only by the bay containing lift and stairs [164]. The steel frame enabled the architect to use most of the surface for huge windows to give maximum daylight. The solid wall area is therefore almost linear and the whole frontage becomes a stimulating and complex pattern of rectangular glass spaces.

In London, too, some architects were taking experimental steps forward. By far the most important of these was the Kodak Building of 1910–11 in Kingsway, by J. J. Burnet [165–166]. Burnet had now opened a London office as well as his old Glasgow base, and the Kodak Building was designed in collaboration with his young London partner Thomas Tait. One building press comment of the time was that it was designed 'with the idea of making a structure suitable in every way for the purpose of a modern office and warehouse, without attempting to copy any style of architecture'.[12] The design has much of Burnet's typical chunky strength, but is stripped of almost all his usual remnant of Classical decoration. The stone of the bottom storeys and the high free cornice give the exterior solidity, but between these the clean strip piers, with dark metal window spandrels between, are a direct expression of the steel frame's simplicity. Some elements of the plan are perhaps influenced by Chicago architecture, particularly that of Sullivan and Burnham,

165 *Kodak Building, Kingsway, London (1910–11), by John Burnet. A famous steel frame building which achieves an impressive functional expression by stripping all decoration from the underlying Classical design, thus linking it with the Stripped Classicism of many later office blocks.*

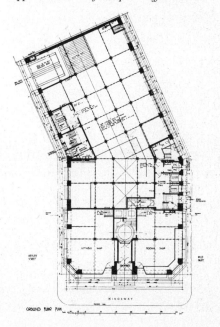

166 *Plan of first floor, Kodak Building (1910–11), by Burnet.*

137

167 Office building, Nos 34–36 Golden Square, Soho, London (1913–14), by Leonard Stokes. The architect developed his own expression of the steel frame structure, while retaining his favourite round arches and varied grid pattern above.

though there is no evidence of contact between them and Burnet. But for the most part the Kodak Building is a logical extension of earlier Burnet designs, with decorative elements eliminated. There is still a touch of the Classical temple about the overall composition and Kodak became a model for large numbers of British office buildings in the 1920s.

Other London architects – and their clients – did not yet feel able to settle for the sheer simplicity of Burnet's grid elevation. Three commercial buildings by architects who had been progressive leaders in the 1890s show the limits felt in expressing steel

frame structure. The office building for A. Gagnière and Co. (now Granada) at Nos 34–36 Golden Square, Soho, was done by Leonard Stokes in 1913–14 [167]. Stokes's large buildings had always employed a strong overall grid, usually combined with round arches on the ground floor. In the Gagnière building Stokes developed this combination boldly and successfully, using remotely Classical features only for surface texture on the stone frontage. During the same years, F. W. Troup built a notably simplified office block called Blackfriars House in New Bridge Street, London.

Dunbar Smith and Cecil Brewer had been through a long Classical phase for large buildings since their pioneering Free Style Mary Ward House of 1895–98. But in about 1914 the leading furniture manufacturer Ambrose Heal commissioned Smith and Brewer to build his firm's new furnishing department store in Tottenham Court Road [168]. The first part of the store was built in 1916, a steel frame structure expressed on the outside by a stone-clad grid. Above the recessed shop windows of the ground floor, three-storey piers frame the pattern in a complicated horizontal rhythm. The design lacks the logical severity of Burnet's Kodak Building, but shows integrity in its treatment of the front elevations to express the structure of the building as well as possessing a certain friendliness suitable for a retail shop. The building was extended, with considerable consistency of style, by Sir Edward Maufe in 1937.

The finest of all these rational buildings of the period was, however, built in Scotland by J. J. Burnet (who became Sir John Burnet in 1914). The Wallace Scott Tailoring Institute at Cathcart in Glasgow was built in 1913–16 for the same Forsyth family whose Edinburgh department store Burnet had already designed. The concept was one which William Forsyth had brought back from America: a garden factory providing facilities for workers' welfare and recreation, built in extensive landscaped grounds (the word Institute was used to emphasize this enlightened capitalism). The Wallace Scott Institute marked the culmination of Burnet's development towards a rational architecture [*169*].[13] The brick-covered steel frame was reflected by the monumental simplicity of the grid walls formed by piers and diapered brickwork spandrels. The power of the composition was increased by the strong corner towers terminating the long frontages. It is unforgivable that Burnet's two finest Free Style buildings, Glasgow's McGeoch's store and the Wallace Scott Institute, have both been destroyed – the first by demolition, the second by mutilating alterations.

After the Wallace Scott building there was a clear shift in the development of functional expression in architecture of any quality in Britain. In 1914–18 the First World War caused a heavy reduction in building work. Burnet – with Holden and Lutyens – later became one of the chief architects to the War Graves Commission. When design and construction work started again, Burnet did not return to the simplicity of expression of his pre-war period. Nor did Holden or Lutyens develop any interest in the expression of structure on the exterior of buildings. Holden's very individualistic free manner became a symbol of reaction after 1930 for progressive idealists influenced by the Bauhaus, while Lutyens's brilliant talents often made such a goal seem irrelevant. The rest of this book will describe the development of the Edwardian Baroque style and the other varieties of Classicism that dominated British architecture during the first quarter of the twentieth century.

168 *Heal's Furniture Store, Nos 196–199 Tottenham Court Road, London (1916, extension 1937), by Dunbar Smith and Cecil Brewer. The Classical roots of the elevation are barely apparent.*

169 *Wallace Scott Tailoring Institute, Cathcart, Glasgow (1913–16), by John Burnet. Now badly altered. A 'garden factory' in landscaped grounds, with much emphasis on workers' welfare. The imposing building was Burnet's last pre-war essay in the simplified yet monumental expression of structure.*

10
High Edwardian Baroque

EDWARDIAN CLASSICISM can be divided into at least two clear phases. Before 1906 it was dominated by bold Baroque forms largely developed from the vigorous British architecture of the early eighteenth century. After that, the influence of French architecture led to more chaste Classical designs, while the necessity of combining stone frontages with steel frame structures produced an intriguing Neo-Mannerism and other variations.

The year 1897 marked Queen Victoria's Diamond Jubilee. It was celebrated in Britain with rather less euphoria than had greeted her Golden Jubilee ten years earlier, but still seemed to crystallize a wide feeling that the nation was reaching a peak of imperial and commercial power. Although the Queen was to die only four years later, the reign of her son Edward VII appeared to extend Britain's heyday throughout the first decade of the new century. The war against the Boers in South Africa brought the country to a high pitch of patriotism and jingoism that increased demand for an outward expression of British might. In economic terms, however, the prosperity of Great Britain and her Empire started to ebb during the Edwardian period, as did the overwhelming privileges of the upper middle classes when confronted with the challenge of the growing trades union movement. But the start of such long-term shifts were not perceptible at the time. The moneyed public wanted to celebrate the aged Queen, the new King, the British

Empire. And it wanted an architectural style to commemorate this feeling of glory.

That style was ready to hand, ripe after the ten years of maturing outlined in chapter four. At the time it was known as English Renaissance (the word Baroque was used only as a pejorative until much later), but we know it today as High Edwardian Baroque. In 1897 a well-known architectural teacher, Professor F. M. Simpson, wrote: 'The movement towards a Classic revival has been steadily gaining ground for years. We see it in many of the public buildings erected lately and it is present in every competition. One of the best examples is Mr. Belcher's Chartered Accountants . . . it is one of the most interesting of modern buildings [59, 64].'[1]

The importance of Belcher and Pite's Institute of Chartered Accountants (1888–93) in the development of a Free Style for large buildings and, again, as the first building of the Arts and Crafts Baroque, has already been noted. Here Simpson is pointing out its importance to the Baroque revival in general, though he overlooks the significance of John Brydon's earlier Wren-influenced work in Chelsea and in Bath.

For, ultimately, the architects of the High Edwardian Baroque (including Belcher himself) followed Brydon's path

170 The great hall under the dome, Old Bailey Criminal Courts, Newgate Street, City of London (1900–06), by Edward Mountford.

171 *St Paul's Cathedral, City of London (1675–1711), by Sir Christopher Wren. The most famous example of English Baroque, close at hand for the many Edwardian architects whose offices were in London.*

rather than the very free development of style suggested by the Institute of Chartered Accountants building. This path was essentially an English nationalist one, the English Renaissance of Wren [*171*] which, as Brydon himself had put it, was about the year 1720 'firmly established as the national style – the vernacular of the country . . . a great mine of artistic wealth'.[2]

This was the appeal of the English early eighteenth-century Baroque to English architects, politicians and clients of around 1900. It was a very *English* Classical style and its buildings were of a splendour that seemed appropriate for the centre of a great empire. A speaker to the Architectural Association in 1898 had this to say of the style's appropriateness to the time.

It is only natural that architects should hark back to the time when architecture in England was on

the progressive wane, and attempt to start afresh from the point when inventive genius gave place to mere copyism. This point would seem to be soon after the Renaissance architecture of Europe became incorporated and joined to English tendencies. . . . The possibilities of the style seem infinite, and there is plenty of evidence that those who have the fortune to build in it are not trammelled with precedents and hard-and-fast lines . . . there is a wonderful originality in such designs and an entire absence of similarity or copying . . . who can say that it may not lead to what must be the desire of us all, namely the formulating of a truly English 20th century progressive architecture?[3]

The earlier architects whose work was used as a source of inspiration for this English Baroque revival were Sir Christopher Wren, Nicholas Hawksmoor, Sir John Vanbrugh and James Gibbs. Their key buildings, in the eyes of their successors of around 1900, appear to have been Greenwich Royal Hospital, St Paul's Cathedral, Blenheim Palace, Castle Howard, Hampton Court garden front, the City of London churches, St Martin's-in-the-Fields and some Oxford and Cambridge buildings such as the Radcliffe Camera.

With hindsight, one can see that during the earlier 1890s many of the successful designs for large public buildings tried to escape from 'copyism' by a free eclectic mixture of historical styles which they attempted to blend into an overall harmony, with more or less success. T. G. Jackson's Jacobean and other work at Oxford has been mentioned in chapter three. Gibson and Russell's County Buildings at Wakefield, Yorkshire (1894), are a good example of such attempts at originality, mixing Classical, Baroque, Jacobean and even Gothic details into a convincing whole.

The English Baroque revival carried this approach further, using one particular English style for its base, adapting its features to current needs with varying degrees of freedom and originality, and occasionally bringing in the influence of other Baroque manners. The winning designs of the competitions in 1897 for three important civic buildings illustrate the very different results that were possible. One was won by John Belcher, an established leader of the revival, the others by previously unknown young architects who were to become major figures in Edwardian Baroque architecture.

The first of the three 1897 competitions was for the City Hall of Belfast, the capital of Northern Ireland, and the winning design was much the closest of the three to its source of inspiration. Its architect was A. Brumwell Thomas (1868–1948) and his Belfast City Hall (1897–1906) [*172*] is a palace in an architectural style based on Wren's St Paul's Cathedral. The plan, which seems almost intent on rejecting the clarity of contemporary French planning, is a hollow rectangle around a large court-yard. It is adequately practical, but Brumwell Thomas did little to relate the forms of the outside of the building to the importance of the spaces inside. Thus the dome is over entrance halls, rather than above the ceremonial banquet hall and the council chamber – which are on either side – while the enormous public hall is tucked away on another side of the courtyard. The dome itself is a free variation on those of St Paul's and of the Greenwich Hospital. The splendid corner cupolas are again freely derived from the west towers of St Paul's, while the interior of the council chamber [*173*] might be from one of Wren's City churches.

In spite of possible complaints about the plan and some aspects of the detailing, this

172 *Belfast City Hall, Donegall Square, Belfast (1897–1906), by A. Brumwell Thomas. The winner of the first of the major competitions for municipal buildings in 1897, Brumwell Thomas used a free variation of the manner of St Paul's Cathedral.*

173 *Council chamber, Belfast City Hall (1897–1906), by Brumwell Thomas. The Wren style predominates in the rich official rooms of the building.*

143

surprising that Wren's buildings in London were the predominant inspiration for works such as the Belfast City Hall. But as the 1890s passed and the Baroque revival grew, other early Baroque works outside London became easily available for study by architects through the publication of a number of books.

Following Mackmurdo's book on *Wren's City Churches* (1883), John Brydon, through his buildings and lecturing in the following decade, campaigned for the revival of Wren's reputation, though he did not publish a book on the subject. Norman Shaw, too, designed in his own version of the Wren manner, without writing about it. But the revival of interest in English Classicism soon produced its own literature: first, *The Architecture of the Renaissance in England* (1894) by J. A. Gotch, then *A History of Renaissance Architecture in England 1500–1800* (1897) by Reginald Blomfield,

174 Colchester Town Hall, High Street, Colchester, Essex (1897–1902), by John Belcher. The success of Belcher's design in a competition assessed by the great Norman Shaw did much to establish the prestige of the free 'English' Baroque.

175 Council chamber, Colchester Town Hall (interiors redesigned 1899).

massive building is one of the splendours of Edwardian Baroque architecture; the very acceptance of the term Baroque entails enjoyment that can be obtained only at the price of the suspension of purist Classical ideas of proportion and detail.

Brumwell Thomas, like most of the successful Edwardian Baroque architects, had a London-based practice. So it is not and later a major illustrated source book in folio-size volumes, *Later Renaissance Architecture in England* (1898–1901), by John Belcher and Mervyn Macartney.[4] Blomfield's book was well-timed and established him as a leader of the revival. Belcher and Macartney had travelled widely around England for years in preparing their book, and its readers were presented with a wide range of buildings intended to inspire contemporary architecture.

Belcher believed strongly in the original objectives of the Art Workers' Guild of uniting the best of the arts of architecture, painting and sculpture in buildings. He was an opponent of scholastic copyism in architecture, regarding buildings of the past as a source only for original creative work. It is indeed ironic that, while he was a leader of the Baroque movement which was to destroy for a long time the development of a British Free Style in large buildings, he held deep convictions so close to those of the Free Style architects. The explanation is that 'unity of the arts' can take many different forms, and Lethaby's school developed the same ideal very differently from Belcher's.

The second important competition of 1897 was for a smaller site and a smaller town than Belfast. This was the competition for the Town Hall of Colchester in Essex, assessed by Norman Shaw, already mentioned in chapter four. The winning design of September 1897 by John Belcher was extensively altered before the building was constructed in 1898–1902 [*174*].

On the restricted site for the Colchester Town Hall there was no room for clarity in the horizontal planning of the chief rooms. Belcher therefore arranged the major spaces vertically, the routine offices on the ground floor leading up to the council chamber and Mayor's parlour on the first floor, and above that to the big moot hall for public meetings. He expressed these important rooms on the outside as a two-level *piano nobile*, emphasized by one of the dominant features of the design: three giant aedicules embracing the two storeys, three couples of Corinthian columns standing out from the wall, with alternating round and pointed Baroque pediments above.

In contrast to Brumwell Thomas's dependence on Wren at his Belfast City Hall, these aedicules illustrate Belcher's free approach to Baroque sources. There is no historical precedent for them, though the idea may have been inspired by the aedicule by Hawksmoor (or perhaps Vanbrugh) on the east side of the King William Block of Greenwich Hospital, or even by the portico of Hawksmoor's Christ Church, Spitalfields. Whatever the source, it gives Colchester a splendidly rich frontage, echoed by an equally inventive high Baroque tower. This tower is topped by a steeple with hints of Wren's steeple for Christ Church, Newgate Street, though the bell stage below has the elongated aedicules which became a favourite Belcher feature and which seem to echo Borromini. The interiors are worthy of a visit, too. The council chamber [*175*] and moot hall were redesigned in 1899 during building work (possibly by Belcher's new young assistant, J. J. Joass), the former being light and almost frivolous, the latter a grave and restrained tunnel-vaulted space.

The tall bell-tower was absent from the Belfast City Hall, but seems to have become *de rigueur* in most of the Baroque municipal buildings. This in itself departed from the precedent of large English Baroque secular buildings of around 1700 in which domes, pediments, or even urns and balustrades were the topmost features. But Wren had adapted the Gothic tower and steeple to his Classical parish churches and this seems to

176 Cardiff City Hall, Cardiff (1897–1906), by Lanchester, Stewart and Rickards. The third great Baroque success in the major competitions of 1897. The style used by Rickards, however, drew its inspiration more from continental European Baroque than from English sources.

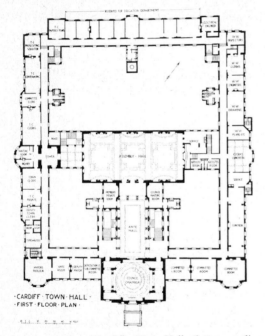

177 Plan, Cardiff City Hall (1897–1906). Lanchester's plan, unhampered by restrictions of space, was exceptional among Edwardian Baroque buildings for its clarity. Stewart's role in the firm's work, until his death in 1904, is unclear.

146

have provided the Edwardians with the idea of putting up towers that would be dominating landmarks. This development may even be viewed as a desire to symbolize the substitution of local government for church authority as the most important influence in the life of a town.

Tower and dome were combined in the winning design of the third major competition of 1897, for the City Hall and Law Courts of Cardiff. The competition was assessed in December and the winning design was by H. V. Lanchester and E. A. Rickards [176]. 'The Cardiff competition was quite a young architects' success, for all the best positions were taken by our younger men,' wrote the editor of one magazine at the time.[5] Of the partnership, which became one of the most successful of the Baroque period, Lanchester (1863–1953) was the planner and engineer, while Rickards (1872–1920) was the immensely inventive draughtsman who brought vitality to the firm's designs. Edwin Rickards came from a background of Cockney poverty and rose to eminence through his restless energy and brilliance as a talker, caricaturist and architectural designer.[6] His work shows a facet of Edwardian Baroque not found in the work of most of his contemporaries. For he was exceptional in that he drew inspiration more from Austrian and French sources than from English Baroque buildings.

The plan of Cardiff City Hall (1897–1906) is evidence of Lanchester's mastery of his sphere; it is clearly thought-out and articulated, and expressive of the functions of each part [177]. In this case the architects had one great advantage in that there was no restriction of space, for a large area was allocated as a civic centre which was nevertheless close to the Castle and the centre of Cardiff. However, it is the exuberant forms and decoration devised by

Rickards on Lanchester's plan that give Cardiff City Hall its special flavour. The tower is an eruption of sheer inventiveness, as is the composition that builds up to the dome topped by its huge Welsh dragon. And the interiors carry the style through with integrity, most of all in the frothing plasterwork of the big barrel-vaulted assembly hall.

The year following the Cardiff competition saw the recognition of the Baroque style by central government as well as local government. In 1898 two immense Whitehall buildings in Westminster were commissioned. One was the general Government Buildings on the corner of Parliament Square which occupied a straightforward rectangular site running through to St James's Park [*178*]. The architect appointed was John Brydon, whose work at Chelsea and Bath has already been described.

Brydon worked to a plan with a fine circular court at its centre (there is surely an intentional echo of the Inigo Jones and John Webb Whitehall Palace scheme here) and several other rectangular courtyards within the large site to give daylight to the offices. The designs were completed in 1898 and the foundations started in 1900, but Brydon died in May 1901 before the building got above ground level. In spite of protests by Brydon's friend Leonard Stokes, the government architect Sir Henry Tanner was appointed to complete the building. Tanner, not a man of high artistic reputation, followed Brydon's designs in general. After part of the building was opened in 1908, *The Architectural Review* commented: 'There are features about it – notably the circular court at the centre – which are tribute enough to the ability of the late Mr. Brydon; but the architect never lived to complete his work and as it stands, it is shorn of some features which would have

178 *Government Buildings, Parliament Square, Westminster, London (1898–1912), by John Brydon. The English Baroque of Wren, Vanbrugh and Hawksmoor in a building commissioned by the government. The design was the last by one of the originators of the Baroque revival, and was completed with unfortunate alterations after Brydon's death in 1901.*

added greatly to its dignity, while the intrusion of another hand less inspired than the original designer is plainly evident.'[7]

Although it is a shame that Brydon's last work was not allowed to live up to the high quality of his Bath designs, the Government Buildings are a handsome enough addition to the Whitehall scene, with high cupola turrets in the centre of the long frontages that were Brydon's favourite free adaptation of the west towers of St Paul's Cathedral. The buildings were finally

147

completed in 1912 and have since then been used by several government departments, most recently the Treasury at the Parliament Street end.

The other large government department building commissioned in 1898 was the War Office, further up Whitehall [*179*]. Here the architect appointed was William Young.[8] A Scot like Brydon, Young had designed and built the Glasgow Municipal Buildings in the 1880s, then built up an extensive country house practice in England. Young worked to a plan for the War Office already prepared by the Department.[9] The foundations were completed in 1899–1901, while Young was still preparing the working drawings. These were ready by the autumn of 1900, but in November of that year Young, like Brydon, died before the superstructure was even started. His son, Clyde Young, was appointed, together with the Office of Works architect Sir John Taylor, to complete the building in 1901–06.

Young was a less talented architect than Brydon, but he was a man of integrity. The story is told by his son of Young's procedure after being asked

by H.M. Office of Works to prepare sketches. . . . My father's first thought on receiving the commission was, very naturally, of the style to be adopted for the new building; and the position of the site . . . quickly decided him upon a Classic treatment. The question whether that treatment should be free or orthodox was a problem more difficult to solve. The influence of the Banqueting House, was, however, too great to be resisted and he decided on the more difficult and dangerous course (one, too, more likely to provoke criticism) of trying to produce a design which would harmonise with its beautiful neighbour . . . The dimensions of the order, the level of the cornice and the height of the building (80 feet) were accordingly made to line with the

Banqueting House as nearly as the internal arrangements would permit.[10]

When it was opened, the building certainly provoked criticism. Indeed, the way in which the aedicules are pushed tightly against the corner towers is unsatisfying. Yet Young's design has much to be said in its defence. One comment at the time made the point: 'A huge building with its best front to Whitehall, but one which nevertheless draws much adverse criticism, more particularly in its corner turrets and the treatment of the windows behind the colonnade; be it noted however that the corner turrets mask the fact that there is not a right-angle on the site.'[11] To this it may be added that the corner turrets give a splendid focus ahead as one goes northwards up Whitehall, before the direction of the road alters slightly and the focus shifts to Nelson's column. Finally, it is worth pointing out that there are striking similarities between Young's Whitehall frontage, with its corner turrets, and Wren's designs of 1698 for Whitehall Palace.[12]

Whatever their merits and faults, the commission of Baroque buildings for the government expressed official approval for the style. For the next few years nearly every large building commissioned, with the exception of churches, was designed in that manner. The year 1899 saw Baroque designs selected for the Hull Central Library (Wills and Anderson), the Guernsey Public Buildings (Edward Mountford won the competition, but Frank Atkinson's second prize design was built), the Cartwright Library at Bradford (Simpson and Milner-Allen), the Plumstead (later called Woolwich) Municipal Buildings (A. Brumwell Thomas), the Imperial College of Science (Aston Webb) and the Royal Naval College at Dartmouth (Aston Webb).

148

Aston Webb (1849–1930, later Sir Aston) was the establishment architect *par excellence* and probably had the largest architectural practice in England at the end of the century, most of it carried out in partnership with E. Ingress Bell. The son of a successful watercolour painter, Webb was troubled by none of the idealistic problems that confronted his Arts and Crafts namesake Philip Webb (who was no relative). Sir Aston moved easily from style to style, performing ably enough in each, and from large commission to large commission – many of them won in competitions. His Victoria Law Courts at Birmingham (1887–91) were designed in an early Renaissance manner, 'the French style of Francis I', and are a successful example of their kind. His Victoria and Albert Museum in London (1891–1909) is a ponderous eclectic mixture of Renaissance and Romanesque, but with some marvellous spaces inside. Christ's Hospital School in Sussex (1893–1902) is again eclectic with many Elizabethan features, while the splendid Birmingham University (1900–09) is loosely Byzantine in style. From 1899 onwards, however, most of his buildings were variations on the fashionable Grand Manner Baroque.

In 1900 Aston Webb gave a paper on 'Design' to the Architectural Association in London,[13] in which he criticized the 'simplicity of design' which he said had become a popular catch-phrase of late. He gave instances of large buildings of 'extremely elaborated elevation' but which nevertheless had overall 'restfulness and repose'.

Webb's own Royal Naval College at Dartmouth had been designed in the year before he gave his paper and was completed in 1903. It is an example of Edwardian Baroque on an immense scale, spreading across a hillside high over the river Dart in

179 *The War Office, Whitehall, Westminster, London (1898–1906), by William Young. The second of the two giant central government buildings in the Baroque style commissioned from London-Scot architects in 1898. Young, like Brydon, completed his designs but died before the work had progressed beyond the foundations.*

Devon. Somewhere, a long way in the background, the inspiration of Wren's Chelsea Hospital can be seen in Webb's palatial composition [*180*]. But the repose of Wren's design is submerged in Webb's work by the restless insertion of stone bands in the areas of brickwork and by curiously Mannerist detailing of the turrets and skyline pediments in some of the ranges.

In July of the following year, 1900, the result of the competition for another major national building was announced. This was the new Central Criminal Courts at the Old Bailey in the City of London, and the

149

manner and his subsequent High Baroque buildings before his early death are among the most self-confident of the period.

Some of the architectural magazines welcomed the result of the Old Bailey competition in 1900. 'Mr. Mountford's design was undoubtedly the best,' declared *The British Architect*.[14] But *The Architectural Review* took the opportunity to launch the Free Style architects' last great assault on Edwardian Baroque. In an unsigned editorial,[15] presumably by that genius of Arts and Crafts free design Henry Wilson (who had edited the magazine since its start in 1896), all the designs entered in the competition were torn to pieces. After first allowing that the site was a difficult one, the article continued,

With a building, however cramped and distorted the site, we would be able to tell at a glance what it is, and know its purpose. . . . Do any of these designs look like a Sessions House? Have they the special character which should stamp such a building, so that it may be known at a glance what it is? We think not. And if this be so, how can they possibly have any artistic expression or value whatever?

After setting out the method by which a true expression should have been sought, and dubbing the plans with 'the spirit with which one solves a puzzle into which human feeling does not enter', the editorial goes on,

if the plans are lacking in imagination and artistic feeling, so must be the outward appearance. . . . Here it is that the worst feature of these designs is to be found. Hardly one of them accurately and sincerely expresses its internal arrangements. . . . Take as an example Mr. Brydon's or Mr. Hare's . . . Which are we to admire – the plan or the elevation? It is impossible to admire both, for they contradict one another, with the result that we admire neither.

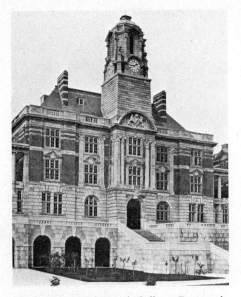

180 Detail, Royal Naval College, Dartmouth, Devon (1899–1903), by Aston Webb. In his design for the vast college buildings overlooking the river Dart, Webb used the Baroque manner in an individualistic way.

winner was Edward Mountford. The project was an emotionally loaded one, for it involved the demolition of George Dance's Newgate Prison, a masterpiece of English eighteenth-century architecture. In exchange, however, London received the best of its giant Edwardian Baroque official buildings, at least as far as the frontages and principal interiors were concerned [*181*]. The planning of the building was more open to attack.

Edward Mountford (1855–1908) has already been mentioned, for his Sheffield (1890) and Battersea (1892) Town Hall designs were early if still eclectic moves towards an English Baroque revival. By 1898 his Liverpool Technical School was designed in a big Vanbrugh-inspired

The uncompromising attack may have contributed to Wilson losing his job when *The Architectural Review* was reorganized a year later and an editorial board appointed which included some of those architects whom his magazine had attacked.

Mountford did in fact slightly revise his 1900 Old Bailey design [*182*] before building started (1902–06),[16] but not in a way that would have placated Wilson. Indeed Wilson's demands could only have been met by the use of a Free Style that would have been generally unacceptable at the time, or by a clearly articulated Classical plan in the French Beaux-Arts tradition that would have been inherently unsuited to such a cramped site (an interesting comparison is provided here by Lanchester and Rickards's successful articulation in plan on the big site at Cardiff). As it is, Mountford expressed the level of the courts themselves as the *piano nobile* and the plan is adequately functional, if unclear and wasteful in the big hallways and staircase. The exterior is a self-assured Portland stone period piece of great splendour, rising to a central dome. The interiors are richly decorated with sculpture by Gilbert Seale and F. W. Pomeroy, painting by Gerald Moira and Sir William Richmond, and *verde antico* marble with columns of Greek cipollino [*170*]. It is to be regretted that the entrance portico, with its twin pediments, does not advance more boldly from the wall; but this again was an attempt to use the limited site fully.

High Edwardian Baroque continued to dominate English public buildings for six or more years after the Old Bailey competition. Henry Hare's Henley Town Hall in Oxfordshire (1900–04) is a charming example of the style on a smaller scale, with a fine example of the barrel-vaulted public hall typical of Edwardian architecture. The Walsall Town Hall near

181 Central Criminal Courts, Old Bailey, Newgate Street, City of London (1900–06), by Edward Mountford. One of the most successful of the major Baroque public buildings.

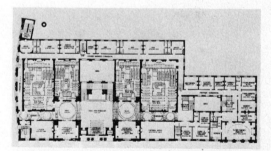

182 Original plan of 1900 for the Old Bailey Criminal Courts, by Mountford. Mountford's plan, and its relevance to the elevations, was bitterly attacked by The Architectural Review under Henry Wilson's editorship.

183 The board room, Norwich Union Head Office, Surrey Street, Norwich (1903–05), by G. J. and F. W. Skipper. This Norwich firm of architects did some of the best Baroque buildings of the period.

Birmingham (1901–05) by Gibson and Russell is another notable example, with an extraordinary tower and swirling sculptural decoration that shows strong influence of Michelangelo. The Deptford Town Hall (1902) by Lanchester and Rickards is an original and delightful display of Rickards's talent.

The style was soon taken up by commerce, too. The Liverpool Cotton Exchange by Matear and Simon (now demolished) and Electra House in Moorgate, in the City of London, by John Belcher were both Baroque business palaces started in 1900. More significantly in the long run, Edwin Lutyens's building of 1904 for *Country Life* magazine, in Covent Garden, was the first big Grand Manner building by the last great exponent

of the style. Insurance was a rapidly growing business of the period and the Norwich Union headquarters in Surrey Street, Norwich (1903–05), is a notable example of the work of George and F. W. Skipper, a local firm who did much other bold Baroque work in that city [*183*]. In London, Belcher's Royal London House in Finsbury Square (1904–05) [*185*] and Norman Shaw's Alliance Assurance at No. 88 St James's Street (1904–06) are other typical versions of Baroque insurance offices. In Scotland a more restrained Classical manner was widely used, but J. J. Burnet's corner section of the Clyde Trust in Robertson Street, Glasgow (1905–08), is as exuberant as any English Baroque, and other architects did similar work in the early years of the century in several Scottish cities.

184 School of Art, Hull, Yorkshire (1904), by Lanchester and Rickards. The quality and originality of Rickards's draughtsmanship and sculptural design put much of the firm's work in a class of its own.

185 Detail, Royal London House, Finsbury Square, London (1904–05), by John Belcher. One of the architect's most florid works.

187 Detail, Piccadilly Hotel, Piccadilly, London (1905–08). The façades only – here and on Regent Street – were designed by Norman Shaw. As with other styles, Shaw used the Baroque freely and with brilliance.

186 Coliseum Theatre, St Martin's Lane, London (1902–04), by Frank Matcham. Matcham, together with his former pupils W. G. R. Sprague and Bertie Crewe, dominated Edwardian theatre architecture. They used a wide variety of Classical styles, of which the Coliseum is the best High Baroque example.

153

again – or perhaps Brumwell Thomas's Belfast City Hall – in the splendid Mersey Docks Building on the Pier Head in Liverpool (1903–07), designed by Sir Arnold Thornely) [*188*]. As at Belfast, however, the detailing is unimaginative compared with the best Baroque work of the time.

Returning to public and municipal buildings designed in the last years of High Edwardian Baroque, before the tide turned against its extravagance in about 1906, the work of Brumwell Thomas himself deserves further mention. His last and most exhilarating major building of the period

188 Mersey Docks Building, Pier Head, Liverpool (1903–07), by Arnold Thornely (with Briggs and Wolstenholme). High Edwardian Baroque outside a steel frame for the Mersey Docks and Harbour Board. The quadrangular tower in the background is the ventilator shaft of the Mersey Tunnel built in 1925–34.

189 Stockport Town Hall, Wellington Road South, Stockport, Cheshire (1904–08), by A. Brumwell Thomas. The third and the most completely self-assured of Brumwell Thomas's major public buildings. The interiors are extreme examples of the Baroque Grand Manner.

In other types of building, Lanchester and Rickards used a delicate Baroque for the Hull School of Art (1904) [*184*], Frank Matcham employed a full-blooded version for his Coliseum Theatre in London (1902–04) [*186*] and Norman Shaw gave a stunningly inventive example in the Piccadilly Hotel, London (1905–08) [*187*]. The style spread all over England and the Empire in buildings of most kinds, with the exception of churches and houses. Canada and Australia are particularly rich in Baroque provincial and state government edifices.

In 1903 Sir William Emerson designed a vast Baroque memorial to Queen Victoria for Calcutta, where it still brings an Italianate version of St Paul's Cathedral to the crowded Indian city. We see St Paul's

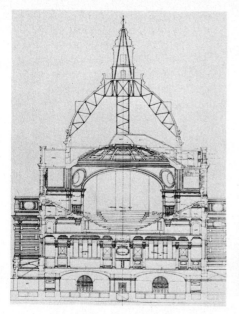

190, 191 Section and perspective of the final design of 1905 for Central Hall (Methodist), Storey's Gate, Westminster, London (opened 1911), by Lanchester and Rickards. The front towers were unfortunately never built. Even without them, the building and its interiors carry total conviction.

was the Town Hall for Stockport, near Manchester (1904–08) [*189*]. This is another big palace of a building, better planned than his Belfast work, with the main council rooms grouped behind a powerful Baroque double portico. Above this centre rises an exuberantly inventive tower like a magnified variation of a late Wren church steeple. Inside, the scale of the entrance is well managed, dignified yet not so grandiose as to intimidate visitors. A double stairway rises to the council suite, with a successful council chamber and a resoundingly self-assured Baroque hall, barrel-vaulted and with huge volutes on either side of the proscenium.

In 1905 Lanchester and Rickards won the competition for their last really big building, the Central Hall at Westminster, commissioned by the Methodist Church [*190–191*]. It is another convincing demonstration of Rickards's talent, drawing on continental rather than English Baroque for inspiration. The building was opened in 1911, though the planned twin towers on the entrance frontage have never been built. Lanchester and Rickards's most extraordinary design of all was an entry for the London County Council's County Hall competition in 1907. Rickards's sketch for the building depicts a giant curving frontage with an ambitious screen across it and a wildly Baroque tower rising in stages behind [*192*]. But by 1907 the days of extreme extravagance had passed and a depression had hit both the building industry and the British economy in general. Rickards's design was rejected in favour of the more restrained, but still grandiose, County Hall by Ralph Knott that can be seen today.[17]

155

192 Competition design of 1907 for London County Council's County Hall, South Bank, London, drawing by E. A. Rickards of Lanchester and Rickards. Not built.

193 Lancaster Town Hall, Dalton Square, Lancaster (1906–09), the last major work by Edward Mountford. The style is still Baroque, but noticeably more restrained than that of his earlier buildings.

The change in taste goes back a little earlier. In 1906 *The Architectural Review* poured scorn on the '*Barocco*' of the Milan International Exhibition, as well as on the 'reprehensible degeneration into the lowest depth of *l'Art Nouveau*'.[18] In that year the same influential magazine started a series called 'The Practical Exemplar of Architecture'.[19] The examples illustrated were for the most part details of eighteenth-century English Classical architecture. Thus the series represented an extraordinary swing away from the emphasis on originality in late Victorian and early Edwardian Baroque towards the set rules of Palladianism or other past styles.

The call for a new Classical purism was taken up by many, notably by Reginald Blomfield (who was on the magazine's editorial board). Thus what had happened in the 1720s was happening again in the 1900s: a period of powerful and inventive Baroque architecture was being followed by a reaction against it and a turning towards Good Taste.

The contrast is well illustrated by two large buildings of the time built in Lancaster. Both were paid for by the local industrial tycoon, Lord Ashton, both were by leading Edwardian Baroque architects and both were opened in 1909. Edward Mountford's Lancaster Town Hall (1906–09) was his last work and was designed at the time when public taste was turning to a graver and more restrained Classical manner [*193*]. The Town Hall presents to the city a small clock tower and a straightforward temple portico, relieved only by the sumptuous sculpture of Edward VII enthroned in the pediment. The interior, too, with its solemn staircase leading up to the council chamber and public hall, is all dark oak and sombre gravity.

John Belcher's Ashton Memorial, on the

194 The Ashton Memorial, Williamson Park, above Lancaster (designed 1904, built 1907–09), by John Belcher. Designed two years before the Lancaster Town Hall, this was Belcher's last and most triumphant High Baroque work.

other hand, had been designed two years earlier, in 1904 [*194*]. The memorial is probably the last of the buildings by the Baroque master's firm which Belcher himself designed. It rises exuberantly on its hilltop site, dominating the city of Lancaster, a monument to Lord Ashton's family's success in business and a splendid final masterpiece of the High Edwardian Baroque period. The composition is put together freely and inventively, with strongly moulded forms and sculptural decoration. These characteristics were typical of the work of Belcher, Mountford, Rickards and others in the High Baroque years between 1897 and 1905. Thereafter, Edwardian Baroque was gradually replaced by other forms of the Grand Manner, as will be seen in the following chapters; sometimes in the elegant French Beaux-Arts styles, sometimes in styles that attempted to adapt Classicism to the new steel and concrete frame structures.

11
The Beaux-Arts Influence on Edwardian Classicism

EDWARDIAN 'Grand Manner' architecture is a term which embraces several different approaches to Classical design. The influence of French Classicism hardly appears in Edwardian buildings before 1906. The Baroque of the turn of the century, usually a free adaptation of the specifically English style of about 1700, was followed by a reaction against its flamboyance. By 1906 there was a move in public fashion towards refinement, and a development within the architectural profession towards purer Neo-Classical composition and planning. The model for such a change was close at hand across the Channel, in the long established system of education in design and architecture of the Ecole des Beaux-Arts in Paris. Indeed, the system had had its advocates in England for decades and had made some headway.

The early attempts to introduce the French educational system into Britain have been well described by Robert Macleod in his book *Style and Society*,[1] from the papers by R. Phené Spiers and William White delivered to the Royal Institute of British Architects in 1884, to the establishment of the first professorship of architecture by the University of Liverpool in 1894. Other organized courses in architecture soon started in Glasgow and London, so that throughout the time of the High Baroque fashion, the groundwork was being laid for a more formalized approach to architecture.

The Ecole des Beaux-Arts was inter-

nationally famous and several British architects – most notably J. J. Burnet – studied there before 1880. It is a curious fact, and a measure of the different attitudes in the two countries, that the researches into the history of the Ecole by Richard Chafee[2] have shown that hardly any British students studied there during the last two decades of the nineteenth century.

The Beaux-Arts system which Phené Spiers admired consisted of a central school for examination purposes and a number of independent *ateliers*, each with its own *maître*, where almost all teaching was done. The Ecole's approach to architecture laid heavy emphasis on clear formalized planning (in contrast to current English thought) and taught architects to work up their designs through a series of project stages, employing the Classical orders with correct proportions once the plan was fully developed. The aim of every ambitious student was to win the 'Grand Prix de Rome' competition, which would entitle him to years of study in that city and a secure salaried career when he returned to France.

The Beaux-Arts educational system was much changed when the first formal architectural courses were started in Britain, for the courses had to fit in with the

195 Inveresk House, Aldwych, London (1906–07), by Mewès and Davis for the Morning Post *newspaper. The architects at their most elegantly Parisian. The building has now been spoiled by the addition of upper storeys.*

196 La Bagatelle, Bois de Boulogne, Paris (1777), by Bélanger. A charming eighteenth-century example of the type of French Classical architecture which became fashionable in Europe around 1900 and in England after about 1905.

structure of the universities which housed them, and in any case there was widespread suspicion of French ideas in Victorian England. Nor did the French forms of Neo-Classical architectural style find many English enthusiasts in the high days of Edwardian Baroque between 1897 and 1906.

Here and there, signs of a clarity of planning worthy of the French tradition could be found. The fine plan of the Cardiff City Hall design of 1897 by H. V. Lanchester of Lanchester and Rickards is a good example. Lanchester had no Beaux-Arts training and his ability in planning appears to have been in the tradition of Alfred Waterhouse, the most distinguished large-scale planner among Victorian architects and, incidentally, the assessor of the Cardiff competition. In general, however, large Edwardian Baroque buildings show a disinterest in the clear articulation of main and connecting spaces of the Classical planning tradition, and an actual distaste for symmetry. This was

160

partly caused by a hostility towards foreign ideas, but an equally important factor was the cramped sites often provided for buildings such as the Colchester Town Hall and the Old Bailey Criminal Courts. The architects were required to cram many large ceremonial or official rooms, on several storeys, into these small irregular sites and this was hardly conducive to clear Beaux-Arts planning.

Apart from the plans, the elevations and detailing of contemporary French Classical buildings showed styles strikingly different from the English Baroque of about 1900. Architectural historians tend to refer to the 'Beaux-Arts style' as if it were a single type of Neo-Classicism. But in reality, at least three major strands of French Classical architecture were to appear in Edwardian buildings in England. The chaste but grand Neo-Grec of the Paris Palais de Justice (rebuilt in the 1830s by Louis Duc) and the Grand Palais of the 1900 Paris Exhibition represent one general type. The inventive splendour of Charles Garnier's famous Opéra in Paris (1861–75) shows another more exuberant side of French Classicism. The third type displays a lighter feeling of elegance and gaiety which can be traced back to French buildings such as A. J. Gabriel's Petit Trianon (1762–66) and the little château called La Bagatelle, built in the Bois de Boulogne for the Comte d'Artois by Bélanger in 1777 [196]. Here there can be seen the use of banded Classical wall surfaces, without strongly projecting pilasters or columns, which entered the vocabulary of English architects such as Arthur Davis, Reginald Blomfield and Frank Verity after the reign of the Francophile King Edward VII had reached its half-way point.

Writing on the variations appearing in Edwardian Classical buildings in 1907, the editor of *The Architectural Review* noticed a recrudescence of the French Renaissance. On the purely decorative side it has never left us, but the Ritz Hotel and the new Morning Post building are essentially Gallic; the reconstructed 'Playhouse' carries us back to the period of Watteau; one or two of our West End mansions have been reconstructed on Louis Seize lines . . . let us hope that, excepting the planning, there will be very little Modern French 'Renaissance' with it.[3]

This reference to Modern French 'Renaissance' presumably refers to the version of the Beaux-Arts Classical style that became widely fashionable in Europe after the Paris Exhibition of 1900. That exhibition has sometimes been referred to as the highest point of Art Nouveau success.[4] But it was the Classical exhibition buildings which made a greater impression on visiting architects: the grave Grand Palais, the more light-hearted Petit Palais and the Pont Alexandre III. Richard Chafee has also pointed out that it was only at this time that the Neo-Classical buildings along the great boulevards laid out by Haussmann under Napoleon III were reaching completion and the full effect of the giant rebuilding of Paris could be appreciated.

Certainly it seems that the spread throughout Europe of a version of the French manner, often frivolous but of great charm, dates from about the time of the Paris Exhibition. As far as England is concerned, the very word 'Edwardian' is still associated with the splendid hotels, theatres and casinos built during that reign in London, Normandy, the French and Italian Rivieras and elsewhere. The French influence reached London through the Ritz Hotel and the other work of its architects Mewès and Davis, a very different French style from the purer Classicism of the Grand Palais which was to produce its own effect in England later.

Arthur J. Davis (1878–1951) was the London-born son of a wealthy Jewish businessman with European connections. Davis had a brilliant career at the Ecole des Beaux-Arts in Paris and the established hotel architect Charles Mewès (designer of the Paris Ritz) made the Englishman his London partner in 1900 at the age of twenty-two. Their first London jobs were a palm court and other interiors for the Carlton Hotel (now destroyed), and then the Ritz Hotel in Piccadilly.

The exterior of the Ritz (1903–06) is very Parisian indeed with its high Mansart roofs, street arcade and simplified Classical stone walls [*197*]. It was one of the earliest major steel frame buildings in London. The design is largely Mewès's, but Davis had a hand in it and a stronger influence still on the brilliant interiors which are its chief splendour [*198*]. From the main door in Arlington Street a broad space sweeps the length of the ground floor, past the spiralling staircase, winter garden and hall which open off it. Spaces flow into other spaces, big mirrors increase the impression of opulent breadth, and the public rooms come to their climax in the glorious dining-room overlooking Green Park.

After the building of the Ritz, Davis played an increasingly dominant part in his firm's designs for England. Inveresk House for the *Morning Post* (1906–07) stands at the end of the Aldwych, facing across Waterloo Bridge [*195*]. 'The design is a modern rendering of Louis Seize,' noted *The Architectural Review* in 1908.[5] This was the most elegant of all these Beaux-Arts London buildings, though its proportions were later marred by the addition of two attic storeys. The Royal Automobile Club, designed by Davis and built in Pall Mall in 1908–11, was intended to be the club to end all West End clubs [*199*]. The imposing exterior is echoed in a series of grand public

197 *The Ritz Hotel, Piccadilly, London (1903–06), by Mewès and Davis. The first arrival of Edwardian Beaux-Arts Classicism in the streets of London, the Ritz was also one of the capital's first large steel frame buildings.*

rooms on the largest scale with interior decoration typical of one branch of French Classicism [200]. Davis also carried out work at Luton Hoo in 1903 and Polesden Lacey, Surrey, in 1906, which almost amounted to a complete rebuilding of these large country houses in the fashionable styles of the time.

In London and other major British cities, the French Edwardian hotel style soon became a symbol of the pleasures and luxury of the upper middle classes on holiday. Palm courts, promenades and spacious dining-rooms are keynotes of these marvellous confectionery palaces (the London Waldorf Hotel by A. G. R. Mackenzie, son of Marshall Mackenzie, is a good example [201]), decorated by mile upon mile of the cast plaster mouldings and sculpture produced by such workshops as Messrs George Jackson and Sons. At the

198 *Dining-room, Ritz Hotel (1903–06), by Mewès and Davis. The sumptuous climax to the* well-planned series of public rooms on the ground floor.

199 *Royal Automobile Club, Pall Mall, London (1908–11), by Mewès and Davis. Davis's design for this London super-club expresses supreme self-confidence.*
200 *Entrance hall, Royal Automobile Club (1908–11), by Mewès and Davis.*

201 *The palm court lounge, Waldorf Hotel, Aldwych, London (1906–08), by A. M. and*   *A. G. R. Mackenzie. The idea of the palm court became identified with Edwardian hotel luxury.*

163

202 Interior, Albery (formerly the New) Theatre, St Martin's Lane, London (1902–03), by W. G. R. Sprague. The architect's numerous London theatres are incomparable for their lavish but refined Classical interiors and foyers.

dogmatic man. From about 1895 onwards he waged perpetual war against any non-Classical form of expression in architecture, although he had been a member of the Art Workers' Guild. His book *A History of Renaissance Architecture in England 1500–1800*, published in 1897, was one of the most influential texts of the revival of Classicism in England, and also on the Baroque work of the decade before 1906. His own designs up to the end of the century were largely for country houses in a restrained Wren-like Baroque. In 1907 Blomfield was appointed Professor of Architecture at the Royal Academy and his inaugural lectures of February and March that year are revealing. He devoted much time to the history of architecture, attacking the Gothic revival and belittling the ideas of William Morris, while praising

203 United University Club, Pall Mall East, Westminster, London (1906–07), by Reginald Blomfield. By 1907 the movement led by Blomfield towards purer Classicism on the French model was gaining ground over the Baroque.

same time a series of magnificent theatres were being built in London and other cities by the architect Frank Matcham and his brilliant pupils W. G. R. Sprague and Bertie Crewe, who soon started their own practices [202].[6]

Other more idealistic architects were influenced by the Beaux-Arts styles, too. Chief among them was Reginald Blomfield (1856–1942). Son of a clergyman and nephew of a well-known church architect, Blomfield took a first-class degree in Greats at Oxford and played for the University Rugby football team occasionally. Blomfield was a scholar and a designer of talent and elegance, though an aggressive and

204 Piccadilly Circus western side and Regent Street quadrant, London. The overall design of c. 1913 by Sir Reginald Blomfield for the façades includes the buildings on the corners of Lower Regent Street and Piccadilly. The various buildings were carried out (and their interiors designed) by various architects; the block shown on the left here by J. J. Joass, that on the right by Ernest Newton, following Blomfield's elevations.

the Renaissance and English architects such as Sir William Chambers. In summing up, he said: 'Architectural forms are old just as are the words of a language. Still, no one asserts that the possibilities of the English language are exhausted, and it is equally so in architecture. The architect's invention and originality are shown in the use he makes of accepted forms.'[7]

From 1903 onwards, when he did a most delicate Classical music room for Hatchlands in Surrey, Blomfield moved steadily towards a Beaux-Arts Classical style. At the same time he was working on his *History of French Architecture*, the first volume of which was published in 1911. Blomfield's United University Club in Pall Mall East (1906–07) is a refined work [*203*], but his refacing of the Carlton Club in Pall Mall (original design 1913, executed 1922 and now demolished) and his Menin Gate war memorial were splendid. Blomfield's *chef d'œuvre*, however, is the elevation for the whole western part of Piccadilly Circus [*204*]. The designs were accepted in about 1913 after a long controversy over alternative schemes. They include the buildings on left and right at the top of Lower Regent Street, the whole angle block between Piccadilly and Regent Street, both sides of the great curving quadrant of Regent Street (apart from Norman Shaw's Baroque Piccadilly Hotel of 1905–08 in the centre) and the domed Westminster and County Insurance build-

165

205 East frontage, Buckingham Palace, London (1912–13), by Aston Webb (Queen Victoria Memorial designed by the sculptor Sir Thomas Brock). Webb used a refined Classical style in replacing this façade, in contrast with his generally heavier work.

ing that faces back down Lower Regent Street. The interiors of the buildings were designed, and their construction supervised, by various architects over the following years: the Swan and Edgar corner block by J. J. Joass in 1917–24, and the County Insurance building by Ernest Newton in 1924. But the overall exterior design, with its curving French cupolas, is Blomfield's largest and most dignified Beaux-Arts inspired work.

It was Blomfield who led the campaign for a new French-inspired discipline in Classical architecture, but other architects followed him in this direction. Sir Aston

Webb had altered the style of the designs produced by his office from the Baroque of the Royal Naval College at Dartmouth and the Imperial College of Science, South Kensington (1900–06), to a more refined Classicism. Aston Webb was knighted as early as 1904 – more for the vast number of his public buildings, one might think sceptically, than for their aesthetic qualities. Nevertheless, he was a supremely competent architect. In 1901 he was commissioned to turn The Mall approach to Buckingham Palace into a memorial to Queen Victoria. His original scheme was revised over the next few years and he was forced to include a large amount of Admiralty office space in the triumphal arch planned for the entry from Trafalgar Square. The result was the Admiralty Arch built in 1908–09, a heavy amalgam of arch and building. At the other end of the newly broadened boulevard of The Mall, Webb's plans for a *rond-point* were carried out with Sir Thomas Brock's Queen Victoria Memorial in the centre. Then, in 1913, Webb rebuilt the main public façade of Buckingham Palace[8] in a delicate and pretty Classical manner, although the accents of the three porticos seem too weak for the splendid position of the frontage [*205*].

The chief London building that was named in memory of Edward VII himself was the product of the Grand Manner work of a more distinguished architect than Webb, J. J. Burnet. In 1904 the trustees of the British Museum decided to enlarge their buildings and invited twelve archi-

tects to submit samples of their past work. From these they selected J. J. Burnet, the most celebrated Scottish architect of the time, and he prepared a vast scheme of four buildings around a courtyard. Only one range was built, that known as the King Edward VII Galleries. Burnet was knighted when it was completed in 1914.

The King Edward VII Galleries was Burnet's first London building [*206*]. In its design he returned, from all his excursions into various styles in Scotland, to a Beaux-Arts influenced Classical purity that would have pleased his old Parisian master, Jean-Louis Pascal. The plan of the galleries and stairways displays a clarity that carries great

206 King Edward VII Galleries, British Museum, Bloomsbury, London (1904–14), by John Burnet. The most elegant of the Beaux-Arts influenced Edwardian Classical buildings in London, it won a knighthood for Burnet.
207 First floor plan, King Edward VII Galleries (1904–14), by Burnet.

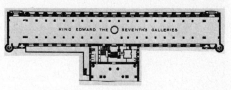

167

208 Selfridge's department store, Oxford Street, London (first section 1907–09, the whole block completed 1928), by Francis Swales, Daniel Burnham, Frank Atkinson and J. J. Burnet. The well-known Chicago architect, Burnham, was appointed consultant for this building whose splendid elevation was designed by another American architect, the young Beaux-Arts trained Francis Swales.

conviction [207]. The fine Ionic colonnade of the exterior is echoed in the Neo-Greek detailing inside (though some of the best Burnet rooms have already been destroyed).

A giant colonnade of a very different nature is to be seen in Selfridge's department store in Oxford Street, London. The owner, Gordon Selfridge, asked Daniel Burnham – the American architect of many enormous Chicago

buildings – to be consulting architect and the manner of the exterior is certainly close to Burnham's [208]. But the elevation was apparently done in England in about 1907 by a young American called Francis Swales, who had recently been studying at the Ecole des Beaux-Arts in Paris, in the atelier Pascal (where Burnet, too, had studied thirty years earlier).

The steel frame structure inside was the work of Burnham's representative, Albert D. Miller, in consultation with Burnet and R. Frank Atkinson. Initially the construction was supervised by Atkinson and the first ten bays in Oxford Street were opened in 1909. Sir John Burnet was then given charge of constructing the rest of the immense building, which was completed in stages up to 1928.

The Beaux-Arts influence is seen more straightforwardly in the numerous blocks of luxury flats in London designed by Frank

Verity (1864–1937) and his talented assistant A. E. (later Sir Albert) Richardson. In blocks such as No. 7 Cleveland Row (1905), beside St James's Palace, there is a disciplined use of Classical proportions with very little ornamentation that might well be the work of a Beaux-Arts architect in Paris itself [*209*].

By 1911, Richardson had left Verity's office and, in independent practice, he became a regular contributor to *The Architectural Review*. One article of his in that year, entitled 'The Style Neo-Grec',[9] protested against the impurity of English Classical monumental architecture, as against the inventiveness within pure Classicism of French work. Richardson held up C. R. Cockerell (1788–1863) as the English representative of Greek Classicism in the previous century and pointed out that Cockerell had 'paid the greatest respect to the works of Sir Christopher Wren, but he knew better than to repeat the classical meretricious ornaments of this master'.

Discipline in Classical design continued to be the cry of Sir Reginald Blomfield, and he campaigned actively in the Royal Institute of British Architects, in the pages of *The Architectural Review* and in the new architectural schools for the introduction of a Beaux-Arts type of education. The Professor of Architecture at the important Liverpool University school, C. H. Reilly, later acknowledged[10] that 'its teaching at the beginning of the new century was largely based on Sir Reginald's. His books became text-books for professors and students alike.'

In 1913, Blomfield, helped by Arthur Davis, H. V. Lanchester and others, actually went so far as to establish an architectural *atelier* in London on the model of the Ecole des Beaux-Arts. But the days of the French fashion were coming to an end. The London *atelier* closed in 1914 with the outbreak of war and did not reopen. The lasting effect on British architecture of the period of Beaux-Arts influence was that a more organized system of education did emerge (although it was much more varied than in France) and that some elegance of proportion was retained by many of those who designed in the so-called Stripped Classical style before and after the First World War.

209 Flats, No. 7 Cleveland Row, St James's, London (1905), by Frank Verity. Verity was a successful commercial architect who introduced the simplified French Classical manner in many blocks of luxury flats in London.

The Neo-Georgian House

WHILE PUBLIC and other large Edwardian buildings were passing through the decade of High Baroque and the following years of French Classical influence, another much quieter revival of Classicism was developing into a version of English domestic architecture which has proved far more lasting. This revival is usually called the Neo-Georgian and the general style is still being used in houses being built today.

Like the Baroque revival of the 1890s, the Neo-Georgian domestic revival was started by architects close to Norman Shaw and to the Arts and Crafts movement. Houses in the Georgian manner were built from time to time throughout the Victorian period, but the start of the real revival can be attributed to the new respect for Sir Christopher Wren which emerged in the 1880s.

The revival of interest in Wren has already been described in chapter four. The theme of Mackmurdo's influential book of 1883 on the City of London churches was taken up in views such as those expressed by Philip Webb, the architect high priest of the Arts and Crafts movement, that Wren's work was truly English rather than imported Italian in character.[1] Of the early Wren revival buildings by John Brydon and Norman Shaw, it is Shaw's No. 170 Queen's Gate in Kensington (1887–88) that is of most concern in this chapter, for this large London house combining Wren and Dutch motifs was a precursor of much that happened in England ten years later [62].

The varied types of Arts and Crafts houses that were built during the early 1890s show little more than the occasional Classical detail included in the design. For example, Lethaby himself included a Venetian window in his 1893 house, The Hurst. It was two other founders of the Art Workers' Guild who are generally accepted as the leading spirits in the Neo-Georgian revival, Ernest Newton and Mervyn Macartney, although Reginald Blomfield built a generally Wren-inspired house as early as 1892.

Newton's well-known house of 1895, Redcourt, shows the influence of Lethaby more than that of any other architect and is definitely non-historicist in style [13]. The truth seems to be that several of the Art Workers' Guild architects moved towards a very free Wren type of house design in the last two years of the century. Thus at Pangbourne in Berkshire in 1898, Leonard Stokes built Shooter's Hill House overlooking the river Thames [210]. The house has an experimental skew plan, but the main river elevation is detailed in a style that is undeniably free Neo-Georgian. On the other hand, some architects soon moved

210 Shooter's Hill House, Pangbourne, Berkshire (1898), by Leonard Stokes. River frontage. An example of the free approach of Arts and Crafts architects to the Neo-Georgian style, a domestic parallel to the inventive Baroque of contemporary large buildings.

211 Sketch design by James Ransome for a house to be built in the New Forest (exhibited at the Royal Academy in 1899). The doll's-house look of this design contrasts with the flexible Neo-Georgian work of architects such as Newton, Macartney and Stokes.

212 Frithwood House, Northwood, Middlesex (1900), by Mervyn Macartney. Garden front. Macartney's Neo-Georgian designs were quiet and restrained in their use of Classical features.

213 Design for a house near Cambridge (1900), by Horace Field.

towards more compact plans and symmetrical façades; James Ransome's sketch design for a house in the New Forest, exhibited at the Royal Academy in 1899, is an example of this trend [211].

By 1900, many Neo-Georgian house designs were appearing in the architectural magazines and in the architecture section of the Royal Academy summer exhibition. Good examples of that year include Mervyn Macartney's Frithwood House at Northwood [212], Horace Field's design for a house near Cambridge [213], and Ernest George and Yeates's Holwell in Hertfordshire [215]. Macartney's design has a quiet simplicity typical of that sensitive if uninspiring architect and Field's has elements of eccentricity. But Holwell is not too far from a reproduction of a small early Georgian manor house. The same firm showed how a Wren-like manner could be used for a block of flats in their Queen Alexandra's Court, Wimbledon (1902–04) [216].

The Neo-Georgian style reaches a new self-confidence, however, in Ernest Newton's house called Steep Hill, built in 1902–04 near St Helier in the Channel Islands [214]. Newton's favourite delicate lattice-work and a bold Arts and Crafts chimney are still there,[2] but otherwise the house is completely Georgian revivalist in appearance. Another notable house contemporary with Steep Hill, is Red House at Chapel Allerton near Leeds, built in 1902–03 by the Yorkshire architects Francis Bedford and Sydney Kitson [217]. Here a simple brick Neo-Georgian exterior conceals a bold plan designed around a big two-storey living-room, with overhead daylight, in the centre of the building.

By 1902 Lutyens, too, was moving away from the Free Style towards the Neo-Georgian, though his miniature Baroque living-room at Little Thakeham in Sussex is

215 *Design for Holwell House, Hertfordshire (1900), by Ernest George and Yeates.*

214 *Steep Hill, near St Helier, Jersey, Channel Islands (1902–04), by Ernest Newton. Garden front. Newton, whose earlier houses employ an Arts and Crafts vernacular approach, was the master of freely Neo-Georgian domestic architecture.*

216 *Queen Alexandra's Court, St Mary's Road, Wimbledon, London (1902–04), by Ernest George and Yeates. The Neo-Georgian domestic style employed in a block of flats.*

217 *Interior, Red House, Chapel Allerton, near Leeds, Yorkshire (1902–03), by Francis Bedford and Sydney Kitson. The unusual top-lit interior is contained within a simple brick Neo-Georgian exterior.*

another brilliant game with solids and voids, filigree metalwork and variations of level. The levity of some of the Classical detailing contains the seeds of the architect's sustained wit in his many big buildings of the following decades.

Four years later, in 1906, Lutyens built a completely Classical house called Heathcote, near Ilkley in Yorkshire [218]. Again the spirit is light-hearted and Baroque rather than Neo-Georgian. Lutyens liked to refer to his Classical architecture as 'the High Game' and one sees why, even at this stage before his most fascinating series of complex geometrical conjuring tricks had started.

A far wilder version of the Classical domestic revival is Halsey Ricardo's unique house for Ernest Debenham at No. 8

Addison Road, North Kensington (1905–07). Ricardo was a talented and fairly wealthy architect, a zealous adherent of the Arts and Crafts movement, who spent more time writing about architecture than practising it. Most of the Arts and Crafts men had personal obsessions as well as their shared ideas: for example, Lethaby's symbolism and Prior's insistence upon local materials. In Ricardo's case, the obsession was with coloured glazed exteriors. He extolled the aesthetic and practical advantages of coloured tiles in a number of talks and articles. 'We have tried mass and form, and light and shade, might we not now have an attempt at colour?' he wrote in 1902 in an article entitled 'Enamelled Tiles'.[3]

The Debenham house gave Ricardo a chance to bring his ideal to the streets of London. The style of the exterior is itself astonishing, for it is an extremely personal type of Arts and Crafts Classicism, with the windows of the two middle storeys recessed beneath an arcade. But the materials used are almost unique in England. The basement is of blue-grey semi-vitrified

218 Heathcote, near Ilkley, Yorkshire (1906), by Edwin Lutyens. Garden front. A Baroque variation of the Neo-Georgian, showing much originality and wit.

brick, while the projecting Classical features above are of pink-cream glazed 'Carrara-Ware' terracotta. The panels between these Corinthian pillars and arches are of glazed brick, a deep green below and a bright blue above. The interiors are equally startling, with many intriguing spatial effects [*219*]. Ricardo was helped here by several others leading members of the Art Workers' Guild: Edward Prior designed some of the glass, the plasterwork was by Gimson, the carving by W. Aumonier and there are de Morgan tiles in many parts of the house. The result is an extraordinary treasury of Arts and Crafts decoration in an exotic version of a Classical style.

Such extremism in the use of Classical features was a rarity. Ernest Newton's calm Neo-Georgian mastery shown in his mature houses such as Luckley in Berkshire (1907), with a few original touches to prevent the serenity from becoming dull, is an example of the style at its best [*220–222*]. And in Scotland, Robert Lorimer's design for Wemyss Hall in Fife (1905–07) showed that the Neo-Georgian manner was perfectly capable of adaptation to local traditional materials [*223*].

The fashion was swinging quickly back towards more correct copyism of historic styles. In April 1906 the most influential building design magazine of the day, *The Architectural Review*, started an important new regular feature called 'The Practical Exemplar of Architecture', mentioned briefly in chapter ten. The introductory article,[4] presumably by Mervyn Macartney (who became editor in 1905), stated:

To be frank with our readers, our intention is by photographs and measured drawings to place before architects an absolutely reliable and correct reproduction of all that pertains to architecture so that any architect could reproduce any given subject, from a chimney

219 The hall, Debenham House (now the Richmond Fellowship), No. 8 Addison Road, North Kensington, London (1905–07), by Halsey Ricardo. On both exterior and interior of this house the architect used glazed coloured tiles and played extraordinary games with Classical architecture. In this room, the lower walls are of deep blue glazed tiles, with detailing in green and white marble. Glass designed by Edward Prior.

stack to a door knob. It is not intended that the host of adapters should be increased, so much as to ensure that the adaptations should be correct.

And the series started with nine pages of Classical gate piers, followed by nine pages of chimney stacks and eight pages of doorways in the next issue of the magazine, with the emphasis on the English eighteenth century. It continued for many

220 Luckley, Wokingham, Berkshire (1907), by
Ernest Newton. Garden front. A mature and lovely
example of Newton's Neo-Georgian work.

221 Plan of Luckley (1907), by Newton.

222 Drawing-room hearth, Luckley (1907), by
Newton. The new swing of fashion towards Classical
Good Taste is apparent in this interior.

years and doubtless contributed much to the establishment of a Neo-Georgian style which has been fondly loved by several generations of British house-buyers. The style took much British domestic architecture into a backwater after the exciting rapids of Arts and Crafts originality, but the backwater was an attractive one.

Leading furniture shops were soon promoting this new Good Taste. In 1909 Messrs Heal and Son published a booklet called *An Aesthetic Conversion*, in whose introduction it was stated that, 'among recent revivals in the domestic arts none was possessed of more vigour than that of the furniture craftsman. Its purpose has been fulfilled – it has created a distaste for what was undoubtedly a bad period . . . That purpose served, it has vanished to unknown limbos and *l'art nouveau* seems to us now a weary, old and tiresome fashion.' The booklet went on to illustrate examples of the refined historical styles of interior design and furniture to which its readers were now expected to aspire – Palladian, Adam and many others [224].

This revival of Good Taste, with its curious echoes of the similar campaign by the English Palladian school of about 1720, is a matter of historical fact and it pervaded the furnishing and interior decoration of English upper middle-class houses for decades. Whatever may be the verdict on it, and on the Classical details on rows of brick boxes which contractors describe as Neo-Georgian, one important distinction should be made. The Neo-Georgian house as designed by architects of quality throughout the twentieth century is quite apart from the cynical mass-production of the type; it represents an attempt of convincing integrity to produce a comfortable house in a modern adaptation of a traditional English type which the users, as much as the architects, found pleasing.

223 *Wemyss Hall, Cupar, Fife (1905–07), by Robert Lorimer. Terrace front. The architect retained elements of Scottish vernacular work in this very personal rendering of Classical domestic architecture.*

224 *The new Good Taste in 1909. An illustration from the booklet* An Aesthetic Conversion, *published by Heal and Son.*

13
Palaces of Prosperity – Variations on the Grand Manner

THE REIGN of Edward VII saw the summit of the British Empire's splendour: a time of business well-being in Britain, and of expansion in commerce and industry. Temples were built for the god of prosperity. Grandiose office buildings, palatial hotels, banks and other buildings – almost all in one or other of the newly revived Classical styles – were erected in the major cities. Insurance offices, in particular, proliferated after 1895, at first in the Baroque style (see chapter ten), then in other Classical styles. The boom in insurance became so noticeable that in 1905 the architect Paul Waterhouse wrote of 'the appearance in our streets of vast palaces dedicated to the business of the great corporations who make their money by relieving people of risk'.[1]

The particular building Paul Waterhouse was writing about was the Royal Insurance Company building in Liverpool, a design by J. Francis Doyle which had won a competition in 1896. Another entry for the same competition is of even greater interest. It was by John Belcher and Beresford Pite, and it heralded the appearance of the Neo-Mannerism of a Michelangelesque type that was to flourish for a time in the following decade [226].

This 1896 design shows every sign of being chiefly by Pite, who was fascinated by Michelangelo.[2] In 1898 he wrote of the Laurenziana library staircase in Florence that architects of the day would 'find its suggestiveness attractive enough to induce

more constant reference than other popular fountains of inspiration'. Pite's early buildings have already been described in chapter four and elsewhere. They were free Baroque, but moving towards an anti-rational use of Classical features that is reminiscent of Italian Mannerism.

Some explanation of the relevance of Italian Renaissance Mannerism to English Edwardian architects is necessary here. In the 1520s Michelangelo in Florence and Giulio Romano in Mantua produced buildings whose expression was that of a powerful new variation of Classical architecture but which used architectural features in a clearly non-structural way – a style which modern historians have dubbed early Mannerism. In the early twentieth century there was still more reason to make it clear that a Classical exterior of a building was irrelevant to its internal structure. The new steel frames were cheaper and provided more free internal space than mass masonry or other traditional methods, but the clients of prestige buildings usually insisted on Classical façades. A small group of successful architects led by Beresford Pite, Charles Holden (of Percy Adams's firm), J. J. Joass (John Belcher's chief

225 Common-room fireplace, the Law Society library block, Chancery Lane, London (1903–04), by Charles Holden. The receding tiers of buttress pilasters echo the exterior of the building. Frieze panel sculpture by Conrad Dressler.

226 Competition design of 1896 for the Royal Insurance building, Liverpool, by John Belcher and Beresford Pite. Norman Shaw assessed the competition, but this design was not placed. The drawing shows Pite's new interest in Michelangelo's Mannerism.

227 Library block, the Law Society, Chancery Lane, London (1903–04), by Charles Holden. Holden here picked up Pite's Neo-Mannerism and combined it with his own strong liking for piled-up geometrical masses.

assistant) and Walter Thomas produced a series of buildings that pushed the Mannerist approach still further. These buildings are best described as Neo-Mannerist.

Pite was interested in this style more for its freshness than for the expression of a new type of structure (structural experiment bored him). It was Holden who designed the first of these Neo-Mannerist steel frame Classical buildings in London. This was a library wing for the Law Society in Chancery Lane (1903–04), which had to harmonize to some extent with the Society's earlier building beside it [227]. So Holden, who had worked for a year with the Arts and Crafts designer Ashbee, used Classical architecture for the first time. But the detailing employed by Holden, especially that of the corner niches and the round ground-floor arches, reflects Beresford Pite's Neo-Mannerism. The pillars in the arches show clearly that they are not structural, for they support only sculpted figures, again Michelangelesque in feeling. The overall shape of the building is a typical Holden exercise in the build-up of chunky rectangular masses (Frank Lloyd Wright's Unity Temple of 1906 is a similar composition, perhaps also showing the impact of the 1898 Secessionist building in Vienna). And the rich interior of Holden's library contains echoes of the outside elevations, especially in the piling-up of stumpy pilasters over the fireplace [225].

There followed three other striking London buildings by Holden in the next five years: Norwich House at No. 127 High Holborn (1904), Rhodesia House at No. 429 Strand (1907–08), and Evelyn House at No. 62 Oxford Street (1908). All of them may be described as Neo-Mannerist but, particularly in the case of Rhodesia House, the Classical features are so freely and powerfully used that they are close to a completely Free Style of architecture [*228*].

Meanwhile a Highland Scot named John James Joass (1868–1952), trained in Burnet's Glasgow office and Pite's successor as John Belcher's chief assistant, had taken up the Neo-Mannerist style too. It first appeared in Belcher and Joass's work on the steel frame upper storeys of Winchester House in London Wall (1904–05, demolished 1966). This was followed by three of the most notable buildings in the style in London: Mappin House at No. 158 Oxford Street (1906–08), Mowbray's Bookshop at No. 28 Margaret Street (1907–08), and the Royal Insurance building on the west corner of St James's Street and Piccadilly (1907–08).

Belcher, one of the leading Edwardian Baroque architects did little design work for his firm after the Ashton Memorial of 1904. He discussed each design with his assistant, but a member of his staff later wrote that it was Joass 'who detailed all the buildings of those days and gave us that curious elongated classical form with pendant blocks and wreaths'.[3] Of the Belcher and Joass Neo-Mannerist buildings, Mappin House is perhaps the most elegant British office building of its period [*229*]. Its steel frame leaves free the maximum amount of space inside the structure, as the plan shows [*230*]. At the same time, the light skin of Athenian Pentelikon marble, with its high arches and witty Mannerist detailing, makes it clear that this is no traditional load-bearing stone structure.

The Royal Insurance building is, however, the most sensational of these Mannerist designs. Again, the steel frame is expressed on the exterior by the fierce vertical emphasis and by the high ground-level columns which leave the street frontages clear for show windows. In the

228 *British Medical Association building (now Rhodesia House), No. 429 Strand, London (1907–08), by Holden. The new steel frame structures of the time made Classical architecture seem irrelevant to some architects. Holden and others expressed this by using Classical features in an anti-rational way.*

three floors above there is an astonishing outburst of detailing and sculpture on the Pentelikon marble frontages, with Classical features used in an anarchistic way [*231*]. Among the thrusting series of strongly vertical bays, there are pendant blocks with overlapping keystones and swags, then blank niches whose likely occupants, marble cherubs, appear to have climbed up to carry with their hands the weight of the cornice, gallery and roof storeys. Joass continued to produce a long succession of Neo-Mannerist buildings over the follow-

229 Mappin House, No. 158 Oxford Street, London (1906–08), by John Belcher and J. J. Joass. The walls consist of glass held in a thin layer of marble, with Neo-Mannerist detailing by Joass, covering the steel frame structure of the building.

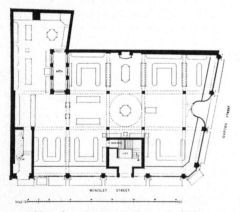

230 Plan of 1906, Mappin House, Oxford Street, by Belcher and Joass. The increased area made available for use by the steel frame structure contrasts with the area occupied by solid wall in older buildings.

ing twenty-five years, and indeed in the late 1920s produced two works as vertically expressive as the Royal Insurance.[4]

Outside London, one of the few important architects who tried a similar type of expression for large buildings using the new structural techniques was Walter Thomas in Liverpool. Thomas's best-known and mammoth work, the Liver Building for the Royal Liver Friendly Society, on the Pier Head in Liverpool (1908–11), is a huge quadrangular block with a frame of reinforced concrete, relieved by projecting vertical accents and the fantastic towers, domes and sculptured Liver birds on top [233].

The aggressive Neo-Mannerist style, however, was no more acceptable to the pundits of the new Classical Good Taste at the end of Edward VII's reign than was the Free Style itself. In 1910 *The Architectural Review* denounced those architects 'who unquestionably possess ability, but who are obsessed with the idea of doing something fresh ... They take the Orders, elongate and compress them, cut off cornices and mouldings and then, with an infusion of their own ideas, they produce a new style – the Ugly Style. This is the true cult of beauty!'[5] By this time *The Architectural Review* was actively promoting a return to a purer use of Classical architecture, so well exemplified by the French Beaux-Arts tradition described in chapter eleven.

The strangest of all the Edwardian Mannerist designs in London came from the unpredictable Beresford Pite. In his Carnegie Public Library in Thornhill Square, Islington (1906–08), and in his big building in Euston Square for the London, Edinburgh and Glasgow Assurance Company (1906–12), Pite used elements of Classical Greek architecture in as iconoclastic and Mannerist a way as Holden and Joass were treating Renaissance details in the

231 Detail, *Royal Insurance building, Piccadilly and St James's Street, London (1907–08), by Belcher and Joass. The most extreme example of Joass's Neo-Mannerist detailing.*

233 *The Liver Building, Pier Head, Liverpool (1908–11), by Walter Thomas for the Royal Liver Friendly Society. An early reinforced concrete frame, clad in grey granite, with free Neo-Mannerist detailing and exotic towers.*

232 *Entrance hall, London, Edinburgh and Glasgow Assurance, Euston Square, London (this section 1906–08), by Beresford Pite. The architect played with individual features of Classical Greek architecture in this extraordinary building.*

same years. In particular, the hallway of the Euston Square building (now government offices) is a wild extravaganza on the Greek theme [232]. The wing which Pite added to the building in 1912 on the Euston Road frontage shows a far more restrained type of Neo-Greek style.

Turning to Scotland, the Classical traditions of Alexander 'Greek' Thomson (1817–75) in Glasgow and William Playfair (1789–1857) in Edinburgh had not died out, although developments there and in England affected the types of Classicism

234 *New Library, St Andrews University, Scotland (1907–09), by Robert Lorimer. An elegant building in a chaste Classical style.*

in fashion. In Edinburgh, Burnet's originality in the use of Classical detail was not followed by other architects, except perhaps in the fine Boroughmuir School (1910–14) by J. A. Carfrae. Burnet's bold Civil Service and Professional Supply building in George Street (1903–07) and Forsyth's department store in Prince's Street (1906–10) stand out from the work of men such as George Washington Browne (1853–1939), though Browne's eclectic work has its moments of inspiration. In 1904 the Midlothian County Buildings were completed in Parliament Square, close to St Giles's Cathedral. Their architect, J. Macintyre Henry, showed in his design of 1899 an awareness of contemporary English work which is reflected in the sculptured frieze behind the colonnade and in the blocked columns of the Venetian windows. But the overall design displays a chaste and restrained Palladian manner. The same can be said of the Edinburgh Life Assurance building on the corner of George Street and Hanover

Street, built in 1908–09 by J. M. Dick Peddie (1853–1921), although the corner dome brings a touch of Baroque spirit to the design [235]. Nevertheless, the buildings associated with the rebuilding of the North Bridge, by various architects, are perhaps the most exciting group done at the turn of the century in Edinburgh.

Outside Edinburgh, Glasgow's typical individualism can be seen in the way its less famous architects used Classical architecture. A good example of this is the National Bank of Scotland in St Enoch Square, built by the architect Alexander N. Paterson (1862–1947) in 1906–08, which expresses the equivalent of English Neo-Mannerism in the stone frontage over its steel frame.

However, perhaps the most important event of these years for Scottish Classical architecture was that the talented Robert Lorimer (1864–1929) took the same step as Lutyens in England. Like Lutyens, Lorimer had designed many excellent houses on the principles of Arts and Crafts free architecture in the 1890s. But during the first decade of the new century, he took up Classical architecture and used it with rare elegance. Lorimer's New Library for St Andrews University (1907–09) is a particularly delicate design [234], and the architect went on to fame and a knighthood with work in many different styles including the Gothic of the Thistle Chapel in St Giles's Cathedral, Edinburgh (1910), and numerous Baronial country houses.

It is clear from what has been written here that the variations of the Classical Grand Manner took many different forms during the second half of Edward VII's reign after the reaction against High Baroque. Yet another type can be seen in the splendid Florentine palazzo with a reinforced concrete frame that Mewès and Davis designed as the Cunard Building (1914–16) on the Pier Head in Liverpool [236]. The Baroque style itself produced a few last phenomena, notably Ralph Knott's County Hall design of 1907 for the London County Council and the Port of London Authority's flamboyant headquarters (1912–22) beside the Tower of London.

The commission for the Port of London Authority building was won in a competition of 1912 by Edwin Cooper (1873–1942), who had recently started a personal practice after working in a series of partnerships. Cooper's success in the competition of 1911 for the St Marylebone Town Hall was, however, more significant for the future. Reviewing the entries for the competition, the editor of one architectural magazine wrote: 'We cannot help asking ourselves whether all these colossal columns, domes, towers, groups of sculpture and other imposing features are felt by their authors to be the only natural and inevitable expression of the necessities of the case.'[6]

Such criticism of extravagant building was in harmony with general feeling at the time. And the St Marylebone Town Hall built to Cooper's designs shows a greatly simplified use of Classicism, emphasizing the volumes in Holden's way, rather than creating broken Baroque outlines en-

235 *Edinburgh Life Assurance building, George Street and Hanover Street, Edinburgh (1908–09), by J. M. Dick Peddie. A handsome and restrained Classicism, enlivened by the corner dome, that is typical of much Edinburgh architecture of the time.*

236 *Cunard Building, Pier Head, Liverpool (1914–16), designed by Mewès and Davis (executed by Willink and Thicknesse). The majestic stone exterior is built around a reinforced concrete frame.*

185

crusted with sculpture [237]. The mention of Holden's name here is no coincidence. More than anyone else, it was his work that bridged the gap between the attempts at a Free Style and the varieties of Edwardian Classicism. By stripping all but a minimum of ornament from buildings which still retained Classical echoes, Holden pointed the design of large buildings in a new direction.

This – the Stripped Classical – was the path which much British public architecture was to follow for many years. One of its chief exponents, A. E. Richardson (1880–1964), wrote in 1911: 'Today we stand bewildered amidst the Babylonian confusion brought about by the thoughtless reproduction of various historical styles', and went on to call for a new simple

238 No. 7 St James's Square, London (1911), by Edwin Lutyens. The flatness of the elevation, relieved only by porch and cornice, represents a move towards the Stripped Classicism widely used in the following twenty years.

237 St Marylebone Town Hall, Marylebone Road, London (1911–18), by Edwin Cooper. By the end of the first decade of the century, the reaction against extravagance in taste and cost helped to bring in simplified Classical forms.

adaptation of Classical principles.[7] Richardson's own first building of any size was the New Theatre in Manchester (1912) and the requirements of theatrical showmanship gave him little opportunity to put his purist ideas into practice. But he was to produce many Stripped Classical buildings of great excellence shortly after the Great War of 1914–18.

Nevertheless, it is in the work of Edwin Lutyens that the greatest achievements of the Stripped Classical style are to be found. The big London house of 1911 which Lutyens designed at No. 7 St James's Square shows the trend: a Classical use of window proportions on a four-storey brick frontage of extraordinarily flat relief [238]. Only the porch and the cornice at the top give any depth to the wall surface. Then in 1912 Lutyens, with Herbert Baker (who had built many fine buildings in South Africa), was given the job of a lifetime: the design of the government buildings for the capital of India, New Delhi. Baker designed the Legislative Buildings, but it is the Viceroy's House by Lutyens, completed only in 1931, that is the monumental masterpiece of the Stripped Classicism developed from High Edwardian Baroque [239].[8]

British public buildings of the period between the two world wars were dominated by this Classical manner, simplified by the elimination of most decorative features. Other fashions came and went, including phases of ancient Egyptian influence, American monumental Classicism, simplified Scandinavian large-scale architecture and the inspiration of the Dutch work of Berlage and others. Those two decades were as complicated as the period covered by this book, but it was the rationalist ideas of the Bauhaus, brought to England by refugees from German Nazism in the early 1930s, rather than such transient developments that were to have the longest-lasting influence on British architecture.

239 *The Viceroy's House, New Delhi, India (1912–31), by Edwin Lutyens. In one of Lutyens's best Classical buildings the Grand Manner, which had started with the Baroque revival in the 1890s,* reached its most brilliant conclusion. In the Viceroy's House the architect uses simplified Classical forms, with occasional touches of India's own vernacular styles.

187

Notes on the Text

Chapter One

1 The movement's ideology and development have been admirably traced in Gillian Naylor, *The Arts and Crafts Movement* (London 1971) and in Robert Macleod, *Style and Society* (London 1971).

2 *Contrasts* (2nd revised edition, London 1841; first version 1836).

3 *The Seven Lamps of Architecture* (London 1849), chapter 'The Lamp of Truth'.

4 *The Stones of Venice* (London 1851–53), chapter 'On the Nature of Gothic'.

5 *Art of the People*, a speech at Birmingham Town Hall, 1879.

6 *Architectural Association Notes*, Vol. 4, p. 23.

7 *Architectural Association Notes*, Vol. 3, p. 90.

Chapter Two

1 *Collected Works of William Morris* (London 1915), Vol. 22, p. 33.

2 Godwin's paper to the Manchester Architectural Association was printed in *The British Architect*, 29 November 1878.

3 A good account of the philosophical and biological influences on Mackmurdo is given in a thesis by Malcolm Haslam published in précis form in *Country Life*, 27 February and 6 March 1975.

4 See Godfrey Rubens, 'William Lethaby's Buildings', in A. Service (ed.), *Edwardian Architecture and its Origins* (London 1975).

5 See Christopher Grillet, 'Edward Schroeder Prior', in *The Architectural Review*, 1952, Vol. 112, p. 302, reprinted in *Edwardian Architecture and its Origins*. Much more information has been drawn from the first full thesis on Prior being prepared by Lynne Walker, to whom my thanks are due.

6 A complete list of members of the Guild from 1884 to 1934, with their occupations and year of joining, is given in H. J. L. J. Massé, *The Art Workers' Guild* (Oxford 1935), p. 133.

7 *The Architectural Review*, 1903, Vol. 13, p. 188.

8 See A. Service, 'James MacLaren and the Godwin Legacy', in *The Architectural Review*, August 1973.

9 *Architectural Association Notes*, 1889–90, Vol. 4, p. 23. Both Lethaby and Prior gave occasional lectures at the Architectural Association at this time and in the early 1890s, and were clearly held in high esteem. In 1888–89 the President of the Association was Leonard Stokes and the honours list included Detmar Blow, Edwin Lutyens, Owen Fleming and Banister Fletcher.

10 See Walter Godfrey, 'The Work of George Devey', in *The Architectural Review*, 1907, Vol. 21, pp. 22–30, 83–88 and 293–306.

11 The drawings for No. 42 Netherhall Gardens in the R.I.B.A. drawings collection are all by Lethaby.

12 Thesis on E. S. Prior by Lynne Walker, 1975.

13 *Transactions of The National Association for the Advancement of Art and its Application to Industry* (1889). William Morris was in the chair and pointed out, after Prior's address, that 'easy and cheap carriage forced people to use materials not fitted for the district and out of harmony with the surroundings. As for iron architecture, there never was and never could be such.' The Edinburgh Art Congress was one of a series in different cities.

14 Richardson's Quincy Library of 1880 was illustrated in *The British Architect*, 5 January 1883 (attribution corrected 30 March 1883), and this magazine illustrated such American work fairly regularly after that.

15 Voysey lived at 11 Melina Place from 1890 to 1897, Prior at 10 Melina Place from 1894 to 1901.

16 *The Architectural Review*, 1897, Vol. 3, p. 42. For further details about such plans, see Jill Franklin, 'Edwardian Butterfly Houses', in *The Architectural Review*, April 1975.

17 *The British Architect*, 22 February 1895.

18 Illustrated in *The Architectural Review*, 1899, Vol. 6, supplement after p. 32.

19 See *The Builder*, 1898, Vol. 75, pp. 230 and 343, and *The Studio*, 1898, Vol. 13, p. 239.

20 Design illustrated in *The British Architect*, 7 December 1888.

21 Voysey's paper 'The Art of Today' was printed in *The British Architect*, 18 November 1892.

22 See A. Service, 'Arts and Crafts Extremist', in *Architectural Association Quarterly*, 1974, Vol. 6, No. 2, and ibid., 'Charles Harrison Townsend', in *Edwardian Architecture and its Origins*, p. 164.

23 *The Studio*, Vol. 9, October 1896.

24 A full list of Ashbee's buildings is given by Alan Crawford in *Architectural History*, 1970, Vol. 13, pp. 64–76.

25 See James D. Kornwolf, *M. H. Baillie Scott and the Arts and Crafts Movement* (Baltimore 1972).

26 W. R. Lethaby, *Architecture, Mysticism and Myth* (London 1891; republished by Architectural Press, London 1974). The book was perhaps the biggest single written influence on Arts and Crafts architectural ideas in the 1890s; quotations from it by Ricardo, Henry Wilson, Townsend, Mackintosh and others recur again and again.

27 Muthesius published three influential books in Germany reporting on his studies in Britain: *Die Englische Baukunst der Gegenwart* (Leipzig 1900), *Die Neuere Kirkliche Baukunst in England* (Berlin 1901) and *Das Englische Haus* (Berlin 1904–05). Robin Middleton has pointed out to me that another cultural attaché from Germany, Karl Hinckeldeyn, was sent to study American domestic building before Muthesius was in Britain.

Chapter Three

1 *The Architect*, 7 August 1875, p. 344.

2 H. O. Cresswell in *Architectural Association Notes*, 1892, Vol. 7, p. 60.

3 Joseph Nash, *The Mansions of England in the Olden Time* (London 1838–49). Republished in 1906 by *The Studio* with an introduction by C. Harrison Townsend.

4 *The Architectural Review*, 1897, Vol. 3, p. 42.

5 *Transactions of the National Association for the Advancement of Art and its Application to Industry*, 1889, pp. 320–21.

6 W. R. Lethaby, *Architecture, Mysticism and Myth* (London 1891).

7 See *The British Architect*, 5 January and 30 March 1883, and *The Builder*, 22 January 1887.

8 *Architectural Association Notes*, 1888, Vol. 3, p. 9 and 1893, Vol. 8, p. 34. Lululand was designed by Richardson for the artist Herkomer in 1886. Herkomer altered parts of the design before the house was completed in 1894. A fragment still stands in Melbourne Road, Bushey, Herts.

9 *House and Garden*, February 1906, commented on in *The Architectural Review*, 1906, Vol. 19, p. 165.

10 *Architectural Association Notes*, Vol. 4, p. 56.

11 *Architectural Association Notes*, Vol. 8, p. 129.

12 *Architectural Association Notes*, Vol. 8, p. 95.

13 The book is dated 1892 on the title page, though it was actually published in late 1891.

14 *Architecture, Mysticism and Myth*, pp. xx, 6, 7, 8, 35 and 45.

15 *Architecture, Mysticism and Myth*, pp. 65–66.

16 *The Studio*, 1894, Vol. 4, p. 88.

17 See Pevsner and Richards (eds), *The Anti-Rationalists* (London 1973), for a selection of Art Nouveau architecture, especially Sherban Cantacuzino's study of Guimard, who visited London in 1894.

18 See A. Service (ed.), *Edwardian Architecture and its Origins* (London 1975), pp. 162 ff., for the development of Blackheath.

19 See *The British Architect*, 28 June to 12 July 1895, for designs entered in this competition, including entries by Ricardo and Horsley.

20 *The British Architect*, 25 February 1898.

21 Mackintosh's designs were often published in *The British Architect* from the early 1890s onwards, and he doubtless saw the Smith and Brewer design published on 28 June 1895.

22 'Originality in Architecture', a paper given by Townsend to the Architectural Association in London on 1 February 1902, published in *The Builder*, Vol. 82, pp. 133–36. Comment on it by Muthesius in *Architectural Association Notes*, 1902, Vol. 17.

Chapter Four

1 Chelsea Town Hall was extended to the King's Road by Brydon's close friend Leonard Stokes in 1904–08. Stokes commented in *The Architectural Review*, 1909, Vol. 25, p. 150, that 'as far as practicable, the general detail of his [Brydon's] work has been followed'. Brydon's design was illustrated in *The British Architect*, 27 November 1885.

2 *Architectural Association Notes*, Vol. 3, p. 92.

3 Printed in *The Builder*, Vol. 56, pp. 147 and 168.

4 *The British Architect*, 4 January 1889.

5 See A. Service, 'Belcher and Joass', in *The Architectural Review*, November 1970.

6 In 1968–70 William Whitfield extended and refurbished the building, after persuading the Institute not to demolish and redevelop from scratch.

7 See W. J. Loftie, 'Brydon at Bath', in *The Architectural Review*, 1905, Vol. 18, pp. 3, 51 and 147.

8 *Architectural Association Notes*, September 1891, Vol. 6, p. 57.

9 Blomfield's essay on 'The English Tradition' in furniture was published in *Arts and Crafts Essays*

by Members of the Arts and Crafts Exhibition Society (London 1893).

10 See obituary in *The Architectural Review*, 1908, Vol. 23, p. 161.

11 Shaw and Jackson (eds), *Architecture, a Profession or an Art?* (London 1892).

12 *The British Architect*, 17 February 1899.

13 Stokes was the Architectural Association's President in 1890, Mountford in 1893 and Pite in 1896. For Brydon's activities see *Architectural Association Notes*, 1901, Vol. 16, pp. 87 and 99. It should be noted, however, that Prior and Lethaby also lectured at the Association in the early 1890s.

14 See Robert Macleod, *Style and Society* (London 1971), pp. 80–100, for an excellent account of the introduction of French ideas of architectural education to Britain.

15 See A. Service, 'John Belcher's Colchester Town Hall', in *Transactions of the Essex Archaeological Society*, 1973, Vol. 5.

16 Pite, 'The Architecture of Michael Angelo', in *The Architectural Review*, Vol. 4, p. 219 and Vol. 5, pp. 21 and 86.

17 See A. Service, 'Arthur Beresford Pite', in A. Service (ed.), *Edwardian Architecture and its Origins* (London 1975), p. 394.

18 Prior's Medical Schools are extensively illustrated in *The Architectural Review*, 1904, Vol. 15, p. 159. Prior's accompanying comment says: 'Since the building here is a memorial one, it has some elaboration of stonework externally.'

Chapter Five

1 H. S. Goodhart-Rendel, *English Architecture since the Regency* (London 1953).

2 See J. E. Newbery, 'The Work of John L. Pearson R.A.', in *The Architectural Review*, 1896–97, Vol. 1, pp. 1 and 69.

3 Sedding's paper is printed in the supplement to the November 1890 issue of *Architectural Association Notes*, p. 11.

4 J. P. Cooper and H. Wilson, 'The Work of John Sedding', with an appreciation by C. H. Whall, in *The Architectural Review*, 1898, Vol. 3, pp. 35, 125, 188 and 235, and Vol. 4, pp. 33 and 74, largely reprinted in A. Service (ed.), *Edwardian Architecture and its Origins* (London 1975), pp. 258–79.

5 *The Architectural Review*, 1901, Vol. 10, pp. 163 ff. The works by Champneys illustrated here are Gothic by chance, but he was a wide-ranging stylist of some originality. For example, he was among the early users of the Queen Anne style for London Board Schools in the early 1870s.

6 Fully illustrated in Nicholas Taylor, 'Byzantium in Brighton', in *Edwardian Architecture and its Origins*, pp. 281–88.

7 Protests by many leading architects were published in *The Architectural Review*, Vol. 10, p. 163 and elsewhere, while Edward Prior and Professor F. M. Simpson contributed articles on what they considered the approach should be in designing the cathedral on pp. 138–46 of the same volume. Prior's article develops a favourite later theme of his, that modern cathedrals should be built by their craftsmen, working from outline specifications given by the Church authorities, and without a designing architect. Further information about the Liverpool Cathedral competition is given in J. Thomas, 'The Style shall be Gothic', in *The Architectural Review*, September 1975.

8 See Canon B. F. L. Clarke, 'Ecclesiastical Architecture', in *Journal of the Royal Society of Arts*, March 1973, p. 234.

9 See John Betjeman, 'J. N. Comper', in *The Architectural Review*, 1939, Vol. 85, p. 79.

Chapter Six

1 *The Architectural Review*, 1904, Vol. 15, p. 217.

2 For other versions of this plan see Jill Franklin, 'Edwardian Butterfly Houses', in *The Architectural Review*, April 1975.

3 Lawrence Weaver (ed.), *Small Country Houses of Today* (London 1910), quoted by John Archer in 'The partnership of Edgar Wood and J. Henry Sellers', in A. Service (ed.), *Edwardian Architecture and its Origins* (London 1975).

4 James D. Kornwolf, *M. H. Baillie Scott and the Arts and Crafts Movement* (Baltimore 1972), pp. 292–316, gives a good account of Scott's work at Hampstead Garden Suburb and its significance.

5 Fleming was joint editor of the *Architectural Association Notes* in 1891–92 but he and the Architectural Association's President, Leonard Stokes, resigned in protest against the Association's new educational scheme. See *Architectural Association Notes*, Vol. 6, pp. 178 and 208.

6 See D. Gregory-Jones, 'Some Early Works of the L.C.C. Architect's Department', in *Architectural Association Journal*, 1954, pp. 95–105.

7 See article on the Millbank Estate in *The Architectural Review*, 1910, Vol. 27.

8 See Blashill's paper of February 1900 reported in *Architectural Association Notes*, Vol. 15, p. 36.

Chapter Seven

1 Both quoted in Nikolaus Pevsner, *Pioneers of*

Modern Design (London 1960), pp. 106–07.

2 *The Architectural Review*, 1901, Vol. 10, p. 104.

3 *The British Architect*, 14 October 1904, p. 273.

4 *Architectural Association Notes*, 1900, Vol. 15, p. 137.

5 *The Architectural Review*, 1901, Vol. 9, p. 143.

6 But it is ironic that a year later Cross had surrendered to the popularity of Edwardian Baroque; see his Baroque designs for a public dye house and public swimming baths illustrated in *The British Architect*, 25 April and 20 June 1902.

7 See Pevsner, 'Goodhart-Rendel's Roll-Call', in A. Service (ed.), *Edwardian Architecture and its Origins* (London 1975). Goodhart-Rendel appears to have started in architecture about 1905; see his design for a house illustrated in *The British Architect* in July of that year.

8 The design made a strong enough impression to earn a full-page illustration in *The Architectural Review*, 1896–97, Vol. 1.

9 See photographs and plans with article in *The Architectural Review*, 1906, Vol. 19, pp. 277–312.

10 Photographs and plans with article in *The Architectural Review*, 1908, Vol. 24, pp. 234–47. Drawings of the design had been published in *The Builder*, 2 September 1905.

11 *Building*, 1931, p. 396.

12 Robert Macleod, *Charles Rennie Mackintosh* (London 1968), p. 137.

13 *The British Architect*, 4 January 1907, Vol. 67.

14 See David Walker, 'Lamond of Dundee', in *The Architectural Review*, 1958, Vol. 123, p. 269.

15 See *The Builders' Journal*, 25 March 1908, pp. 269–73, quoted in David Walker, 'The Partnership of James Salmon and J. G. Gillespie', in *Edwardian Architecture and its Origins*, p. 245.

Chapter Eight

1 *The Architectural Review*, 1898, Vol. 4, pp. 33 and 74.

2 W. R. Lethaby, *Architecture, Mysticism and Myth* (London 1891).

3 Godfrey Rubens's biography of Lethaby is in preparation at the time of writing. I am extremely grateful to him for the information he has given me and for the discussions we have had about Lethaby's symbolist intentions. It should be noted that the triple lancet and star are not among the symbols discussed in *Architecture, Mysticism and Myth*. But the church was designed a decade after the book was written, and in the interim other works giving Lethaby further information had been published, e.g. that by F. Hulme, *Symbolism in Christian Art* (London 1892).

4 See John Archer, 'Edgar Wood – a Notable Manchester Architect', in *Transactions of the Lancashire and Cheshire Antiquarian Society*, Vol. 73–74, p. 173. At the time of writing the church is in an appalling state and the interior almost gutted, though there are plans to reconstruct it.

5 *The British Architect*, 15 February 1905, and the *The Architectural Review*, 1901, Vol. 10, pp. 143–46.

Chapter Nine

1 *Architectural Association Notes*, Vol. 8, pp. 85–87 and 116.

2 *The Architectural Review*, 1908, Vol. 24, p. 153.

3 *The British Architect*, editorial commenting on the end of the century, 4 January 1901.

4 Martin S. Briggs, 'Iron and Steel and Modern Design', in *The Architectural Review*, 1907, Vol. 21, pp. 221–26.

5 W. R. Lethaby, *Architecture* (London 1912), p. 247.

6 The Stokes and the Brewill and Bailey designs were illustrated in *The Architectural Review*, 1900, Vol. 8, pp. 41 and 183.

7 *The Architectural Review*, 1900, Vol. 7, p. 194.

8 Charles Marsh and William Dunn, *Reinforced Concrete* (3rd revised edition, London 1906).

9 The designs of Holden's Bristol library were published in 1905 and photographs of his Law Society library in *The Architectural Review*, 1906, Vol. 19, pp. 120–27. Both show compositions of piled-up volumes similar to Sellers's central tower at the Dronsfield building and in Wood and Sellers's slightly later schools.

10 *The British Architect*, 25 June, 2 July and 30 July 1909.

11 W. R. Lethaby, 'Some Things to be Done', a paper to the Architectural Association; see *Architectural Association Journal*, April 1913.

12 *The British Architect*, 5 January 1912, reporting that the building had recently been opened, having been 'built in little over a year'.

13 An excellent account of Burnet's development is given in David Walker, 'Sir John James Burnet', in A. Service (ed.), *Edwardian Architecture and its Origins* (London 1975).

Chapter Ten

1 *The Architectural Review*, 1897, Vol. 2, p. 90.

2 *The Builder*, 1889, Vol. 56, pp. 169–70.

3 *Architectural Association Notes*, 1898, Vol. 13, p. 172.

4 All these books were published in London. Belcher's architectural practice suffered a long gap between 1888 and 1897, during which his and Pite's entries for competitions were widely

praised and influential, but failed to gain first prizes or major commissions. He and Macartney used the time well by collecting material for their large book, concentrating on the period between c.1600 and c.1780. The work is dated 1901, but the first volume was published in 1898 and reviewed that year (see *The Architectural Review*, Vol. 3, p. 93). The list of subscribers to the work, printed in the book, is almost a roll-call of the major Edwardian Baroque architects, including Blomfield, Brydon, Burnet, George, Lanchester, Mountford, Newton, Runtz, Shaw, Stokes and Aston Webb as well as Honeyman and Keppie (Mackintosh's firm).

5 *The British Architect*, 7 January 1898.

6 See John Warren, 'Edwin Alfred Rickards', in A. Service (ed.), *Edwardian Architecture and its Origins* (London 1975), pp. 339–50.

7 See *The Architectural Review*, 1908, Vol. 24, pp. 69–83 and 1910, Vol. 28, p. 55.

8 See obituary of Young, in *Journal of the Royal Institute of British Architects*, November 1900.

9 *The Architectural Review*, 1900, Vol. 8, p. 234.

10 *The Architectural Review*, 1906, Vol. 20, pp. 301–16.

11 *The Architectural Review*, 1910, Vol. 28, p. 59.

12 See Kerry Downes, *English Baroque Architecture* (London 1966), plates 74–77.

13 *Architectural Association Notes*, 1900, Vol. 15, p. 162.

14 *The British Architect*, 27 July 1900.

15 *The Architectural Review*, 1900, Vol. 8, p. 3.

16 See *The Architectural Review*, 1900, Vol. 8, p. 3 and 1907, Vol. 21, pp. 136–52, for Mountford's original and final plans.

17 The competition was held in 1907, though the result was announced in early 1908. See *The British Architect* and other magazines throughout January and February 1908.

18 *The Architectural Review*, Vol. 20, pp. 10, 94 and 139.

19 *The Architectural Review*, 1906, Vol. 19, p. 155.

Chapter Eleven

1 Robert Macleod, *Style and Society – Architectural Ideology in Britain 1835–1914* (London 1971), pp. 88–97. Macleod's book, however, does not make clear the long gap between the efforts to introduce the French educational system to Britain in the 1880s and the advent of French influence on British buildings and education in the 1900s.

2 Richard Chafee's book on the Ecole des Beaux-Arts is in preparation at the time of writing and I

owe much to the information he has given me in advance.

3 *The Architectural Review*, 1907, Vol. 22, p. 167.

4 E.g. in Philippe Jullian, *The Triumph of Art Nouveau – Paris Exhibition, 1900* (London 1974).

5 *The Architectural Review*, 1908, Vol. 23, p. 127.

6 See Victor Glasstone, *Victorian and Edwardian Theatres* (London 1975), for an illuminating account of Edwardian theatrical architecture.

7 Blomfield's lectures were printed in full in *The Architectural Review* during 1907 and in book form in *The Mistress Art* (London 1908). I am grateful to Mr Richard Fellows, who has been generous with information from his researches for his thesis on Blomfield.

8 *The British Architect*, 3 January 1913, published the 'approved elevation' of the new design.

9 *The Architectural Review*, July 1911, Vol. 30, pp. 25–28.

10 C. H. Reilly, *Representative British Architects of the Present Day* (London 1931), p. 61.

Chapter Twelve

1 See the comments on the 'sea-change' of Renaissance architecture in St Paul's Cathedral in Webb's letter published in W. R. Lethaby, *Philip Webb and his Work* (London 1935), p. 138.

2 Newton maintained some Arts and Crafts ideals in his Neo-Georgian work, for the description of the house in *The Architectural Review*, 1905, Vol. 17, notes that the oak panelling and the tiles were local work made in Jersey.

3 *The Architectural Review*, 1902, Vol. 11, pp. 92–94 and 117–27.

4 The series begins in Vol. 19, p. 155.

Chapter Thirteen

1 In a review of a book on the Royal Insurance Company's Baroque Liverpool building (designed by J. Francis Doyle, in consultation with Norman Shaw) in *The Architectural Review*, 1905, Vol. 17.

2 *The British Architect*, 1908, Vol. 70, and *The Architectural Review*, 1898, Vols 4 and 5, have papers by Pite on Michelangelo's architecture.

3 Professor Charles H. Reilly, in *Scaffolding in the Sky* (London 1938). Belcher visited America in 1899 and doubtless encouraged his firm's early experiments with steel frames. Joass later said of his old employer (later partner) that 'new ideas appealed to him irresistibly' but that with Belcher's illness in old age 'an increasing proportion of the responsibility of the work of those years naturally fell into my hands'. See

Journal of the Royal Institute of British Architects, 1915, pp. 97 and 121.
4 Abbey House, Baker Street, London (completed 1932), and the central section with tower of Royal London House, Finsbury Square (1927–30). See list of the firm's work in A. Service, 'Belcher and Joass', in A. Service (ed.), *Edwardian Architecture and its Origins* (London 1975), pp. 311–27.

5 *The Architectural Review*, 1910, Vol. 27, article signed 'X'.
6 *The Architects' and Builders' Journal*, 1911.
7 A. E. Richardson, 'American Buildings', in *The British Architect*, 17 March 1911.
8 See Gavin Stamp, 'Indian Summer', in *The Architectural Review*, 1976, Vol. 159, pp. 365–72, for a remarkable account of the work in India of British architects contemporary with Lutyens.

Select Bibliography

ARCHER, J. H. G. 'Edgar Wood – a Notable Manchester Architect', in *Transactions of the Lancashire and Cheshire Antiquarian Society*, Vols 73–74.
Edgar Wood – A Biography (forthcoming).
Arts and Crafts Essays by Members of the Arts and Crafts Exhibition Society (London 1893). Includes essays by Edward Prior, Halsey Ricardo, Reginald Blomfield, William Lethaby, T. G. Jackson and others on various aspects of furniture.
ASHBEE, C. R. *Craftsmanship in Competitive Industry* (Essex House Press 1908).
Modern English Silverwork (Essex House Press 1909; reprinted by Weinreb, London 1974).
Should We Stop Teaching Art? (London 1911).
'Memoirs' (unpublished manuscript in Victoria and Albert Museum, 1938). A valuable source for the views of this leading figure in the Arts and Crafts movement.
ASLIN, E. *The Aesthetic Movement* (London 1969). A good account of a movement which included E. W. Godwin and had much influence on the Arts and Crafts movement, despite clashes of principle.
BAKER, SIR H. *Architecture and Personalities* (London 1944). Memoirs of Lutyens's contemporary, who became a leading figure in Britain in the 1920s.
BEATTIE, S. 'New Scotland Yard', in *Architectural History* (Journal of the Society of Architectural Historians of Great Britain), 1972, Vol. 15, pp. 68–81.
BELCHER, J. *Essentials in Architecture* (London 1907). The views of a leader of the Edwardian Baroque revival.
BELCHER, J., AND M. MACARTNEY *Later Renaissance Architecture in England* (London 1898–1901). A source book for the Edwardian Baroque revival consisting of two illustrated folio volumes on English buildings *c.* 1600–1780.

BETJEMAN, SIR J. 'J. Ninian Comper', in *The Architectural Review*, 1939, Vol. 85, pp. 79–82.
BLOMFIELD, SIR R. *The Formal Garden in England* (London 1893).
A History of Renaissance Architecture in England 1500–1800 (London 1897). One of the main sources of inspiration for the revival of Classicism at the end of the century.
The Mistress Art (London 1908). Royal Academy lectures of 1907 expressing the need for purer Classicism.
History of French Architecture (London 1911 onwards). The expression of Blomfield's long fascination with French Classicism.
Memoirs of an Architect (London 1932).
Richard Norman Shaw R. A. (London 1940). The first biography of Shaw. Blomfield was devoted to Shaw and saw his career as a long progression towards Classicism.
BRANDON-JONES, J. C. F. A. *Voysey* (undated reprint of a special issue of *Architectural Association Quarterly*). See also under Ferriday, P.
BRIGGS, M. S. *Everyman's Concise Encyclopaedia of Architecture* (London 1959). Particularly strong in references to British architects of the period 1900–39, who were the contemporaries of the architect author.
CARLYLE, T. *Past and Present* (London 1843). An influence on Ruskin and Morris.
CHAFEE, R. *Architecture and l'École des Beaux-Arts* (forthcoming).
CLARKE, B. F. L. *Anglican Cathedrals outside the British Isles* (London 1958).
COOPER, N. *The Opulent Eye. Late Victorian and Edwardian Taste in Interior Design* (London 1976).
CRANE, W. *Ideals in Art* (London 1905).
An Artist's Reminiscences (London 1907).
William Morris to Whistler (London 1911).

CRAWFORD, A., AND S. BURY *Life of C. R. Ashbee* (forthcoming).

DARLEY, G. *Villages of Vision* (London 1975). A good history of 'model' villages in the period 1770–1970 in Britain.

DAVISON, T. RAFFLES (ed.) *The Arts connected with Building* (London 1909).

DOWNES, K. *English Baroque Architecture* (London 1966). Illustrates hundreds of the English Baroque buildings of *c.* 1680–1720 which influenced the Edwardians.

EATON, L. K. *American Architecture Comes of Age: European Reaction to H. H. Richardson and Louis Sullivan* (Cambridge, Mass. 1972).

FAWCETT, J. (ed.) *Seven Victorian Architects* (London 1976). Includes essays by D. Lloyd on J. L. Pearson, by D. Verey on G. F. Bodley, by S. Allen Smith on Waterhouse and by R. Gradidge on Lutyens.

FERRIDAY, P. (ed.) *Victorian Architecture* (London 1963). Includes essays by J. Brandon-Jones on Philip Webb and Voysey.

FLETCHER, SIR H. BANISTER *The English House* (London 1910).

FRANKLIN, J. 'Edwardian Butterfly Houses', in *The Architectural Review*, April 1975. A good article on the experimental house plans of Edward Prior and his followers.

Gimson, Ernest: His Life and Work (Stratford on Avon 1924). A primary source book of Arts and Crafts work.

GLASSTONE, V. *Victorian and Edwardian Theatres* (London 1975). An invaluable work on an important and little-known aspect of Edwardian architectural flair.

GOMME, A., AND D. M. WALKER. See Walker, D. M., and A. Gomme.

GOODHART-RENDEL, H. S. *English Architecture since the Regency* (London 1953). A brief book by the witty historian who did much to draw attention to Edwardian work.

GOTCH, J. A. *The Architecture of the Renaissance in England* (London 1894). Another important source of inspiration for Edwardian Classicists.

The Growth of the English House (London 1909).

GRADIDGE, R. 'Edwin Lutyens', in J. Fawcett (ed.), *Seven Victorian Architects* (London 1976).

GRAY, A. S. *A Biographical Dictionary of Edwardian Architecture* (forthcoming).

GREIG, D. E. *Herbert Baker in South Africa* (Cape Town and London 1970). An excellent account of Baker's early work.

HARBRON, D. *The Conscious Stone. The Life of E. W. Godwin* (London 1949). A fascinating subject, but the book gives an unsatisfying account of Godwin's architecture.

HILL, OLIVER *Scottish Castles of the Sixteenth and Seventeenth Centuries* (London 1953). Illustrates much of the Scottish vernacular work that influenced architects of Mackintosh's generation.

HITCHCOCK, H. RUSSELL *Architecture: Nineteenth and Twentieth Centuries* (London 1958). The classic account of the international architectural scene that was the background to developments in Britain.

The Architecture of H. H. Richardson (Hamden 1961). A major biography of the great American who influenced much British architecture of *c.* 1890.

HOBHOUSE, H. *Lost London* (London 1971). A sad but valuable record of demolished London buildings, well illustrated.

HOWARD, E. *Garden Cities of Tomorrow* (London 1902). A work of key influence in the history of town planning.

HOWARTH, T. *Charles Rennie Mackintosh and the Modern Movement* (London 1952). The major biography of the great Scottish architect.

HUSSEY, C., AND A. S. G. BUTLER *Lutyens Memorial Volumes* (London 1951). A vast three-volume record of the great architect's work.

HUSSEY, C. *Sir Robert Lorimer* (London 1931). The standard book on the eminent Scottish architect.

JACKSON, SIR T. G. See Shaw, R. Norman, and Sir T. G. Jackson.

JORDAN, R. FURNEAUX *Victorian Architecture* (London 1966). An outline of the Victorian period, touching on the Edwardian.

JULLIAN, P. *The Triumph of Art Nouveau: Paris Exhibition, 1900* (London 1974). A well-illustrated record of an exhibition whose Classical architecture had more influence in England than its Art Nouveau exhibits.

KORNWOLF, J. D. *M. H. Baillie Scott and the Arts and Crafts Movement* (Baltimore 1972). A major biography of Baillie Scott, which perhaps makes him appear a more dominant figure than he was.

LETHABY, W. R. *Architecture, Mysticism and Myth* (London 1891; Architectural Press reprint with introduction by Godfrey Rubens, London 1975). The most important attempt by an Arts and Crafts architect to establish the symbolism underlying architecture of all periods.

Santa Sophia (London 1894). Byzantine architecture and its symbolism interested Lethaby before the style became fashionable in England in the 1890s.

Morris as Work-Master (London 1902).

Medieval Art (London 1904).

Architecture: an Introduction to the History and Theory

of the Art of Building (London 1912).

Architecture, Nature and Magic (originally published as essays in *The Builder* in 1928; republished in book form, London 1956). The subject of Lethaby's first book re-thought and much altered over thirty years later.

Philip Webb and his Work (Oxford 1935). The major source of information on the father-figure of Arts and Crafts architecture.

MACARTNEY, SIR M. *Recent English Domestic Architecture* (London 1908). Illustrates many important houses of the period.

MACKMURDO, A. H. 'History of the Arts and Crafts Movement' (unpublished manuscript in William Morris Gallery, Walthamstow).

Autobiographical notes (unpublished, in William Morris Gallery, Walthamstow). Both works by Mackmurdo listed here are significant, though not always dependable, sources of knowledge for the early years of Arts and Crafts architecture.

MACLEOD, R. *Charles Rennie Mackintosh* (London 1968). A beautifully illustrated short biography.

Style and Society – Architectural Ideology in Britain 1835–1914 (London 1971). A major piece of scholarship on changing ideals in British architecture during the Victorian and Edwardian period, though little coverage is given to Edwardian Baroque.

MADSEN, S. T. *Art Nouveau* (London 1967). A classic study of its subject.

MANSON, G. C. *Frank Lloyd Wright to 1910, the First Golden Age* (New York 1958).

MASSÉ, H. J. L. J. *The Art Workers' Guild* (Oxford 1935). An important record of the first fifty years of this centre of Arts and Crafts activities.

MCARA, D. *Sir James Gowans, Romantic Rationalist* (Edinburgh 1975). Biography of a mid-Victorian Edinburgh architect who showed much eccentric originality.

MORRIS, W. *Collected Works* (London 1910–15). The major corpus of William Morris's writings, edited by May Morris. Some work omitted from this edition has been subsequently published by the Nonesuch Press.

Letters of – to his Family and Friends (London 1950).

MUTHESIUS, H. *Die Englische Baukunst der Gegenwart* (Leipzig 1900).

Das Englische Haus (Berlin 1904–05). The two works by Muthesius listed here illustrate most of the buildings of originality of the time in Britain and were major influences in the spread of Arts and Crafts ideas in the German-speaking countries.

NASH, J. *The Mansions of England in the Olden Time* (London 1838–49; new edition with introduction by C. Harrison Townsend, London 1906). Romantic drawings of Elizabethan and Jacobean buildings, contributing to the vogue for Elizabethan style during the rest of the century.

NAYLOR, G. *The Arts and Crafts Movement* (London 1971). A scholarly and valuable account of the movement's development, though with inadequate attention to architecture, especially in the illustrations.

NEWTON, W. G. *The Work of Ernest Newton R. A.* (London 1923).

PEVSNER, SIR N. *Charles Rennie Mackintosh* (Milan 1950).

The Buildings of England (London 1951–75). In many volumes on the individual counties of England before the reorganization of local government in 1973. Revised volumes still in preparation and other editors are preparing series to cover the buildings of the counties of Scotland and of Wales. Coverage of the Edwardian period was thin in the early volumes, excellent in later and revised volumes.

Pioneers of Modern Design (first published as *Pioneers of the Modern Movement*, London 1936; revised edition, London 1960). The classic book on the development of originality in design and of rationalism from the late nineteenth century onwards.

Studies in Art, Architecture and Design (London 1968). A large collection of essays by Pevsner which have appeared in various periodicals and publications over the years.

PEVSNER, SIR N., AND SIR J. RICHARDS (eds) *The Anti-Rationalists* (London 1973). Well-illustrated essays on Art Nouveau architects such as Guimard and Berenguer as well as on craft work.

REILLY, SIR C. H. *Representative British Architects of the Present Day* (London 1931). Includes essays on Edwardian figures such as Blomfield, Arthur J. Davis, Lutyens and others. The lack of dating for buildings is often frustrating.

Scaffolding in the Sky (London 1938). Useful autobiographical source book by an important figure in architectural education who trained in some of the prosperous Edwardian firms.

RENSSELAER, M. G. VAN *Henry Hobson Richardson and his Works* (New York 1888). Important contemporary biography of the American 'Romanesque' architect.

RICHARDS, SIR J. See Pevsner, Sir N., and Sir J. Richards.

RICHARDSON, A. E. *Monumental Classical Architecture in Great Britain* (London 1914).

ROBERTS, A. R. N. (ed.) *William Richard Lethaby*

(London 1957).

RUBENS, G. *The Life and Work of William Lethaby* (forthcoming). See also under Service, A. S. D. (ed.), and Lethaby, W. R.

RUSKIN, J. *The Seven Lamps of Architecture* (London 1849).
The Stones of Venice (London 1851–53). The two works by Ruskin listed here were major influences on William Morris and on the Arts and Crafts movement in general.

SAINT, A. *Richard Norman Shaw* (Yale 1976). The definitive biography of the great architect.

SCOTT, M. H. BAILLIE *Houses and Gardens* (London 1906). Baillie Scott's illustrated book on his own houses up to about 1905. No dates, and often no house names, are given. But J. D. Kornwolf (q.v.) has traced most of these.

SCOTT, M. H. BAILLIE, AND A. E. BERESFORD *Houses and Gardens* (London 1933).

SCOTT-MONCREIFF, W. *John Francis Bentley* (London 1924).

SEDDING, J. D. *Art and Handicraft* (London 1893).

SERVICE, A. S. D. 'Arts and Crafts Extremist', in *Architectural Association Quarterly*, 1974, Vol. 6, No. 2.
'John Belcher's Colchester Town Hall', in *Transactions of the Essex Archaeological Society*, 1973, Vol. 5.

SERVICE, A. S. D. (ed.) *Edwardian Architecture and its Origins* (London 1975). Includes introductory chapters and illustrated essays on James MacLaren, Charles Harrison Townsend, John Belcher and J. J. Joass, A. Beresford Pite, the L.C.C. Architect's Department, and Mewès and Davis by the editor. Essays on R. Norman Shaw, Charles Holden, Sir Edwin Lutyens and H. S. Goodhart-Rendel by Sir Nikolaus Pevsner. Essays on Sir John Burnet, Charles Rennie Mackintosh, James Salmon and J. Gaff Gillespie by David Walker. Essays on Henry Wilson and Sir Albert Richardson by Nicholas Taylor. Essays on Philip Webb by George Jack, on W. E. Nesfield by J. M. Brydon, on Edward Godwin by Dudley Harbron and by H. Montgomery Hyde, on E. R. Robson by David Gregory-Jones, on William Lethaby by Godfrey Rubens, on Edward Prior by Christopher Grillet, on C. F. A. Voysey by Sir John Betjeman, on J. D. Sedding by J. P. Cooper and by Henry Wilson, on Edwardian ecclesiastical architecture by B. F. L. Clarke, on Sir Aston Webb by H. Bulkeley Creswell, on E. A. Rickards by John Warren, on Leonard Stokes by H. V. M. Roberts, on Edgar Wood and J. Henry Sellers by John Archer, and on the garden city by Ernest Newton and by Sir Mervyn Macartney. Many of these essays were originally published in *The Architectural Review*, while nine essays and the introductory chapters were newly written for the book.

SHAW, R. NORMAN, AND SIR T. G. JACKSON (eds) *Architecture, a Profession or an Art?* (London 1892). The major expression of the protest against professionalism in architecture with essays by Shaw, Jackson, Prior, Lethaby, Gerald Horsley, J. T. Micklethwaite and others.

SPIERS, R. PHENÉ *The Orders of Architecture* (London 1890). An important early effort to re-establish correct Classicism in England.

STAMP, G. 'Indian Summer', in *The Architectural Review*, 1976, Vol. 159, p. 365. An illuminating article on some of the architects who followed Lutyens to New Delhi and other parts of India. Mr Stamp is also preparing a biography of Sir Giles Gilbert Scott and of the earlier members of that notable family of architects.

STATHAM, H. H. *Modern Architecture* (London 1897). An account of late nineteenth century architecture by the editor of *The Builder* magazine.

STEVENSON, J. J. *House Architecture* (London 1880). The 'Queen Anne' style house promoted by one of the style's early exponents.

SUMMERSON, SIR J. 'British Contemporaries of Frank Lloyd Wright', in *Studies in Western Art* (Princeton 1963). A seminal paper on British architecture of 1890–1914.
The Turn of the Century: Architecture in Britain around 1900 (W. A. Cargill memorial lecture 1975, Glasgow University Press). A crisp and illuminating summary of the period.

TAYLOR, N. See under Service, A. S. D. (ed.).

THOMAS, J. 'The Style shall be Gothic', in *The Architectural Review*, September 1975. A good account of the background and the entries for the Liverpool Cathedral competition of 1903.

WALKER, D. M. 'Lamond of Dundee', in *The Architectural Review*, 1958, Vol. 123, p. 269.
Edinburgh in The Buildings of Scotland series (in preparation).
See also under Service, A. S. D. (ed.) for essays on Burnet, Mackintosh, Salmon and Gillespie.

WALKER, D. M., AND A. GOMME *The Architecture of Glasgow* (London 1968). The definitive architectural book on the city that produced much of the best work in the Edwardian period.

WALKER, L. *The Life and Work of Edward S. Prior* (in preparation).

WARREN, E. 'The Life and Work of George Frederick Bodley', in *Journal of the Royal Institute of British Architects*, 1909–10, pp. 305–36.

WEAVER, L. (ed.) *Small Country Houses of Today*

(London 1910). Illustrates houses by many important architects including Lethaby, Barnsley and Edgar Wood.

WILDE, O. *The Soul of Man under Socialism* (available in *Essays by Oscar Wilde*, edited by Hesketh Pearson, London 1950).

WINMILL, J. M. *Charles C. Winmill* (London 1946). A biography by his daughter of one of the leading architects of the early years of the L.C.C. Architect's Department.

Other useful articles in periodicals are mentioned in the footnotes of this book. Of the magazines of the late nineteenth and early twentieth centuries, the following will be found especially valuable. *The Architect* was one of the most widely read architectural magazines of the time and published a series 'The Architectural Illustration Society' in 1890–94 which illustrated progressive work of the time. *The Architectural Review* was first published in 1896; under the successive editorships of Henry Wilson, D. S. McColl, Mervyn Macartney, Ernest Newton and then his son W. G. Newton it became the influential establishment magazine of Edwardian architecture, leading the campaign for purer Classicism after 1906 and introducing a regular feature on town planning in 1908. *The British Architect* was the most determinedly progressive architectural magazine from the 1870s onwards, with strong reporting of Scottish work as well as English; it published many of the designs of Godwin, Voysey, Mackintosh, Edgar Wood and others who showed originality. *The Builder* under the editorship of H. H. Statham was probably the magazine with the largest circulation of the period; it published a wide range of work of all types. *The Studio* was first published in

1893 and is an important source of information on Arts and Crafts domestic architecture, as well as on the decorative arts. *Academy Architecture* featuring the architectural designs exhibited at each year's Royal Academy exhibition was first published in 1889; it is invaluable. *The Journal of the Royal Institute of British Architects* is a main source on activities and views within the R.I.B.A., while *Architectural Association Notes* gives valuable insights into what was being taught to students and young architects from 1887 onwards. *The Builders' Journal, Building News, The Architects' and Builders' Journal* and other less important building magazines of the period often contain illustrations etc. of buildings and designs not published elsewhere.

Further research is needed on some aspects and on many individual architects of the period. Among the latter particular mention should be made of Sir George Washington Browne, J. M. Brydon, John A. Campbell, Basil Champneys, T. E. Collcutt, Sir Edwin Cooper, H. Bulkeley Creswell, Sir William Emerson, Owen Fleming, William Flockhart, James G. Gibson, H. T. Hare, E. Vincent Harris, Sir T. G. Jackson, William Leiper, Sir Mervyn Macartney, Temple Moore, Reginald Morphew, Edward Mountford, Sir Charles Nicholson, Ernest Newton (who deserves a book to himself), Sir C. H. Reilly, R. Weir Schultz (who changed his name to R. S. Weir after 1914), Sir Giles Gilbert Scott, George Sherrin, Sir John Simpson, A. Dunbar Smith, H. H. Statham, Sir Walter Tapper, Sir A. Brumwell Thomas, Sir Arnold Thornely, Frank Verity, Sir Aston Webb and William Young. Many of these were successful architects of the Edwardian Baroque revival, and subsequent practitioners of Classical work, who have received much less attention than their Arts and Crafts contemporaries.

Leading Architects
and Some of Their Buildings 1890–1914

This list is intended to help those who want to go and see buildings of the period 1890–1914 by some of the leading architects. It would be impractical to include all the talented architects of the time, and the lists of buildings are not intended to be complete records of each architect's work within these years.
Italic numbers within square brackets refer to buildings illustrated in the main text.

Adams, H. PERCY. See Holden,

Charles, of Adams, Holden and Pearson.
Adshead, STANLEY D. (1868–1946). *Born at Altrincham, Cheshire. Worked for George Sherrin 1890, then for Sir Ernest George and for William Flockhart. Own practice c. 1901. A celebrated draughtsman. Appointed Professor of Civic Design at Liverpool University 1909–15, the first university chair in town planning in Britain. In architectural partnership with Stanley C. Ramsey 1912 onwards.* 1903–04 Royal Victoria Pavilion, Sea

Front, Ramsgate, Kent; 1903–04 Public Library, Guildford Lawn, Ramsgate, Kent; 1908 Warehouse, Tooley Street, London; 1912–13 Interior, Playhouse Theatre, Williamson Square, Liverpool; 1913 St Anselm's Church, Kennington Road, London (with Ramsey); 1913–14 Terrace cottages in Cardigan Street and Courtenay Street, and Old Tenants' Hostel with cloister in Black Prince Road, Lambeth, London (with Ramsey, for Duchy of

Cornwall estate).

Anderson, ROBERT ROWAND (later Sir R. Rowand) (1834–1921). *Born at Forres, Morayshire. Served in Royal Engineers studying construction before turning to architecture. Private practice in Edinburgh 1875 onwards. First President of Scottish Institute of Architects. Knighted 1902. Royal Gold Medal 1916. Early work included Medical Schools of Edinburgh University (1875–88) and the completion, with dome, in 1886 of Old College, Edinburgh University.*
1885–90 Scottish National Portrait Gallery, Queen Street, Edinburgh; 1891–92 Morningside South Church, Cluny Drive, Edinburgh; 1897 McEwan Hall, Teviot Place, Edinburgh; 1897 Pollokshaws Burgh Buildings, No. 2025 Pollokshaws Road, Glasgow; 1903 Pearce Institute, No. 840 Govan Road, Govan, Glasgow.

Ashbee, CHARLES ROBERT (1863–1942). *One of the most impressive figures, as designer and as writer, of the Arts and Crafts movement. Born in London, studied history at King's College, Cambridge. Articled to G. F. Bodley 1886. Founded the Guild of Handicraft in the poor East End of London 1888, making a wide range of furniture etc., often to Ashbee's designs. Founded Essex House Press 1898. By 1902 the Guild of Handicraft had 50 craftsmen working members. On expiry of its Mile End lease, Ashbee moved the Guild, with craftsmen and families amounting to another 100 people, to Chipping Campden, Gloucestershire. The Guild was dissolved after a financial crisis in 1908, but survived as a Trust with reduced activities until 1914. By then Ashbee had accepted the potential of the machine. Ashbee's early architecture showed striking originality. His buildings at Chipping Campden, on the other hand, are barely distinguishable from old vernacular work. His remarkable houses in Chelsea, London, at No. 37 Cheyne Walk (1894), Nos 72–73 Cheyne Walk (1897) [27], No. 75 Cheyne Walk (1902) and No. 71 Cheyne Walk (1912–13) have been destroyed and only Nos. 38–39 Cheyne Walk (1899–1901) survive. (Research by Alan Crawford and Shirley Bury.)*
1895–97 Chapel and additions, Wombourne Wodehouse, near Wolverhampton, Staffordshire; 1899–1901 Nos 38–39 Cheyne Walk, Chelsea, London [28–29]; c. 1902 New wing, Coombe End, Whitchurch, Oxfordshire; 1902–06 Rebuilt many derelict cottages at and near Chipping Campden, Gloucestershire; c. 1905 Little Coppice, Iver Heath, Buckinghamshire; c. 1905 The Shoehorn, Orpington, Kent; c. 1905 Stanstead House and Five Bells, Dromenagh Estate, Iver Heath, Buckinghamshire; 1905 Norman Chapel,

Broad Campden, Gloucestershire (conversion of chapel into his own house); 1906 52 industrial cottages around Birchfield Road, Ellesmere Port, Cheshire; 1907 Byways, Yarnton, Oxfordshire; 1907 Villa San Giorgio, beside San Pancrazio church, Taormina, Sicily; c. 1909 Manor Gate Cottage, Ockley, Surrey; 1911 Houses, Nos 1049–1054 Squirrel's Heath Avenue, Romford, Essex; 1912–13 Sidcot, near Winscombe, Somerset.

Atkinson, R. FRANK (1869–1923). *A distinguished practitioner of the Wren-influenced variety of Edwardian Baroque. Trained by J. Macvicar Doyle in Liverpool and became an ardent disciple of Norman Shaw. Started his own practice in London 1901.*
1904 Laurie and McConnal shop and building, Fitzroy Street, Cambridge; 1905–06 Bromley Town Hall, Tweedy Road, Bromley, Kent; 1906 Waring and Gillow department store, Nos 164–188 Oxford Street, London; 1907 Office building, No. 151 Great Portland Street, London; 1908 Shop and office building, No. 11 Great Marlborough Street, London; c. 1908 Exhibition buildings, Olympia, Kensington, London; 1908–14 Adelphi Hotel, Lime Street, Liverpool (further extensions later); 1912–21 Whiteley Model Village, plan, entrance lodges and houses in West Avenue, near Cobham, Surrey; 1913 Redcot, No. 78 Warren Road, Blundellsands, north of Liverpool.

Baker, HERBERT (later Sir Herbert) (1862–1946). *Born at Cobham, Kent. Articled to Arthur Baker, worked for Sir Ernest George 1882–90, where he met Lutyens. Practised in South Africa initially at Cecil Rhodes's suggestion 1893–1912 (partners included Francis Masey and F. L. H. Fleming), after which he and Lutyens were appointed architects for the main buildings at New Delhi. His many South African buildings before 1912 include the government Union Buildings, Pretoria (1910–12). After the 1914–18 war, Baker practised successfully in England. Knighted 1923. Royal Gold Medal 1927. (Research by Doreen Greig.)*

Barnsley, ERNEST (1863–1926) and SIDNEY (1865–1926). *Born in Birmingham, Ernest trained under Sedding, Sidney under Norman Shaw. Established a guild crafts workshop at Pinbury Park and at Daneway Park, Sapperton, Gloucestershire, with Ernest Gimson c. 1900.*
Some buildings by Ernest Barnsley.
c. 1900 Interiors at Pinbury Park, near Duntisbourne Rouse, Gloucestershire; c. 1901 Upper Dorvel House, Sapperton, Gloucestershire; 1909–26 Rodmarton Manor and cottages, Rodmarton, Gloucestershire; 1912 Village Hall, Sapperton, Gloucestershire; date?

Cottages at Minchinhampton Common and at Coates, Gloucestershire.
Some buildings by Sidney Barnsley.
1891 St Sophia's, Lower Kingswood, Surrey; c. 1901 Beechanger Sapperton, Gloucestershire (for himself); c. 1913 Gyde Almshouses, Gloucester Road, Painswick, Gloucestershire; date? Blocks of cottages, Miserden, Gloucestershire.

Belcher, JOHN (1841–1913), with A. Beresford Pite 1885–97 and with John James Joass 1898 onwards. *Belcher was born in London and succeeded to his father's established practice. His work went through several phases of style – French Classical, Gothic and Shaw-influenced vernacular before arriving in 1888 at the Baroque of which he became, with his partners, a leading exponent. Royal Gold Medal 1907.*
1888–93 Institute of Chartered Accountants, Moorgate Place, City of London (with Beresford Pite) [59, 64]; 1897–1902 Colchester Town Hall, High Street, Colchester, Essex [frontispiece, 174–175]; 1900–02 'Birmingham Post building, No. 88 Fleet Street, London; 1900–03 Electra House, No. 84 Moorgate, City of London; 1902 Portico and entrance wing, Cornbury Park, Oxfordshire; 1904–05 Royal London House, Finsbury Square, London (first section) [185]; 1904–09 The Ashton Memorial, Williamson Park, Lancaster [194]; (Subsequent buildings were designed almost entirely by J. J. Joass) 1906–08 Mappin House, Nos 158–162 Oxford Street, London [229–230]; 1907–08 Mowbray's Bookshop, No. 28 Margaret Street, London; 1907–08 Royal Insurance building, corner of Piccadilly and St James's Street, London [231]; 1909–12 Whiteley's department store, Queensway, Bayswater, London; 1910–12 Holy Trinity Church, Kingsway, London; 1910–12 Royal Society of Medicine, Henrietta Place, Marylebone, London; 1910 Offices for Zoological Society, Outer Circle, Regent's Park, London; 1912 House, No. 31 Weymouth Street, Marylebone, London; 1913 The Mappin Terraces, London Zoo, Regent's Park, London.

Bell, E. INGRESS (1826–1914). See Webb, Sir Aston.

Bentley, JOHN FRANCIS (1839–1902). *Born at Doncaster, Yorkshire. Worked for an engineering firm in Manchester, a builder in London and the architect Henry Clutton in 1858. Converted to Roman Catholicism in 1862 and developed a distinguished practice in Roman Catholic architecture in the Gothic style, most notably the Church of the Holy Rood, Watford (1883–90) [79].*
1891–93 Redemptorist Monastery, Clapham, London; 1895–1903 West-

minster Roman Catholic Cathedral, Victoria Street, London [*78*, *87*]; 1897–98 St Luke's Church, Chiddingstone Causeway, Kent; 1898 Church of St Francis, Convent Lane, Bocking, Essex.

Bidlake, WILLIAM HENRY (1862–1938). *Educated in Wolverhampton and at Christ's College, Cambridge. Articled to R. W. Edis, then worked for G. F. Bodley and for R. R. Anderson. Started to practise in Birmingham 1888, where he became the leading Arts and Crafts architect.*

1892–99 St Oswald's Church, St Oswald's Road, Small Heath, Birmingham; 1898 Withens, No. 5 Barker Road, Four Oaks, Birmingham; 1899 St Patrick's Church, Salter Street, Earlswood, Birmingham; 1899–1901 St Agatha's Church, Stratford Road, Sparkbrook, Birmingham [*86*]; *c.* 1900 Woodgate, No. 37 Hartopp Road, Four Oaks, Birmingham; 1901 Emmanuel Church, Walford Road, Sparkbrook, Birmingham; 1901 The Garth, Edgbaston Park Road, Birmingham; 1904 Bishop Latimer Church, Handsworth New Road, Winson Green, Birmingham; 1904 Warehouse, Great Charles Street, Birmingham; 1907 St Andrew's Church, Oxhill Road, Handsworth, Birmingham; 1908 Vicarage, No. 84 Cato Street, Birmingham; 1909–16 Emmanuel Church, Birmingham Road, Wylde Green, Sutton Coldfield.

Blomfield, REGINALD (later Sir Reginald) (1856–1942). *Born in London, educated at Haileybury and at Exeter College, Oxford. Articled to his uncle, Sir Arthur Blomfield. Own practice 1884 onwards. At that time close to the Arts and Crafts movement, but steadily became a convinced Classicist. His books, lectures and buildings contributed much to the more refined Classicism and French influence that followed the High Baroque period. Knighted 1919. Royal Gold Medal 1913.*

1892 Swiftsden, near Etchingham, Sussex (early Neo-Georgian); 1895 No. 20 Buckingham Gate, London; 1895 Mystole House, near Chartham, Kent (east side added to older house); 1896 Wordsworth Building, Lady Margaret Hall, Oxford University; 1896–99 Parish Institute, Fratton Road, Portsea, Hampshire; 1897 Headmaster's house, St Edmund's School, Canterbury, Kent; 1897–1910 Heathfield Park, Heathfield, Sussex; 1900 Stansted House, Stansted, Sussex; 1900 Warehouse for Army and Navy Stores, Greycoat Place, off Victoria Street, London; 1900–02 Saltcote Place, Rye, Sussex; 1902–26 Sherborne (Girls') School, Bradford Road, Sherborne, Dorset; 1901 Elwyns House, Felsted School, Essex; 1905 Barclays Bank, Tindal Square, Chelmsford,

Essex; 1906 Public Library, Lincoln; 1906–07 United University Club, Pall Mall East, London [*203*]; 1908 Moundsmere Manor, Nutley, Hampshire; 1909 Carrington Building, Sherborne (Boys') School, Dorset; 1912–13 Building for Barker's department store, Kensington High Street, London; 1913 Rebuilt in altered form Waldershare Park, Kent (after fire); *c.* 1913 Elevation designs for west side of Piccadilly Circus, London, including both corners of Lower Regent Street, both corners of Piccadilly, the corners of Regent Street, the Regent Street quadrant (excluding Norman Shaw's Piccadilly Hotel in its centre) and the County Fire Office on the north side of the Circus [*204*]. Executed by various architects up to 1930.

Blow, DETMAR (1867–1939). *A devoted member of the Arts and Crafts movement at the turn of the century, and disciple of Ruskin, Lethaby, Gimson and Prior, Blow became architect to the Duke of Westminster's Grosvenor Estate c. 1910. He was architect of Government House, Salisbury, Rhodesia.*

1894 Additions, Heale House, Woodford, Wiltshire; 1898 Restoration of Lake House, Wilsford, Wiltshire (with Philip Webb); 1900 Happisburgh House, Happisburgh, Norfolk [*100*]; 1904 Fonthill House, in grounds of Fonthill Abbey, Wiltshire; 1906 Playhouse Theatre, Craven Street, Westminster, London (with F. Billerey); 1906 Christ Church, Thorney Hill, near Avon Tyrell, Hampshire; 1911–12 Cheam School, Kingsclere, Hampshire (with Billerey); 1912 Harewood House, No. 13 Hanover Square, Mayfair, London; 1912 Houses, Nos 45–51 Park Street, Mayfair, London; 1912 Office building, Nos 103–109 Wardour Street, Soho, London; 1912 Horwood House, Little Horwood, Buckinghamshire (with Billerey); 1914 Hilles, Harescombe, Gloucestershire (for himself).

Bodley, GEORGE FREDERICK (1827–1907). *Born at Hull, Yorkshire. Pupil of Sir George Gilbert Scott. Independent practice 1860, in partnership with Thomas Garner (1839–1906) from 1869. Founded the church furnishing firm Watts and Co. in 1870 with the younger George Gilbert Scott and Garner, and designed most of its plate. Bodley was one of the finest Victorian Gothic architects.*

1889–91 St John the Baptist, High Street, Epping, Essex (with Garner); 1892 All Saints' Church, Danehill, Sussex (with Garner); 1894–95 Gatehouse and school for Bodley's earlier church of St Augustine, Pendlebury, Lancashire; 1897–98 St Matthew's Church, Wood Lane, Chapel Allerton, Leeds, Yorkshire; 1902–04 Holy Trinity Church, Prince Consort Road,

Kensington, London (completed later) [*83*]; 1903 Assessor of Liverpool Cathedral competition and acted as advisor to the appointed architect, Giles Gilbert Scott, until his own death in 1907; 1903–04 St Edward's Church, Brown Lane, Holbeck, Leeds, Yorkshire; 1907–09 Tower of St John the Baptist, Epping, Essex; 1907–09 Monument to Lord Salisbury on north side of nave, Westminster Abbey, London.

Brewer, W. CECIL (1871–1918). See Smith and Brewer.

Brierley, WALTER H. (1862–1926). *Trained by his father, later worked for architects in Warrington and Liverpool. A talented Yorkshire architect whose houses are usually in an Arts and Crafts Tudor manner, while his churches are Gothic and his public buildings individualistic Neo-Georgian.*

1891 North Cliff, Black Cliff Head, Filey, Yorkshire; 1894–96 St Mary's Church, Goathland, Yorkshire; 1895 The Close, near Brompton-in-Allerton, Yorkshire; 1896 Scarcroft Road School, York; 1900 School principal's house and other buildings, King's Manor, Exhibition Square, York; 1900–02 St Luke's Church, Burton Stone Lane, York; 1903 Interior of Heslington Hall, now University of York; 1904 Poppleton Road School, York; 1904 Haxby Road School, York; *c.* 1904–06 County Hall, Northallerton, Yorkshire; 1908 The Garth, Sim Balk Lane, Bishopsthorpe, Yorkshire; *c.* 1909 Thorpe Underwood Hall, south-east of Boroughbridge, Yorkshire; 1911 Lumley Barracks, Burton Stone Lane, York; 1912–13 Sion Hall, Kirby Wiske, Yorkshire; 1914 Purey Cust Nursing Home, Minster Precinct, York.

Briggs, ROBERT A. (*c.* 1858–1916). *Articled to G. R. Redgrave in London c. 1876, started practice in 1884. A largely domestic architect whose designs were within the Arts and Crafts tradition but subject to whimsy. His book* Bungalows and Country Residences *earned him the nickname of 'Bungalow Briggs'.*

c. 1890 4 bungalow houses, Bellaggio, Surrey; *c.* 1895 Screen of the Jesus Chapel, Worcester Cathedral; *c.* 1900 Houses in Dormans Park, Dormansland, near Lingfield, Surrey; *c.* 1900 Rebuilt Cowley Manor, Gloucestershire; 1903 The Old Mill, on the sea front, Aldeburgh, Suffolk.

Briggs and Wolstenholme. See Thornely, Sir Arnold.

Browne, GEORGE WASHINGTON (later Sir George) (1853–1939). *One of the most successful Edinburgh architects of the period, often working in a 'François Premier' or in an eclectic manner. In partnerships successively as R. R. Anderson and Browne, Wardrop, Anderson and*

Browne, and Dick Peddie and Washington Browne 1895–1907.
1887–90 Central Public Library, George IV Bridge, Edinburgh; 1905 British Linen Bank, No. 69 George Street, Edinburgh; 1908 School library (former art room), Daniel Stewart's College, Queensferry Road, Edinburgh; 1914–15 Y.M.C.A. building, No. 14 St Andrew Street, Edinburgh.
Brydon, JOHN M. (1840–1901). *Born at Dunfermline, Fife. Trained in Liverpool, then with David Bryce and Campbell Douglas in Glasgow. Worked with Nesfield and with Norman Shaw in London. Own practice 1880. His St Peter's Hospital, Henrietta Street, Covent Garden, London (1883–84), is in the 'Queen Anne' style, but in 1885 he won the Chelsea Town (Vestry) Hall competition with a Wren/Gibbs design [60]. From then on he became an enthusiastic and distinguished designer in the English Baroque style, lecturing on its excellence in 1889. Brydon built several important buildings in Bath, but died before his major commission (the Government Buildings in Parliament Square) had risen above foundation level. The building was completed inadequately by another architect.*
1891–95 Chelsea Public Library and Polytechnic, Manresa Road, Chelsea, London; 1891–95 The Guildhall, High Street, Bath (retaining only central frontage of original 1766–75 building by Thomas Baldwin) [66–67]; 1892 Village Hall, Forest Row, Sussex; 1894–96 Buildings to surround the rediscovered Roman Baths, and Concert Hall, Stall Street etc., Bath; 1896 School of Medicine for Women, Handel Street, London; 1896–97 Municipal Art Gallery, corner of Grand Parade and Bridge Street, Bath [68]; 1898–1912 Government Buildings, Parliament Square and Parliament Street, Westminster, London (detail altered during completion of the building under Sir Henry Tanner) [178].
Burnet, JOHN JAMES (later Sir John) (1857–1938). *Born in Glasgow and after training at the Ecole des Beaux-Arts in Paris 1874–77 entered partnership in his father's successful practice. In partnership with J. A. Campbell 1886–98, with Thomas Tait and Francis Lorne in London after 1905. The most celebrated Scottish architect of his time, he excelled in most styles to which he turned his hand. Knighted 1914. Royal Gold Medal 1923.*
1890 Garmoyle, near Dumbarton, Dunbartonshire (with J. A. Campbell); 1890–91 Charing Cross Mansions, Nos 2–30 St George's Road, Glasgow (with Campbell); 1891–92 Athenaeum Theatre, No. 179 Buchanan Street, Glasgow (with Campbell) [70]; 1894 Glasgow Stock Exchange, No. 63 West George Street, Glasgow; 1895–96 Savings Bank of Glasgow,

No. 99 Glassford Street, Glasgow; 1896–1900 Gardner Memorial Church, Brechin, Angus; 1899 Atlantic Chambers, No. 43 Hope Street, Glasgow; 1901 Elder Library, No. 228 Langlands Road, Govan, Glasgow; 1903–07 Civil Service and Professional Supply building, George Street, Edinburgh [157]; 1904–14 King Edward VII Galleries, British Museum, London [206–207]; 1904–06 Fairnalie, Selkirkshire; 1905–10 McGeoch's store, No. 28 West Campbell Street, Glasgow (demolished) [133]; 1906–10 Forsyth's department store, Prince's Street, Edinburgh; 1909–11 General Buildings, Aldwych, London; 1910–11 Alhambra Theatre, No. 43 Wellington Street, Glasgow (demolished); 1910–11 Kodak Building, Kingsway, London (with Thomas Tait) [165–166]; 1913–16 Wallace Scott Tailoring Institute, No. 42 Spean Street, Cathcart, Glasgow (with Norman Dick, now mutilated) [169].
Butterfield, WILLIAM (1814–1900). *Born in London, became one of the greatest High Victorian Gothic architects. By the 1890s he was practising little, though, for example, the steeple of his St Andrew's Church, Rugby, was added in 1895–96.*
Campbell, JOHN ARCHIBALD (1859–1909). *Trained with Burnet and Son, then at the Ecole des Beaux-Arts in Paris 1880–83. In partnership with J. J. Burnet 1886–97, then started independent practice and designed a number of striking buildings before his early death. See J. J. Burnet list for some of his buildings in partnership with Burnet.*
Some buildings in independent practice. 1898 Office building, Nos 164–168 Buchanan Street, Glasgow; 1902 Office building, Nos 157–167 Hope Street, Glasgow; 1904 Edinburgh Life Assurance building, No. 124 St Vincent Street, Glasgow; 1905 No. 50 Argyle Street, Glasgow; 1908 Northern Insurance building, Nos 84–94 St Vincent Street, Glasgow [164].
Caröe, WILLIAM D. (1857–1938). *Born in Liverpool, educated at Trinity College, Cambridge, articled to J. L. Pearson. His work was largely ecclesiastical.*
1897 St Stephen's Church, Bobbers Mill Road, Nottingham; 1897–1900 St David's Church, St David's Hill, Exeter, Devon; 1898–1902 Boarding houses, Wycombe Abbey School, High Wycombe, Buckinghamshire; 1901–03 Coleherne Court, Old Brompton Road and Redcliffe Gardens, Kensington, London; 1901 St Michael Bassishaw, Hertford Road, Edmonton, Middlesex; 1902 St Barnabas's Church, St Barnabas Road, Walthamstow, London; 1903 St Aldhelm's Church, Silver Street, Edmonton, Middlesex; 1903 Church Commissioners' office block, No. 1

Millbank, Westminster, London; c. 1903 Houses, Nos 37–43 Park Street, Mayfair, London; 1906 St Edward's House, Great Smith Street, Westminster, London; 1907–09 Bishop's Palace, Southwell, Nottinghamshire; 1913 (consecration) St Ninian's Church, Douglas, Isle of Man.
Champneys, BASIL (1842–1935). *Born in London, educated at Trinity College, Cambridge, articled in Llandaff. Private practice 1867. His Indian Institute at Oxford (1884) brought him fame, and he followed T. G. Jackson's manner in several Oxford buildings. Royal Gold Medal 1912.*
1890–99 Rylands Memorial Library, Deansgate, Manchester [82]; 1898 Chapel, Mill Hill School, Mill Hill, London; 1898 St Luke's Church, Kidderpore Avenue, Hampstead, London; 1898 Memorial Buildings, Winchester College, Hampshire; 1900–02 St Andrew and St Michael, Blackwall Lane, Greenwich, London; 1903 Library, Somerville College, Oxford; 1903 King Edward VII Grammar School, King's Lynn, Norfolk; 1910–13 Bedford College, University of London, Regent's Park, London.
Collcutt, THOMAS E. (1840–1924). *Born at Oxford, articled to R. E. Armstrong, worked for G. E. Street. Independent practice 1872. Royal Gold Medal 1902. In partnership with Stanley Hamp c. 1903 onwards. His most typical design manner combines brickwork and terracotta in an eclectic style, but he also showed much sensitivity working in other styles.*
1887–93 The Imperial Institute, Kensington, London (demolished except campanile) [1]; 1889–91 Savoy Hotel, Thames Embankment, London; 1890 Wigmore Hall, Nos 38–40 Wigmore Street, London; 1890 Palace Theatre, Cambridge Circus, London; 1890 Office building, Nos 45–47 Ludgate Hill, City of London; 1900–03 Lloyd's Shipping Register, Fenchurch Street, City of London; 1907 Winterstoke Library and Murray Scriptorium, Mill Hill School, Mill Hill, London.
Comper, J. NINIAN (later Sir Ninian) (1864–1960). *Born in Aberdeen, articled to G. F. Bodley. Specialized in church restoration and furnishing, but built several important churches which develop eclecticism into what Comper called 'Unity by Inclusion'. Knighted 1950.*
1893 Lady Chapel, Downside Abbey, Somerset; 1898 St Margaret's Church, Braemar, Aberdeenshire; 1901–03 St Cyprian, Clarence Gate, west of Regent's Park, London [96]; 1906 Holy Trinity, Southchurch, Southend-on-Sea, Essex (adding to Norman aisle); 1906–30 St Mary, Knox Road, Wellingborough, Northamptonshire [97]; 1909–11 St Mary, Toad Lane, Rochdale, Lancashire; 1909–11 St

Michael, Newquay, Cornwall; 1913 St Martin's Chapel, Heritage Crafts School, Chailey, Sussex.

Cooper, EDWIN (later Sir Edwin) (1873–1942). *Born at Scarborough, Yorkshire, articled to Hall and Davis, later a partner. Independent practice 1897, in partnership with S. B. Russell until 1910, then by himself. Knighted 1923. Royal Gold Medal 1931.*

1898 Scarborough College, Filey Road, Scarborough, Yorkshire (Hall, Cooper and Davis, in a free Tudor style); 1903–14 The Guildhall, Alfred Gelder Street, Hull, Yorkshire (Russell and Cooper, competition assessed by John Belcher); 1905 Medway College of Art, Corporation Street, Rochester, Kent (Russell and Cooper); 1907 Royal Grammar School, Eskdale Terrace, Newcastle-upon-Tyne; 1910–12 Public Library, Dunning Street, Middlesbrough, Yorkshire (Russell and Cooper); 1911–18 St Marylebone Town Hall, Marylebone Road, London [237]; 1912–22 Port of London Authority building, Tower Hill, City of London.

Creswell, H. BULKELEY (1869–1960). *Educated in Bedford and at Trinity College, Dublin. Articled to Sir Aston Webb 1890, own practice 1900. His best-known building is the Willens and Robinson factory at Queensferry, North Wales (1901) [126], but he also designed houses, the Parthenon Room in the British Museum, the Law Courts in Sierra Leone and the College of Agriculture in Mauritius.*

Crewe, BERTIE (d. 1936). *A successful theatre architect, trained in the office of Frank Matcham from c. 1892. Own practice 1894 onwards.*

1894 Metropole Theatre, Camberwell, London (with W. G. R. Sprague); 1900 New Victoria, Broughton, Manchester; 1904 Palace of Varieties, Glasgow; 1910–11 The Stoll Opera House, Kingsway, London (demolished); 1910–11 Shaftesbury Theatre, corner of Shaftesbury Avenue and High Holborn, London; 1913 Palace Music Hall, Manchester; 1913 The Hippodrome, Golders Green, London.

Davis, ARTHUR J. (1878–1951). See Mewès and Davis.

Dawber, E. GUY (later Sir Guy) (1861–1938). *Born at King's Lynn, Norfolk, worked for Sir Thomas Deane and Sir Ernest George. Own practice in London 1891 onwards, specialized in sensitive vernacular house designs. Royal Gold Medal 1928. Knighted 1936.*

1890 Extension to Millbrook House, Broadwell, Gloucestershire; 1898 White House, High Street, Moreton-in-Marsh, Gloucestershire; 1898 Court House, Church Street, Broadway, Worcestershire; 1899 Post Office, High Street, Broadway, Worcester-

shire; 1901 Westhope Manor, 5 miles south of Church Stretton, Shropshire; 1904 Bibsworth, near Broadway, Worcestershire; 1906 Solom's Court, near Banstead, Surrey; 1907 Conkwell Grange, Winsley, Wiltshire; c. 1909 Nether Swell Manor (now Hill Place School), Swell, Gloucestershire; 1910 Eyford Park, near Upper Slaughter, Gloucestershire; c. 1910 Wells Folly, Evenlode, Gloucestershire; 1910–12 Hamptworth Lodge, near Landford, Wiltshire; 1911 Burdocks, near Fairford, Gloucestershire; c. 1911 Housing at Hampstead Garden Suburb, London (including Nos 38–48 Temple Fortune Lane, No. 20 Hampstead Way, Nos 5–6 Ruskin Close).

Douglas, CAMPBELL (1828–1910). *Trained in England and Glasgow. Practice in partnership with J. J. Stevenson 1860–70, with James Sellars 1870–88, alone until 1903, with A. N. Paterson 1903–10. A hugely prosperous practice and his office became a breeding ground for some major architects of the next generation, but built much less after 1890, e.g. 1896 Discharged Prisoners' Aid Society, Nos 28–32 Cathedral Square, Glasgow; 1906 National Bank, Nos 22–24 St Enoch Square, Glasgow (Douglas and A. N. Paterson).*

Douglas, JOHN (1829–1911). *Widely known as 'John Douglas of Chester', his domestic and church designs of the 1880s were distinguished and bold for their time. Trained by E. G. Paley (who later formed the notable partnership of Austin and Paley) in Lancaster. In partnerships as Douglas and Fordham 1885–97 and Douglas and Minshull 1898–1911.*

1890 Ford Lane Farm, near Aldford, Cheshire; 1890 Obelisk, Belgrave Avenue, Eaton Hall estate, Cheshire; 1891 St James Church, Haydock, Lancashire; 1893 Post Office, Warburton, Cheshire; 1894 Eccleston Lodge and gates, Eaton Hall estate, Cheshire; 1895–99 East side (including Martin's Bank) of St Werburgh Street, Chester; c. 1895 St Oswald's Chambers, St Werburgh Street, Chester; 1896 Walmoor Hill, Dee Banks, near Chester (for himself, now fire brigade); c. 1897 Rebuilt Shoemakers' Row, Chester; 1897–99 Diamond Jubilee Clock, Eastgate, Chester; 1898 Congregational Church, Eshe Road North, Great Crosby, Lancashire; c. 1900 Gardeners' cottages by the kitchen gardens, Eaton Hall estate, Cheshire; 1902–03 St John Evangelist, Sandiway, Cheshire, and Sandiway Manor nearby; 1902–03 Lombard Bank and adjoining houses, Bath Street, Chester; 1902–05 South aisle and spire of his earlier church, St Paul, Boughton, Chester.

Dunn and Watson. William Dunn (1859–1934) and Robert Watson (d. 1916). *Dunn worked for William*

Flockhart, then both Dunn and Watson worked with James MacLaren and formed a partnership which succeeded to MacLaren's practice after the latter's early death in 1890. They followed MacLaren's Arts and Crafts vernacular in their early Scottish works, but did Neo-Georgian designs for city buildings after the end of the century. Dunn became a writer of textbooks on steel and concrete frame construction. W. Curtis Green joined the firm c. 1910 and later inherited the practice.

c. 1890 Rebuilt Glenlyon House, Glenlyon, Perthshire; 1891 Fortingall Inn, Fortingall, Perthshire; 1900–05 St John's Institute, Larcom Street, Walworth, London; 1902 No. 46 Great Marlborough Street, London; 1905 Cottages, Abinger, Surrey; 1906 Shottebrooke Park, Maidenhead, Berkshire; 1908 Scottish Provident Institution, south side of Lombard Street at junction with King William Street, near Bank of England, City of London.

Emerson, WILLIAM (later Sir William) (1843–1924). *Born at Whetstone, north London, articled to William Burges. After 1864 spent many years in India, designing and supervising major buildings there.*

1890 Nos 178–179 Queen's Gate, Kensington, London; 1892 Clarence Wing, St Mary's Hospital, Paddington, London; 1898–1901 Hamilton House, Victoria Embankment, London; 1902 Royal Caledonian Asylum, Aldenham Road, Hertfordshire; 1903–21 Queen Victoria Memorial, Calcutta, India; 1910 Façade designs for northern end of Waterloo Place, St James's, London (interiors by various architects).

Field, HORACE (1861–c. 1950). *An inventive designer of Neo-Georgian houses and office buildings. Born in London. A pupil of J. J. Burnet, then articled to R. W. Edis. In partnership with Michael Bunney as Horace Field and Bunney.*

1900–06 North Eastern Railway Headquarters, near the Railway Station, York; 1903 Church Times building, Portugal Street, by Law Courts, London; 1905 House, No. 4 Cowley Street, Westminster, London; 1905 Houses, Nos 10–15 Great College Street, Westminster, London; 1908 Lloyds Bank, Fore Street, Okehampton, Devon; 1909 House, No. 8 Barton Street, Westminster, London.

Flockhart, WILLIAM (c. 1850–1915). *A talented Scottish architect who practised much in England. Trained by Campbell Douglas in Glasgow before settling in London c. 1885.*

1891 House, No. 2 Palace Court, Bayswater, London; 1894 Pasture Wood, near Dorking, Surrey; 1901–04 Rosehaugh, Avoch, Ross-shire; c. 1903 Lansdowne House, Lansdowne Road, Ladbroke Grove, London (flats); c. 1903 Studios, Nos 89–91 Ladbroke

Road, Ladbroke Grove, London; 1904–05 Presbyterian Church House, St Marylebone, London; c. 1905 Houses, Nos 3 and 31 Hertford Street and Nos 12 and 38 Hill Street, Mayfair, London; 1908 Boucheron building, No. 180 New Bond Street, London; 1912 New façade, Old Customs House, Southampton.

George, ERNEST (later Sir Ernest) (1839–1922). *Born in London, articled there to Samuel Hewitt, started practice with Thomas Vaughan 1861. Later in partnership with Harold Peto and finally with Alfred Yeates. Royal Gold Medal 1896. Knighted 1907. A notable watercolourist and draughtsman.*

1891 Limnerslease, Compton, Surrey (for G. F. Watts); 1893–94 Additional great hall and gardens, North Mimms House, Hertfordshire; 1894–97 Claridge's Hotel, Brook Street, Mayfair, London (George and Yeates); 1900–04 Eynsham Park, near Eynsham, Oxfordshire (George and Yeates); c. 1905 Shiplake Court (now College), Shiplake, Oxfordshire (George and Yeates); 1905 Golders Green Crematorium, Hoop Lane, Golders Green, London (George and Yeates); 1906 Busbridge Hall, near Godalming, Surrey (George and Yeates); 1907–10 Royal Exchange Buildings, off Threadneedle Street, City of London (George and Yeates); 1910–11 Putteridge Bury, Lilley, Hertfordshire (George and Yeates); 1910–11 Royal Academy of Music, Marylebone Road, London (George and Yeates); 1911 Garrard's building, corner of Albemarle Street and Grafton Street, Mayfair, London (George and Yeates); 1914 The houses in Hornbeam Walk and Heather Walk, Whiteley model village, near Cobham, Surrey.

Gibson, JAMES G. S. (1861–1951), and Gibson and Russell. *Gibson was born in Dundee and articled to the firm of Ireland and Maclaren there. He worked in Thomas Collcutt's office in London from the early 1880s, own practice 1889, partnership with S. B. Russell 1890–99. He then practised alone until 1909, when he took W. S. A. Gordon into partnership practising as J. S. Gibson and Partners.*

1891 L.C.C. Hostel for Working Men, Parker Street, Covent Garden, London; 1894–98 West Riding County Hall, Wood Street, Wakefield, Yorkshire (Gibson and Russell); 1895–98 West Ham College of Technology (with library and museum), Romford Road, West Ham, London (Gibson and Russell); 1900–01 Central Library, Albion Street, Hull, Yorkshire (Baroque); 1901–05 Walsall Town Hall and Library, Leicester Street, Walsall, Staffordshire (Baroque); 1906–13 Middlesex Guildhall, Parliament Square,

Westminster, London (free Gothic); 1907–09 Debenham and Freebody department store, Wigmore Street, London (Baroque); 1910 Arding and Hobbs department store, Lavender Hill, Battersea, London (Baroque).

Gillespie, JOHN GAFF (1870–1926). See Salmon, James.

Gimson, ERNEST (1864–1920). *Born in Leicester where he met William Morris 1884. Trained by J. D. Sedding, became friendly with Philip Webb, William Lethaby and other Arts and Crafts leaders. Founded Kenton and Co., furniture craftsmen, with Lethaby and others 1890. In 1900 he moved with the Barnsley Brothers to the Cotswolds, where together they established a crafts workshop at Sapperton for the next 25 years.*

1892 Inglewood, Ratcliffe Road, Knighton, Leicester (for himself); 1897 White House, North Avenue, near London Road, Leicester; 1898–99 Stoneywell Cottage, off Polybott Lane, Ulverscroft, Leicestershire [17–18]; 1900 Lea Cottage, Polybott Lane, Leicestershire; c. 1901 The Leasowes, Sapperton, Gloucestershire (for himself); 1907 Waterlane House, south-east of Waterlane, Gloucestershire; 1908 Rockyfield, Polybott Lane, Ulverscroft, Leicestershire; c. 1913 Interior, Drakestone, Stinchcombe, Gloucestershire; c. 1914 2 cottages and Village Hall (not executed until 1928), Kelmscott, Oxfordshire.

Green, W. CURTIS (1875–1960). *Studied engineering, then at Royal Academy Schools. Worked for John Belcher, own practice c. 1907, became partner in Dunn and Watson (successors to James MacLaren's practice) 1910, and inherited the firm as sole partner 1918. He subsequently built a notable series of London banks, office blocks, hotels (including the Dorchester) and flats. A celebrated draughtsman. His pre-1914 works include a house at Shelford near Cambridge (c. 1907) and, with Dunn and Watson, No. 116 Pall Mall, London (c. 1911).*

Hall, Cooper and Davis. See Cooper, Edwin.

Hare, HENRY T. (1860–1921). *One of the outstanding and (so far) underrated designers of large buildings of the period in all the styles of the time. Born at Scarborough, Yorkshire, and articled there. Studied in Paris, worked for King and Hill in London, own practice 1891 onwards. Successful in many competitions.*

1892–95 Stafford County Buildings, Martin Street, Stafford (free Baroque); 1892–97 Oxford Town Hall, St Aldgate's, Oxford (Jacobean); 1897 Old White House public house, Abingdon Road and White House Road, Oxford; c. 1898 Tower House and Midland Bank, north-west corner of Carfax, Oxford; 1899–1902 Westminster College (Presbyterian), Queens' Road,

Cambridge (free Elizabethan) [48]; 1900–02 Public Library, Garrick Street, Wolverhampton, Staffordshire (eclectic Free Style) [122]; 1900–04 Henley Town Hall, Market Place, Henley-on-Thames, Oxfordshire (restrained Baroque); 1900 Technical College, Victoria Circus, Southend-on-Sea, Essex (Baroque); 1902 Springfield St Mary, No. 121 Banbury Road, Oxford; 1903–04 Public Library, Brook Green Road, Hammersmith, London (Baroque); 1904 Carnegie Library and Art Gallery, Harrogate, Yorkshire (Baroque); 1905–06 Public Library, Holloway Road, Islington, London (Baroque); 1905–11 University College of North Wales, Bangor (monumental Free Style) [132]; 1906 Central Public Library, Victoria Avenue, Southend-on-Sea, Essex (Baroque); 1906 Public Library, Lillie Road, Fulham, London; 1908–09 Public Library, Fulham Road, Fulham, London.

Harris, E. VINCENT (1879–1971). *Born at Plymouth, Devon, and articled there. Worked for Leonard Stokes and Sir William Emerson. Own practice 1908. Won many competitions for government and municipal buildings throughout his career until retirement in 1954, employing an individualistic monumental Stripped Classical style. Royal Gold Medal 1951.*

1908 Glamorgan County Hall, Cardiff; 1910 Nos 1 and 2 Duke Street, St James's, London; 1912 Fire Station, Cardiff; 1915–61 Government Office Buildings (including Ministry of Defence), Victoria Embankment and Whitehall, Westminster, London.

Holden, CHARLES H. (1875–1960), of Adams, Holden and Pearson. *Born in Bolton, Lancashire, articled in Manchester. Worked for C. R. Ashbee for a year 1898, then joined H. Percy Adams and soon took over most of the firm's design work, becoming a partner 1907. Firm of Adams, Holden and Pearson 1912 onwards. A huge practice, specializing in hospitals, office and transport buildings. Royal Gold Medal 1936.*

1900–03 Belgrave Hospital for Children, Clapham Road, Kennington Oval, London [128]; 1903–06 King Edward VII Sanatorium, Easebourne Hill, north of Midhurst, Sussex [129]; 1903–04 Library block, The Law Society, Chancery Lane, London [225, 227]; 1904 Norwich House, No. 127 High Holborn, Bloomsbury, London; 1905–07 Bristol Central Library, Deanery Road, Bristol [130]; 1906–11 Royal Infirmary buildings, Marlborough Hill, Bristol [131]; 1907–08 British Medical Association (now Rhodesia House), No. 429 Strand, London [228]; 1908–10 Evelyn House, No. 62 Oxford Street, London; 1910–14 Sutton Valence School, Sutton Valence, Kent; 1914 Queen Mary's Hostel for King's College, University of London, Duchess of Bedford Walk, Notting Hill, London.

Honeyman, JOHN (1831–1914), of Honeyman and Keppie. *Born in Glasgow and articled there, private practice 1854. Honeyman had a profound knowledge of Gothic and designed some good churches until the 1880s. In 1889 the firm became Honeyman and Keppie (John Keppie) and employed Charles Rennie Mackintosh as draughtsman. Subsequently Honeyman did little or no design work. Of the firm's Glasgow work from 1890 onwards, Keppie designed the Fairfield Shipbuilding offices (1890), additions to No. 6 Rowan Road, Dumbreck (1892), and the Savings Bank at No. 1456 Gallowgate, Camlachie (1908). The rest was predominantly designed by Mackintosh (q.v.). (Research by David Walker and Andor Gomme.)*

Horsley, GERALD (1862–1917). *Worked for Norman Shaw 1879–82. One of the founders of the Art Workers' Guild. Started his own practice 1889.*

1889–90 Church of England School, Arundel, Sussex; 1896 Chapel and offices, Universities Mission to Central Africa, Dartmouth Street, Westminster, London; 1896 Nos 24–25 King William Street, City of London; 1899 Ballroom wing, Balcombe Place, Balcombe, Sussex; 1902–06 St Chad's Church, Longsdon, near Leek, Staffordshire; 1900–04 St Paul's Girls' School, Brook Green, Hammersmith, London [77]; 1904 Coombe Field, near Godalming, Surrey; 1904 Framewood, near Stoke Poges, Buckinghamshire; 1912 Harrow and Pinner Railway Station, off Lower Road, Harrow, Middlesex; 1913 Extension to Baring Brothers, Nos 10–12 Bishopsgate, City of London (demolished 1975); 1914 Music school, St Paul's Girls' School (see above); 1914 The Links, near Hythe, Kent.

Jackson, T. GRAHAM (later Sir Thomas) (1835–1924). *Born in London. Educated at Wadham College, Oxford, then articled to Sir George Gilbert Scott 1858. Own practice 1862. Won competition for Oxford University Examination Schools (1876–82) and started a fashion for freely Jacobean style in university buildings. Joint editor with Norman Shaw of the 1892 book* Architecture, a Profession or an Art?, *arguing against professionalism in architecture. Royal Gold Medal 1910. Baronet 1913.*

1886–1909 New Quad, Brasenose College, High Street, Oxford [33]; 1887–1913 Hertford College, Catte Street, Oxford; 1887–90 St John Evangelist Church, Northington, Hampshire; 1893 Nos 2–3 Hare Court, Temple, off Fleet Street, London; 1893 The King's Mound, Mansfield Road,

Oxford (house); 1901 Cricket pavilion, Agar's Plough, Eton College, Eton, Buckinghamshire; 1901 Radcliffe Science Library, South Parks Road, Oxford; 1904–11 The Law School, Archaeology, Ethnology and Geology Museums, off Downing Street and Pembroke Street, Cambridge; 1907 St Augustine's Church, North Lane, Aldershot, Hampshire; 1908–09 Temple Speech Room for Rugby School, Barby Road, Rugby, Warwickshire; 1908 House, No. 54 Ridgeway, Wimbledon, London; 1908–10 Electrical laboratory, South Parks Road, Oxford; 1910–11 New nave and north aisle, St Michael's Church, Church Hill, Aldershot, Hampshire; 1912 St Mary's Church, Eastrop Lane, Basingstoke, Hampshire.

Joass, JOHN JAMES (1868–1952). See Belcher, John.

Keppie, JOHN (1863–1945). See Honeyman, John, and Mackintosh, C. R.

Knott, RALPH (1878–1929). *Born in London, articled to Woodd and Ainslie. While working for Sir Aston Webb, Knott won the 1908 competition for the County Hall building for London County Council and went into private practice. The first section of County Hall was opened in 1922, but Knott died before its completion.*

Lamond, WILLIAM GILLESPIE (1854–1912). *An architect who produced some interesting Free Style and Baroque buildings in Dundee. Born at West Calder, Midlothian, trained in Dumfries and Northampton. After his own practice in Arbroath failed, he worked in Dundee, producing designs for Charles Ower 1896–98, T. M. Cappon 1898–1904 and J. H. Langlands 1904–12. (Research by David Walker.)*

c. 1897 Pearl Insurance building, beside Royal Exchange, Dundee (Gothic); 1899 Whitehills Hospital, Forfar, Angus; 1900 Towers of St Mary's Roman Catholic Church, Forebank, Dundee; 1901 Wishart Church, Dundee; 1904 Roman Catholic Church, Broughty Ferry, Angus; 1905 Ancrum Road School, Dundee; 1907 Stobswell School, Dundee; 1907 Baroque façade of the Technical Institute, Dundee; 1907 Dens Road School, Dundee; c. 1907 Eastern School, Broughty Ferry, Angus; c. 1908 Glebelands School, Dundee.

Lanchester and Rickards. Lanchester, Henry V. (1863–1953), in partnership with E. A. Rickards (1872–1920) from c. 1896 until Rickards's death in 1920. *In its early years the firm was called Lanchester, Stewart and Rickards, but the third partner, James A. Stewart, died in 1902. Born in London and trained by his father H. J. Lanchester, Lanchester worked for several architects including George Sherrin, where he met Rickards. A distinguished architectural planner, engineer*

and, later, town planner. Royal Gold Medal 1934. Rickards was perhaps the most brilliantly inventive of all Edwardian Baroque draughtsmen and elevation designers. Born in Putney, London, of a working-class family. Trained under R. J. Lovell, Dunn and Watson, Leonard Stokes and Howard Ince, and then worked for George Sherrin 1892–96. A close friend of Arnold Bennett, the novelist (Research by John Warren.)

1897–1906 Cardiff City Hall and Law Courts, Cardiff [176–177]; 1898 Flats, Handel Street, Bloomsbury, London; 1902–04 Deptford Town Hall, New Cross Road, Lewisham, London; 1902–04 Hull School of Art, Anlaby Road, Hull, Yorkshire [184]; 1905–11 Central Hall (Methodist), Storey's Gate, Westminster, London [190–191]; 1907–13 Public fountain and Edward VII Memorial, Bristol; c. 1910 Office block, probably Nos 178–202 Great Portland Street, London; 1910–12 Third Church of Christ Scientist, Curzon Street, Mayfair, London (tower added 1930); 1911–13 Art Gallery (originally Colnaghi's), Nos 144–146 New Bond Street, Mayfair, London; 1911 Knoedler's, No. 14 Old Bond Street, Mayfair, London.

Leiper, WILLIAM (1839–1916). *A distinguished Scottish Gothic architect, trained by Boucher and Cousland. Worked with Campbell Douglas, William White and J. L. Pearson. Apart from his Gothic work, he took up the 1870s manner of Norman Shaw in his many houses in Helensburgh, Dunbartonshire, where he lived.*

1889–90 Templeton's Carpet Factory, No. 62 Templeton Street, Glasgow Green, Glasgow (a polychrome Gothic fantasia); 1892 Sun Life Assurance building, Nos 147–151 West George Street, Glasgow; 1903 St Columba's Church, Kilmacolm, Renfrewshire.

Lethaby, WILLIAM R. (1857–1931). *Born at Barnstaple, Devon. Articled locally to Alexander Lauder. Worked for Norman Shaw 1879–90. A founder of the Art Workers' Guild. Started own practice 1891, but stopped practising after 1902 and devoted himself to teaching and writing. Leading ideologist of Arts and Crafts architecture. Principal of the Central School of Arts and Crafts, London, 1896–1911. Professor of Design, Royal College of Art, 1900–18.*

1891–92 Avon Tyrell, Thorney Hill, south of Ringwood, Hampshire [11]; 1893 The Hurst, Four Oaks, Sutton Coldfield, Birmingham (demolished except lodge) [12]; 1898–1902 Melsetter House, with chapel and estate buildings, Hoy Island, Orkney, Scotland [32]; 1899–1900 Eagle Insurance Buildings, Colmore Row, central Birmingham [49–50]; 1900–01 High Coxlease, south of Lyndhurst, Hampshire

[99]; 1901–02 Church of All Saints, Brockhampton, near Ross-on-Wye, Herefordshire [137–139].

Lorimer, ROBERT S. (later Sir Robert) (1864–1929). *One of the most notable Scottish architects of the first three decades of the century. Born in Edinburgh, articled to Sir R. R. Anderson, worked for Bodley in London before starting own practice in Edinburgh 1892. Among his many buildings of all types, country houses are the most numerous. His early houses show strong influence of the Arts and Crafts movement. Later he designed with consistent brilliance in a wide range of styles, including Gothic and Classical. Knighted 1911.*
1893 Cottage, No. 23 Pentland Avenue, Colinton, Edinburgh; 1895 Houses, Nos 14 and 21 Gillespie Road, Edinburgh; 1897 Acharra, No. 3 Spylaw Avenue, Colinton, Edinburgh; 1898 Briglands House, Kinrossshire; 1898 Hermitage, No. 26 Gillespie Road, Edinburgh; 1899 Hartfell, No. 10 Spylaw Park, Colinton, Edinburgh (additions 1905); 1899 Almora, No. 49 Spylaw Bank Road, Colinton, Edinburgh; 1899 Huntly, No. 32 Gillespie Road, Edinburgh; 1899 Church of the Good Shepherd, Murrayfield Avenue, Edinburgh; 1900–02 Rustic cottages, Nos 1–7, around St Cuthbert's Episcopal Church, Westgarth Avenue, Colinton, Edinburgh; 1900–01 Rowans, No. 21 Pentland Avenue, Colinton, Edinburgh; 1901 Westfield, No. 40 Pentland Avenue, Colinton, Edinburgh; 1903–08 Manor House, Barton Hartshorn, Buckinghamshire; 1903–04 Dunderach, Craiglockhart Park, Edinburgh; 1905–07 Wemyss Hall, Cupar, Fife [223]; 1906–07 St Peter's Roman Catholic Church, Falcon Avenue, Edinburgh [148]; 1906 Glenlyon, No. 47 Spylaw Bank Road, Colinton, Edinburgh; 1906–07 Shieldaig, No. 24 Hermitage Drive, Edinburgh; c. 1907–09 Ardkinglas, Argyllshire; 1907–12 Rebuilding and new additions, Lympne Castle, Lympne, Kent; 1907–09 New Library, St Andrews University, St Andrews, Fife [234]; 1910 Thistle Chapel, St Giles's Cathedral, Parliament Square, Edinburgh; 1912–14 Laverockdale House, off Dreghorn Road, Edinburgh; 1914–15 Stonehouse, No. 1 Pentland Road, Colinton, Edinburgh.

Lutyens, EDWIN L. (later Sir Edwin) (1869–1944). *The most famous British architect of the first half of the twentieth century, his achievements were of outstanding quality from the Arts and Crafts Free Style of his domestic work before c. 1903 to the originality of his later Classicism in many large buildings. Born in London, trained with Sir Ernest George 1887, own practice 1889. Knighted 1918. Royal Gold Medal 1921.*
Some works up to 1914. 1889 Cottage at Littleworth, Surrey; 1890 Crooksbury Lodge, east of Farnham, Surrey (east wing 1898); 1896 Munstead Wood, south-east of Godalming, Surrey (for Gertrude Jekyll); 1897 Fulbrook, north of Elstead, Surrey; 1898–99 Orchards, near Munstead, Surrey; 1899 Overstrand Hall, Overstrand, on the north coast of Norfolk; 1899 Tigbourne Court, near Witley, Surrey [19]; 1900 Grey Walls, Gullane, East Lothian; 1901 Deanery Gardens, Sonning, Berkshire [98]; 1901 Marshcourt, near Stockbridge, Hampshire [101]; 1902 Little Thakeham, near Pulborough, Sussex; 1903 Papillon Hall, Lubenham, Leicestershire (demolished); 1903 onwards Restoration of Lindisfarne Castle from a ruin, Holy Island, Northumberland; 1904 Country Life office building, Tavistock Street, Covent Garden, London; 1905 St John's Institute, Smith Square, Westminster, London; 1905 Nashdom, Taplow, Buckinghamshire; 1906 Heathcote, near Ilkley, Yorkshire [218]; 1906 Dorland House, No. 40 Kingsway, London (offices); 1908 Middlefield, Great Shelford, Cambridgeshire; 1909 Les Communes, Varengeville, France; 1909–13 St Jude's Church [147] and Free Church, Hampstead Garden Suburb, London; 1910 Vicarage, manse and houses in North Square, Hampstead Garden Suburb, London; 1910–30 Castle Drogo, near Drewsteignton, Dartmoor, Devon [112]; 1911 House, No. 7 St James's Square, London [238]; 1911 House, No. 36 Smith Square, Westminster, London; 1911 Theosophical Society (now inner courtyard of British Medical Association), Tavistock Square, London; 1912 British School at Rome, Rome, Italy; 1912 House, No. 18 Little College Street, Westminster, London; 1912–31 Viceroy's House and other major buildings, New Delhi, India [239].

Macartney, MERVYN (later Sir Mervyn) (1853–1932). *Born in County Armagh, Northern Ireland, educated at Lincoln College, Oxford, and then trained by Norman Shaw. A founder of the Art Workers' Guild. Editor of The Architectural Review during much of Edward VII's reign and moved it towards the advocacy of town planning as well as purer Classicism. Many of his own buildings were freely Neo-Georgian. Knighted 1930.*
1889–90 House, No. 167 Queen's Gate, Kensington, London; 1893 Sandhills, near Bletchingley, Surrey; 1893 Guinness Trust flats, Vauxhall Walk, Lambeth, London; c. 1900 Shalesbrooke, off Chapel Lane, Forest Row, Sussex; 1907 Phillip's Hill House

(built as Bussock Wood), north-east of Winterbourne, Berkshire; c. 1910 The Court and Kennet Orleigh, on the hill above Woolhampton, Berkshire; 1912 Houses in South Avenue, Whiteley Village, north-west of Cobham, Surrey (see also Frank Atkinson).

Mackintosh, CHARLES RENNIE (1868–1928). *The most inspired of all British architects attempting a Free Style during this period. Born in Glasgow, trained by John Hutchison there. Joined Honeyman and Keppie (q.v.) as draughtsman 1889 and soon became responsible for much of the firm's design work, becoming a partner 1904. Moved to London 1913, to southern France c. 1919, where he painted watercolours.*
1893 Glasgow Herald building, Nos 60–76 Mitchell Street, Glasgow (with Keppie); 1895 Martyrs Public School, No. 11 Barony Street, Townhead, Glasgow (with Keppie); 1896–99 Glasgow School of Art, No. 167 Renfrew Street, Garnethill, Glasgow [56–58]; 1897–99 Queen's Cross Church, No. 866 Garscube Road, Woodside, Glasgow; 1899 Church Hall, Ruchill Church, Maryhill, Glasgow; 1899–1901 Windyhill, Kilmacolm, Renfrewshire; 1902–04 The Hill House, Helensburgh, Dunbartonshire [108, 110]; 1903 Willow Tea-Rooms, No. 217 Sauchiehall Street, Glasgow (lower part of façade altered, interior transferred to Glasgow University Museum); 1904–06 Scotland Street School, No. 225 Scotland Street, Glasgow [134]; 1907–09 Library wing, Glasgow School of Art, Renfrew Street, Garnethill, Glasgow (design started 1905) [135, 136]; c. 1916 Remodelled house, No. 78 Derngate, Northampton.

Mackmurdo, ARTHUR H. (1851–1942). *Founder of the first of the Arts and Crafts movement guilds, the Century Guild, in 1883, Mackmurdo designed some of the most interesting early Arts and Crafts buildings (e.g. Brooklyn at No. 8 Private Road, Enfield, 1886–87 [8] and pavilions at the Liverpool Exhibition 1886), before turning to an idiosyncratic Classicism in the 1890s. Trained by T. Chatfield Clarke, John Ruskin and James Brooks. Own practice 1875. Did little architecture during the last forty years of his life. (Dating of buildings N. Pevsner, corrected after later research by E. Pond and by M. Haslam.)*
1890 House, No. 16 Redington Road, Hampstead, London; 1891 House, No. 12 Hans Road, Knightsbridge, London; 1893–94 House, No. 25 Cadogan Gardens, Chelsea, London; 1899 Old Swanne public house, Sloane Street, Knightsbridge, London; 1900 Cold storage warehouse, Nos 109–113 Charterhouse Street, Smithfield, London; c. 1900 Little Ruffins, Wickham

Bishops, Essex; c. 1904 Great Ruffins, Wickham Bishops, Essex.

MacLaren, JAMES M. (1843–1890). *One of the first Arts and Crafts architects to use a Free Style of design, MacLaren died young at the start of the period covered by this book. Born at Stirling, Scotland, articled to James Salmon the elder, worked for Campbell Douglas and Stevenson in Glasgow and Edward Godwin and Richard Coad in London. Own practice 1886. His work at The Park, Ledbury (1886), Stirling High School (1887–88) [36] and No. 22 Avonmore Road, West Kensington, London (1888), is among the most influential early Arts and Crafts vernacular before 1890. He won the London Eiffel Tower competition in 1890, but only the surrounding ground level buildings were built at Wembley.*

1889–90 Town Hall, Aberfeldy, Perthshire; 1889–90 Santa Catalina Hotel, Las Palmas, Canary Islands; 1889–90 Double house, Nos 10–12 Palace Court, London; c. 1889–90 Cottages (2 blocks), Farm Steading and Farmer's House, Glenlyon House estate, Fortingall, Perthshire [9]; 1890–91 Heatherwood, Crawley Down, Sussex.

Mallows, CHARLES E. (1864–1915). *Articled to F. T. Mercer in Bedford 1879, worked for various architects (including Flockhart) until 1886, when started own practice in partnership with F. W. Lacey. Later partnerships with A. W. S. Cross and with Grocock of Bedford. A particularly fine draughtsman, his domestic work followed the Arts and Crafts approach of E. S. Prior, while his designs for public buildings were Classical.*

1898 Girls' High School (originally Art School), London Road, Newark, Nottinghamshire; c. 1900 St Andrew's Church and All Saints' School, Bedford (Mallows and Grocock); c. 1900 Three houses, King's Corner and Three Gables, No. 17 Biddenham Turn, and White Cottage, No. 34 Days Lane, Biddenham, Bedfordshire; 1904–05 Dower House (now Territorial Army) and lodge, west of Pembury, Kent; c. 1905 Dutch Tea Garden, Eaton Hall, south of Chester, Cheshire; c. 1906–07 Tirley Garth, with lodges and an estate house, east of Willington, Cheshire; 1908 Joyce Grove, Nettlebed, Oxfordshire; 1910 North London Collegiate School for Girls, Canons Park, Stanmore, Middlesex (incorporating older house on the site of Canons); 1912 Working Men's Club, Nettlebed, Oxfordshire.

Matcham, FRANK (1854–1920). *Born at Newton Abbot, Devon, trained in Devon and London, own practice 1878. With his two pupils, W. G. R. Sprague and Bertie Crewe, Matcham was the most successful of the late Victorian and Edwardian theatre architects.*

1891 Redecoration of interior, The Tivoli, Strand, London; 1892 Empire Palace Music Hall, Leeds, Yorkshire; 1899 Richmond Theatre, The Green, Richmond, Surrey; 1899–1900 The Hippodrome, Charing Cross Road, London (interior destroyed 1958); 1901 Auditorium of The Empire Music Hall, Newcastle-upon-Tyne; 1902–04 The Coliseum, St Martin's Lane, London [186]; 1903 The Royal Hall, Ripon Road, Harrogate, Yorkshire; 1904 The King's Theatre, Glasgow; 1905 Olympia Theatre (now Locarno Ballroom), Liverpool; 1910 The Palladium, London; 1911 Victoria Palace, London; 1912 The Hippodrome, Bristol. (Research by Victor Glasstone.)

Mewès and Davis. Mewès, Charles (1860–1914), in partnership with Arthur J. Davis (1878–1951) from 1900 onwards. *Mewès had already established a large practice in designing hotels (including the Ritz in Paris) when he asked Davis to become his London partner. Davis was born in London and went to study in Paris aged sixteen, later entering the Ecole des Beaux-Arts, through which he met Mewès.*

1901 Interiors including palm court, Carlton Hotel, London (destroyed); 1903–06 The Ritz Hotel, Piccadilly, London [197–198]; 1903 Rebuilt Luton Hoo House interiors (all except chapel), south of Luton, Bedfordshire; 1906–07 Inveresk House, Aldwych, London (for the Morning Post, now spoiled by upper storeys added) [195]; 1906 Extended and rebuilt interiors, Polesden Lacey House, near Dorking, Surrey; 1908 Extension for the Cavalry Club, No. 127 Piccadilly, London; 1908–11 Royal Automobile Club, Pall Mall, London [199–200]; 1914–16 Cunard Building, Pier Head, Liverpool (executed by Willink and Thicknesse) [236].

Mitchell, ARNOLD B. (1863–1944). *Articled to Sir Ernest George. Started own practice 1886 after winning Soane Medallion 1885. Practised from Harrow and Chiswick before retiring to Lyme Regis. He built three large railway stations in South America, including the Plaza Constitución station, Buenos Aires, Argentina.*

1897 Westover House (or Old Walls), Park Lane, Milford-on-Sea, Hampshire; 1900 The Orchard, London Road, Harrow-on-the-Hill, Middlesex; 1901 Port Jackson, Lower Bowden, west of Pangbourne, Berkshire; 1902 St Felix's School, Southwold, Suffolk; 1906–07 University College School, Frognal, Hampstead, London; 1907 Additions to The Vineyards, Great Baddow, Essex; 1909–10 School of Agriculture, off Downing Street, Cambridge.

Moore, TEMPLE L. (1856–1920). *One of* the most distinguished Gothic church architects of the Edwardian period. Son of an army general, articled to the younger George Gilbert Scott 1875, with whom he then worked. Own practice c. 1882 onwards. A large practice, especially in Yorkshire.

1892 Church of the Good Shepherd, Lake, near Sandown, Isle of Wight; 1893–94 St Magnus Church, Bessingby, Yorkshire; 1895 St Peter's Church, Brinckman Street, Barnsley, Yorkshire; 1896 St John Evangelist, south-east of Chop Gate, Bilsdale, Yorkshire; 1897 St Mark's Church, Nottingham Road, Mansfield, Nottinghamshire; 1897 St Botolph's Church, Carlton-in-Cleveland, Yorkshire; 1897 St Mary's Church, Sledmere, Yorkshire; 1900–02 St Cuthbert's Church, Newport Road, Middlesbrough, Yorkshire [94]; 1901 The Manor, Bilbrough, Yorkshire (Jacobean); 1901 Town Hall, Market Place, Helmsley, Yorkshire; 1902 St James's Church, Lealholm, Yorkshire; 1902 St Columba's Church, Cannon Street, Middlesbrough, Yorkshire; 1902 Exterior pulpit, St James's Church, Piccadilly, London; 1905–14 St Wilfrid's Church, Duchy Road, Harrogate, Yorkshire (transepts later) [95]; 1905–06 All Saints' Church, Franciscan Road, Tooting, London; 1906 St Luke's Church, Westmount Road, Eltham, London; 1908–09 St Margaret's Church, Cardigan Road, Leeds, Yorkshire; 1908–28 Priory of St Wilfrid, Springfield Mount, Leeds, Yorkshire (Tudor); 1913 St James's Church, Tower Road, Clacton-on-Sea, Essex; 1914 All Saints' Church, Victoria Street, Basingstoke, Hampshire; 1914–26 St Mary's Church, Nunthorpe, Yorkshire.

Morphew, REGINALD (1874–1972). *An architect who produced some original building designs c. 1900. Articled to A. J. Gale, then worked for Ernest Runtz and for Niven and Wigglesworth. Own practice London c. 1899 onwards, mostly small houses, but two notable large buildings. Wounded in Navy during the 1914–18 war and moved to Polperro, Cornwall, where he built about 20 houses. Lived in south of France c. 1935–72.*

Larger buildings. 1900 Office building, No. 112 Jermyn Street, St James's, London; 1902–03 Marlborough Chambers, Nos 70–72 Jermyn Street, St James's, London.

Mountford, EDWARD W. (1855–1908). *Born at Shipston-on-Stour, Worcestershire. Articled to Habershon and Pite 1872, started own practice 1881. One of the most successful Edwardian Baroque architects, though not the most disciplined.*

1890–91 Battersea Polytechnic, Battersea Park Road, London (eclectic); 1890 Public Library, off Lavender Hill,

Battersea, London (Flemish eclectic); 1890–97 Town Hall, Pinstone Street, Sheffield, Yorkshire (eclectic); 1892–93 Town Hall, Lavender Hill, Battersea, London (Baroque with Jacobean touches); 1893 St Olave's Grammar School, Tooley Street, Bermondsey, London (Baroque with eclectic touches); 1896 Northampton Institute, St John Street, Clerkenwell, London (eclectic Renaissance); 1898–1902 Technical Schools, William Brown Street, Liverpool (Baroque); 1900–06 Central Criminal Courts, Old Bailey, City of London (Baroque) [*170, 181–182*]; 1901 Booth's Distillery office building, Cow Cross Street and Clerkenwell Green, London (Baroque); c. 1905 Willett's office building and flats, No. 34 Sloane Square, Chelsea, London (Baroque); 1906 Northern Insurance Co., No. 1 Moorgate, City of London (Baroque); 1906–09 Town Hall, Dalton Square, Lancaster (restrained Baroque) [*193*].

Newton, ERNEST (1856–1922). *Born in London, educated at Uppingham School, articled to Norman Shaw 1873, own practice 1879. A founder of the Art Workers' Guild and leader of the move towards a freely inventive Neo-Georgian. Royal Gold Medal 1918.*

1891 Westwood and other houses, Bird in Hand Lane, Bickley, Kent (tile-hung vernacular); 1891 St Luke's Institute, Southlands Road, Bromley, Kent (free roughcast vernacular); 1892 St Swithun's Church, Hither Green, Lewisham, London; 1893 Vicarage, near St Peter's Church, Prestbury, Cheshire (tile-hung); 1894–95 Redcourt, Scotland Lane, south of Haslemere, Surrey (Arts and Crafts vernacular with Georgian touches) [*13*]; 1893–1910 Many houses on Camden Place estate, west of the Common, Chislehurst, Kent (free vernacular); 1897 Houses, Nos 67–79 Bebington Road, Port Sunlight, Cheshire (styleless); 1897 Glebelands, Glebelands Road, off Rectory Road, Wokingham, Berkshire (free Tudor); 1898 Vicarage, Shrigley Road, Bollington, Cheshire (free Tudor); 1898 Cottage, Hazeley Heath, north-west of Hartley Wintney, Hampshire (for himself, vernacular roughcast); 1898 A row of buildings comprising Martin's (now Barclays) Bank, Royal Bell Hotel and No. 181 High Street, Market Square, Bromley, Kent (eclectic Free Style); c. 1900? Fremington House, Fremington, Devon (Neo-Georgian); 1901 Fouracre, west of Hartley Wintney, Hampshire (freely Neo-Georgian); 1902–04 Steep Hill, near St Helier, Jersey, Channel Islands (freely Neo-Georgian) [*214*]; 1902 Newbies, north of Baughurst, Hampshire (roughcast vernacular); 1902 Little Orchard, Page Heath Lane, Bickley,

Kent (freely Neo-Georgian); 1903 Alliance Assurance building, No. 88 St James's Street, London (with Norman Shaw); 1905 Spire, St George's Church, Bickley, Kent; c. 1905 Bickley Court, Chislehurst Road, Bickley, Kent (Neo-Georgian); 1906 Ardenrun Place, Crowhurst, Surrey (Neo-Georgian, largely burned 1933); 1906 Convent and School of St Juliana, Begbroke, Oxfordshire (Neo-Georgian); 1907 Luckley, near the Lucas Hospital, south-west of Wokingham, Berkshire (Neo-Georgian) [*220–222*]; 1907 Rebuilt Upton Grey House, on the hill above Upton Grey, Hampshire (tile-hung vernacular); 1907 Dawn House, Romsey Road, Winchester, Hampshire (Neo-Georgian); 1908 Scotsman's Field, Burway Hill, Church Stretton, Shropshire (roughcast with bay windows); 1910 Oldcastle, near Dallington, Sussex (vernacular); 1910 Feathercombe, near Hydestyle, north of Hambledon, Surrey (Neo-Georgian); 1911 Lukyns, north-east of Ewhurst, Surrey (Neo-Georgian); 1911 St Gregory and St Augustine Roman Catholic Church, No. 322 Woodstock Road, Oxford; 1911–12 Glebe House, Kettleshulme, Cheshire (Neo-Georgian); 1912 Houses, East Avenue, Whiteley Village, north-west of Cobham, Surrey (see also Frank Atkinson); 1912 Logmore, south of Westcott, near Dorking, Surrey (Neo-Georgian); 1913 Flint House, east of Goring-on-Thames, Oxfordshire (freely Tudor).

Nicholson, CHARLES A. (later Sir Charles, Bart) (1867–1949). *Born in London, educated at Rugby and Oxford, articled to J. D. Sedding, worked with Henry Wilson, own practice 1893. In partnership as Nicholson and Corlette 1895–1914 and Nicholson and Rushton 1927–49. Succeeded to his father's baronetcy 1903.*

1892 Vicarage, St Andrew's Church, Totteridge, Hertfordshire; 1896 St Matthew's, Chalston, Torquay, Devon; 1898–1908 St Alban's Church, Westcliffe-on-Sea, Essex; 1898 St Matthew's Church, Yiewsley, Middlesex; 1904 Burton Manor, Burton, Wirral, Cheshire (Neo-Georgian); 1910–11 St Augustine's Church, Legsby Avenue, Grimsby, Lincolnshire; 1910–12 Chernocke House, Winchester College, Romans Road, Winchester, Hampshire; 1912 St Luke's Church, Heneage Road, Grimsby, Lincolnshire; 1913–14 St Paul's Church, Yelverton, Devon; 1914 St Alban's Church, Copnor Road, Copnor, Portsmouth, Hampshire.

Niven and Wigglesworth. David B. Niven (1864–1942) and Herbert H. Wigglesworth (1866–1949). *A talented firm working in a Free Style and, from*

1893 onwards, in the Neo-Georgian manner. Niven was born in Dundee, trained there and then worked for Aston Webb from 1888. Wigglesworth trained under A. Marshall Mackenzie and Sir Ernest George. Partnership dissolved 1926.

1899 Lynch House, Clarendon Road, Sevenoaks, Kent; 1899 Willingdon House, Station Avenue, Walton-on-Thames, Surrey; 1901 British Sailors' Society Hostel, corner of Commercial Road and Beccles Street, Stepney, London (Arts and Crafts Tudor); 1904 House, No. 54 Harley Street, London; 1905 Salvation Army hostel, Garford Street, Poplar, London (freely Neo-Georgian); 1907 Office building, Nos 19–21 Hatton Garden, Holborn, London (Neo-Georgian); 1910 Ottershaw Park, Ottershaw, south of Chertsey, Surrey (Neo-Georgian); 1910 Swedish Church, Harcourt Street, Marylebone, London (except façade); Hambro's Bank, No. 41 Bishopsgate, City of London (Neo-Georgian).

Parker, BARRY (1867–1947). See Unwin, Sir Raymond.

Pearson, JOHN LOUGHBOROUGH (1817–97). *Born in Brussels, articled to Ignatius Bonomi in Durham, worked for Anthony Salvin and Philip Hardwick, own practice 1843. Royal Gold Medal 1880. Architect of Truro Cathedral in Cornwall (1880–1910) [81], Pearson was one of the greatest Victorian Gothic church architects. Most of his work was designed before the 1890–1914 period. However, the Catholic Apostolic Church in Maida Avenue, Little Venice, London (1889–91), the Incorporated Accountants' Hall, Victoria Embankment, London (1895), St Matthew's Church, Douglas, Isle of Man (1895–1902), All Saints' Church, Ascot, Berkshire (1896–97), and Brisbane Cathedral, Australia (opened 1901), fall into this period.*

Pite, ARTHUR BERESFORD (1861–1934). *Born in London, articled to his father's firm Habershon and Pite, worked with John Belcher from 1884 (including design of Institute of Chartered Accountants 1888–93 [59, 64]), own practice 1897. An early member of the Art Workers' Guild, and Professor of Architecture (Lethaby's selection) at the Royal College of Art.*

1896 House and shop, No. 82 Mortimer Street, London [75]; 1896 Church Home, Nos 46–54 Great Titchfield Street, London; 1897–1903 Christ Church, Brixton Road, Oval, London (central tower added by another architect) [88]; 1897–98 Church hall for Christ Church, Mowll Street, Oval, London; 1898 House and shop, No. 32 Old Bond Street, London; 1898 Church school offices, No. 126 Great Portland Street, London; 1899 House, No. 37 Harley Street, London [74]; c. 1901 Earlywood, near the church, Frinton-on-Sea, Essex; 1902 Chancel of Holy Trinity Church, Clapham Common, London; 1904 Ames House, Great Titchfield Street, London (youth hostel); 1904 Warehouse, No. 21 Little Portland Street, London; 1906–07 Methodist Church and caretaker's cottage, Agincourt Road, Gospel Oak, London (demolished except cottage); 1906–08 Carnegie Public Library, Thornhill Square, western Islington, London; 1906–08 All Souls' School, Foley Street, Marylebone, London; 1906–12 Office building for London, Edinburgh and Glasgow Assurance Co., Euston Square and Euston Road, London [232]; 1911–30 New entrance, Burlington Arcade, Piccadilly, London; 1913–18 Namirembe Anglican Cathedral, Kampala, Uganda [151].

Prior, EDWARD S. (1852–1932). *Arts and Crafts architect of high ideals and extraordinary originality. Son of a barrister, educated at Harrow and Cambridge, articled to Norman Shaw 1872 and worked with him until the late 1880s, though his own practice started c. 1883 (Red House, Harrow). Prior's Pier Terrace of houses at West Bay, near Bridport, Dorset (1885) [51], the nearby small Holy Trinity Church, Bothenhampton (1887–89) [84], and the superintendent's house at Harrow Laundry, Alma Road, Harrow (1887), are among the most striking Arts and Crafts buildings of that decade. A founder of the Art Workers' Guild in 1884, he later published several notable books and became Professor of Fine Art at Cambridge University 1912–32. (Research by Lynne Walker.)*
1891 The New Music School and other buildings, Harrow School, Peterborough Road, Harrow-on-the-Hill, Middlesex; 1892 and 1908 Pembroke College Mission Church and Hall, Barlow Street, Southwark, London; 1896–97 The Barn, Foxhole Hill Road, Exmouth, Devon [14–15]; 1897 South aisle, St Mary's Church, Burton Bradstock, Dorset; 1900–04 Humphry Museum and Medical Schools (now Zoology Building), Downing Street, Cambridge [76]; 1903–04 Music School, Winchester College, Romans Road, Winchester, Hampshire; 1903–05 Home Place (now a convalescent home) and cottage on estate, east of Holt, northern Norfolk [102–103]; 1904–07 St Andrew's Church, Roker, near Sunderland, County Durham [145–146]; c. 1905 The Moorings, near St John's Church, West Bay, near Bridport, Dorset; 1911–12 Greystones, Waterford Road, Highcliffe-on-Sea, Hampshire; 1912 The Small House, Mid Lavant, north of Chichester, Sussex; 1913–16 St Osmund's Church, Bournemouth Road, Parkstone, Poole, Dorset (ex-cept chancel) [150].

Reilly, CHARLES H. (later Sir Charles) (1874–1948). *An important figure in the history of architectural teaching. Born in London, educated at Merchant Taylors' and at Cambridge, trained by his father C. T. Reilly and by John Belcher, own practice, with Stanley Peach. In 1904 appointed Professor at Liverpool University, the first university School of Architecture in Britain, and remained there until 1934. Royal Gold Medal 1943. Knighted 1944. He designed comparatively few buildings.*

Ricardo, HALSEY (1854–1928). *Born in Bath, father (a banker) and mother died when he was young, educated at Rugby, articled to a Cheltenham architect, then worked for Basil Champneys and became fascinated by Philip Webb. Own practice c. 1881, ceramics partnership with William de Morgan 1888–98. Private income enabled him to select his commissions and he became a leading figure in Arts and Crafts architecture, advocating coloured ceramic building exteriors, writing and building occasionally. One of his best buildings, No. 8 Great George Street, Westminster, London (an office building, 1887), was redeveloped as early as 1912.*
1886–92 Foxoak, Seven Hills Road, Burwood, Surrey; 1891–93 Houses, Nos 15–17 Melbury Road, Holland Park, London; 1900–08 Howra Railway Station, Calcutta, India; 1905 onwards Woodside, north of Graffham, near Midhurst, Sussex; 1905–07 Debenham House, No. 8 Addison Road, Holland Park, London [219]; c. 1907 House, Brooke Market, Holborn, London; 1910 Penlee, Post Bridge, Dartmoor, Devon; 1914–15 House, No. 117 Old Church Street, Chelsea, London.

Richardson, A. E. (later Sir Albert) (1880–1964). *Born in London, father a printer. Articled to Victor Page 1895, went to work for Evelyn Hellicar 1898, Leonard Stokes 1902, Frank Verity (for whom he designed detail of several buildings) 1903. Own practice in partnership with C. Lovett Gill 1908, later with E. A. S. Houfe, and became one of the most distinguished practitioners of Stripped Classicism after the 1914–18 war. Royal Gold Medal 1947. Knighted 1956.*
c. 1910 Offices, Nos 10 and 19 Berkeley Street, London (Richardson and Gill); c. 1912 Farms and cottages for Duchy of Cornwall, village halls and Dulverton Town Hall, Duchy Hotel and restoration of Tor Royal for Prince of Wales, Princetown, Dartmoor, Devon (Richardson and Gill); 1912 New Theatre, Manchester; 1914–16 Moorgate Hall, Nos 83–93 Moorgate, City of London (office block, Richardson and Gill).

Rickards, EDWIN A. (1872–1920). See Lanchester and Rickards.

Russell and Cooper. See Cooper, Edwin.

Salmon, JAMES the younger (1873–1924). *Born in Glasgow, son and grandson of architects, trained by William Leiper. Joined his father 1893 and, with John Gaff Gillespie (1870–1926), the firm became Salmon, Son and Gillespie in 1897. Salmon and Gillespie were excelled only by Burnet and Mackintosh in originality of their Glasgow building of the period. Partnership ended 1913.*
1893 Scottish Temperance League, Nos 106–108 Hope Street, Glasgow (Gillespie); 1897 Mercantile Chambers, No. 39 Bothwell Street, Blythswood, Glasgow (Salmon); 1897 and 1901 Marine Hotel, Troon, Ayrshire (Gillespie); 1899 House No. 12 University Gardens, Hillhead, Glasgow (Gillespie); 1899–1900 British Linen Bank, No. 162 Gorbals Street, Glasgow (scheduled for demolition); 1899 British Linen Bank, No. 816 Govan Road, Govan, Glasgow (Gillespie); 1899 Anderston Savings Bank, No. 752 Argyle Street, Anderston, Glasgow; 1899 'The Hatrack', St Vincent Chambers, Nos 142–144 St Vincent Street, Glasgow (Salmon); 1899 Church Hall, St Andrew's East, No. 681 Alexandra Parade, Dennistoun, Glasgow; 1905 Upper storeys, British Linen Bank, Nos 110–118 Queen Street, Glasgow; 1905–06 Lion Chambers, Nos 170–172 Hope Street, Glasgow (Salmon) [156]; 1907 Municipal Buildings, Stirling (Gillespie); 1911 Pollok Golf Clubhouse, Pollok, Glasgow (Gillespie); 1913 Office block for Steel Co. of Scotland, Blochairn, Scotland (Gillespie); 1914 Church hall, Congregational Church, No. 231 Dalmarnock Road, Dalmarnock, Glasgow (Salmon).

Schultz, ROBERT WEIR (R. Schultz Weir after 1914) (1861–1951). *Born in Scotland, trained with R. R. Anderson, then worked for Norman Shaw and Sir Ernest George. Own practice 1891. A notable Arts and Crafts architect, a follower of Lethaby and an advocate of the admission of women to architecture.*
1899–1900 St Michael's Church, Woolmer Green, Hertfordshire; 1903–04 Pickenham Hall, South Pickenham, Norfolk (Neo-Georgian); 1905–06 How Green, north of Hever, Kent; c. 1908 Beaumonts, Edenbridge, Kent; c. 1908 Scalers Hill, Cobham, Kent; 1909 All Saints' Cathedral, Khartoum, Sudan [149]; c. 1912 Chapel of St Andrew, Westminster Cathedral, Victoria Street, London.

Scott, GILES GILBERT (later Sir Giles Gilbert) (1880–1960). *Born in London, son of George Gilbert Scott the younger and grandson of Sir George Gilbert Scott. Educated at Beaumont, articled to Temple Moore until 1903 when he won the* competition for Liverpool Cathedral [91] and started an immensely successful practice. The Liverpool competition assessors were Norman Shaw and G. F. Bodley. Because of Scott's inexperience, Bodley was appointed joint architect and his influence may be seen in some of the design of the Lady Chapel (built 1904–11) [93]. But Bodley died in 1907 and Scott completely redesigned the rest of the cathedral in 1910 [92]; indeed, he continued to revise the design as it was gradually built during the rest of his life. Knighted 1924. Royal Gold Medal 1925. Apart from Liverpool Cathedral, most of his major works date from after the 1914–18 war. But the Roman Catholic Church of Our Lady of the Assumption, The Hill, Northfleet, Kent, was designed in 1914, and St Paul, Derby Lane, Stoneycroft, Liverpool, c. 1916.

Scott, M. HUGH BAILLIE (1865–1945). *Born near Ramsgate, Kent, one of 14 children of a wealthy Scotsman. Educated at Cirencester Agricultural College, articled to C. E. Davis (City Architect of Bath) 1886–89, worked for F. Saunderson in Isle of Man until 1893, when started own practice there. Moved back to England 1901. Established one of the most successful Arts and Crafts domestic practices with designs of much individuality. (Research by James Kornwolf.)* 1892–93 Oakleigh, Glencrutchery Road, Douglas, Isle of Man (half-timbered and tile-hung); 1892–93 Red House, Victoria Road, Douglas, Isle of Man (half-timbered); 1893–94 Ivydene, Little Switzerland, Douglas, Isle of Man (half-timbered); 1894–96 Bexton Croft, Toft Road, Knutsford, Cheshire (half-timbered); 1895–96 Laurel Bank and Holly Bank, Victoria Road, Douglas, Isle of Man (semi-detached, roughcast with timbered gables); 1896–97 Leafield and Braeside, King Edward Road, Onchan, Isle of Man (semi-detached, roughcast with little timbering); 1897–98 Village Hall, Onchan, Isle of Man (roughcast); c. 1897–98 Terrace of 4 houses, Falcon Cliff, Douglas, Isle of Man (roughcast); 1898–99 Blackwell, on Windermere, Bowness, Westmorland (roughcast); 1898–99 White Lodge, in grounds of St Mary's Convent, Denchworth Road, Wantage, Berkshire (roughcast) [30–31]; 1899–1900 White House, No. 5 Upper Colquhoun Street, Helensburgh, Dunbartonshire (roughcast); 1899–1900 Garth House, Miles Lane, Cobham, Surrey (roughcast and exposed brick); 1899–1902 Winscombe, Beacon Road, Crowborough, Sussex (partly open-plan ground floor, roughcast and brick): 1900–02 Police Station, Castle Rushen, Castletown, Isle of Man (stone); 1902 Sandford Cottage, Wormit, Fife; c. 1903 A house in Zurich, Switzerland; 1904

Heather Cottage, off Cross Road, Sunningdale, Berkshire (roughcast); 1904 The Crows' Nest, in Ashdown Forest, near Duddleswell, Sussex (roughcast); c. 1905 Elmwood Cottages, Nos 7 and 7a Norton Way North, Letchworth, Hertfordshire (roughcast with timbered centre) [106]; 1905 Springwood, Spring Road, and 1907 Corrie Wood, Hitchen Road, Letchworth, Hertfordshire; 1906 Tanglewood, No. 17 Sollershott West, Letchworth, Hertfordshire (roughcast with timbered centre); 1906 Greenways, off Devenish Road, Sunningdale, Berkshire; 1906–07 Bill House, Grafton Road, Selsey-on-Sea, Sussex (roughcast, timbering and other materials); 1907 Kirkstead, Church Lane, Godstone, Surrey; 1908–09 Multiple houses, south-east corner of Meadway and Hampstead Way, Hampstead Garden Suburb, London; 1908–09 Waterlow Court, Heath Close, off Hampstead Way, Hampstead Garden Suburb, London (housing court) [116]; 1909 Burton Court, Longburton, near Sherborne, Dorset; 1910–11 Semi-detached houses, Nos 36–38 Reed Pond Walk, Gidea Park, Romford, Essex (open plan) [107]; 1912 Michaels, Palmar's Cross Hill, Harbledown, near Canterbury, Kent; 1912–13 House, No. 14 Western Drive, Short Hills, New Jersey, U.S.A.; 1912–21 Pilgrims, near Pilgrims Way, Chilham, Kent; 1913 Cottage, No. 144 Cooden Sea Road, Bexhill-on-Sea, Sussex; 1914 Gyrt-Howe, No. 30 Storey's Way, Cambridge; 1914 Great Wood, near Annesley Park, Ottershaw, Surrey.

Sedding, JOHN DANDO (1838–91). *A distinguished Gothic church architect and an early advocate of the Arts and Crafts movement. Born at Eton, Buckinghamshire, articled to G. E. Street 1858, then joined brother Edmund Sedding (1836–68) in Penzance practice. Own London practice 1875. The talented Henry Wilson joined his staff in 1888 at a time when Sedding practice grew greatly. At his early death in 1891, many commissions were in hand and had to be completed and sometimes designed by Wilson (q.v.).*

Sellars, JAMES (1846–88). See Douglas, Campbell.

Sellers, J. HENRY (1861–1954). See Wood, Edgar.

Shaw, R. NORMAN (1831–1912). *The pre-eminent architect in England of the late nineteenth century. Born in Edinburgh and articled there to William Burn 1846. Worked in London for Anthony Salvin and then for G. E. Street 1858. Shared own London office with W. E. Nesfield 1862–68, then independently. Developed large practice and became famous, but twice refused Royal Gold Medal as he objected to R.I.B.A. professionalization. Many of his*

works in the 1890–1914 period were in a freely Baroque manner. (Dating by Andrew Saint.) 1887–90 New Scotland Yard police headquarters, Victoria Embankment, Westminster, London [37]; 1887–88 House, No. 170 Queen's Gate, Kensington, London (freely Neo-Wren) [62]; 1889–94 Bryanston, near Blandford Forum, Dorset (freely Neo-Wren) [61]; 1889–93 All Saints' Church, Richards Castle, Batchcott, south of Ludlow, Shropshire (Gothic); 1889–91 Chesters, north of Hexham, Northumberland (Baroque) [63]; 1893–95 All Saints' Church, Galley Hill, Swanscombe, near Uckfield, Kent (Gothic); 1894–95 The Hallams, east of Wonersh, Surrey (tile-hung and timbering); 1894–96 Police Station, Holmes Road, Kentish Town, London (designed 1891, freely Classical); 1895–98 White Star Line building (now Pacific Steam), James Street, Liverpool; 1897–1907 Southern block, including Cannon Row Police Station, New Scotland Yard, Victoria Embankment, London; 1898–1901 Parr's Bank (now National Westminster), Castle Street, Liverpool (executed with Willink and Thicknesse, restrained Baroque); 1901–03 Gaiety Theatre (destroyed) and office block behind, western corner of Aldwych and Strand, London (with E. Runtz); 1904–05 (designed 1901) Alliance Assurance building, south-west corner of St James's Street, London (with Ernest Newton, restrained Baroque); 1905–09 Extension, Bradford Town Hall, Town Hall Square, Bradford, Yorkshire (designed 1902, freely Gothic extension to Gothic Town Hall); 1905–08 Façades, Piccadilly Hotel, Piccadilly and Regent Street, London (Baroque) [187]; 1907–08 Associated Portland Cement Co. offices, No. 8 Lloyds Avenue, City of London (freely Classical).

Sherrin, GEORGE C. (1843–1909). *Own practice c. 1886 onwards included much work for the London Underground Railway and many private houses, especially at Ingatestone, Essex.* 1893–94 Moorgate Underground Station, Moorgate, City of London (above ground building); c. 1895–99 South Kensington, Kensington High Street, Gloucester Road and Monument Underground Railway Stations, London; 1897 Town Hall, Alexandra Road, Farnborough, Hampshire; 1897–98 Orphanage, Holly Place, Hampstead, London; 1897–98 Gardner Mansions, Nos 2–4 Church Row, Hampstead, London (flats); 1898–1902 The Kursaal, Southend-on-Sea, Essex; 1899–1902 St Mary's Roman Catholic Church, Eldon Street, City of London border with Finsbury; 1900–03 Moorgate Chambers, over Moorgate Underground Station, City of London (offices); 1903–04 Alexandra Hotel, Marine Parade, Dovercourt, Essex; 1903 Wynnstow, near Limpsfield, Hampshire; 1907 Eldon House, beside church in Eldon Street, City of London (offices); 1907–08 Spencer House, South Place, City of London border with Finsbury (offices).

Simpson, JOHN W. (later Sir John) (1858–1933). *Born in Brighton, Sussex, son of an architect, trained at Royal Academy Schools. In partnership with Maxwell Ayrton from 1910. Held several public appointments. Knighted 1924, he later became well known for his work at and around Wembley Stadium with the engineer Sir Owen Williams and Ayrton.* 1898–1900 Roedean School for Girls, Rottingdean, near Brighton, Sussex (the chapel 1906, junior school and sanatorium 1908, and art school and library 1911 also by Simpson); 1900–03 Cartwright Memorial Gallery and Museum, Lister Park, Bradford, Yorkshire; 1907 Audley House, Nos 9–12 Margaret Street, Marylebone, London; 1911 Clare College Mission Church, Dilston Grove, Bermondsey, London; 1912–16 Chapel, Gresham's School, Holt, Norfolk (largely by Ayrton); 1914–16 Offices of Crown Agents for Colonies, Millbank, London.

Skipper, GEORGE J. (1856–1948). *Articled to J. T. Lee in London. Own practice 1880. The leading East Anglia architect of the turn of the century, Skipper produced some excellent examples of Edwardian Baroque, as well as work in other styles, notably the Loire château fantasies of his hotels at Cromer.* 1890 Town Hall, Prince of Wales Road, Cromer, Norfolk; 1891 The Grand Hotel, Cromer, Norfolk; 1893 Hotel Metropole, Cromer, Norfolk; 1895–96 Hotel de Paris, Cromer, Norfolk; 1898–1900 Mancroft Towers, south-west of Oulton, Suffolk; c. 1900 Royal Arcade, off Market Place, Norwich [118]; 1903–05 Norwich Union Assurance headquarters, Surrey Street, Norwich [183]; 1903–05 Jarrold's department store, Exchange Street and London Street, Market Place, Norwich; 1904 Norwich Union office building, No. 24 St Andrew's Street, Cambridge; 1906 Telephone House, No. 43 St Giles Street, Norwich; 1908 Sennowe Hall, Guist, south-east of Fakenham, Norfolk.

Smith and Brewer. A Dunbar Smith (1866–1933) in partnership with W. Cecil Brewer (1871–1918). *Smith was articled to J. G. Gibbins in Brighton, before going on to Royal Academy Schools. Started private practice with Brewer when they won the competition for the Mary Ward Settlement (Passmore Edwards buildings), assessed by Norman Shaw, in June 1895.*

1895–98 Passmore Edwards buildings (now Mary Ward House), Tavistock Place, Bloomsbury, London [55]; 1896 Additions, Royal Hospital, Kew Foot Road, Richmond, Surrey; c. 1898 The East Anglian Sanatorium, and chapel 1909, Nayland, near Colchester, Essex; c. 1900 Little Barley End and stables, Aldbury, Hertfordshire; 1904 Ditton Place, south-west of Balcombe, Sussex; 1906 Acremead, Froghole, north-east of Crockham Hill, Kent; 1908 Interiors of Ely House, No. 37 Dover Street, Mayfair, London; 1909 The Malting House, Malting Lane, Cambridge; 1909–c. 1912 National Museum of Wales, Civic Centre, Cardiff; c. 1914–16 Heal's Furniture Store, Nos 196–197 Tottenham Court Road, London [168].

Spiers, R. PHENÉ (1858–1916). *A famous teacher and advocate of Neo-Classicism. Born at Oxford, became Associate of R.I.B.A. in 1861, but made his name as an architectural writer and teacher. Master of the Royal Academy School of Architecture 1870–1906.*

Sprague, W. G. R. (c. 1865–1933). *The most brilliantly versatile and successful of Frank Matcham's pupils from c. 1892, Sprague soon established his own practice and designed many of the best-known London theatres. (Research by Victor Glasstone.)*

1894 Metropole Theatre, Camberwell, London (with Bertie Crewe); 1898 The Coronet Theatre (now a cinema), Notting Hill Gate, London; 1899–1900 The Hippodrome, Balham, London; 1899 Wyndham's Theatre, Charing Cross Road, London; 1901 The Camden Theatre (now broadcasting studios), Camden Town High Street, London; 1902–03 The Albery (originally the New) Theatre, St Martin's Lane, London [202]; 1905 The Strand Theatre, Strand, London; 1905 The Aldwych Theatre, Aldwych, London; 1906 The Globe Theatre, Shaftesbury Avenue, London; 1907 The Queen's Theatre, Shaftesbury Avenue, London; c. 1910 Théâtre Edward VII, Paris, France; 1913 The Ambassadors Theatre, West Street, London; c. 1914 The Empire Theatre, Penge, London.

Stokes, LEONARD A. (1858–1925). *Born at Southport, Lancashire, articled to S. J. Nicholl 1871, then worked for G. E. Street, for Thomas Collcutt and for G. F. Bodley. Own practice 1883. Designed many Roman Catholic and Telephone Company buildings. A characterful and inventive designer, whose originality retained roots in styles of the past. Royal Gold Medal 1919. (Research by Rory Spence.)*

1888–90 House, No. 47 Palace Court, Bayswater, London; 1888–90 St Clare's Church and presbytery, Arundel Avenue, Sefton Park, Liverpool;

1890 Corpus Christi Schools, Miles Platting, Liverpool; 1893–1909 Nazareth House, convent and chapel, Royston Gardens, Bexhill, Sussex; 1895 Pangbourne School, Pangbourne Hill, Pangbourne, Berkshire; 1895–96 All Souls' Church and presbytery, Fitzwilliam Street, Peterborough, Cambridgeshire; 1896 St Mary's Primary School, No. 49 Brook Green, Hammersmith, London; 1898 Shooter's Hill House, Pangbourne, Berkshire [210]; 1898–99 Yew Tree Lodge, No. 2 West Drive, Streatham, London; 1899–1903 All Saints' Convent, Shenley Road, London Colney, Hertfordshire [46]; 1899–1901 College of Further Education, New Inn Hall Street, Oxford; 1900 onwards A series of telephone exchanges for the National Telephone Co., including that at No. 149 Rose Street, Edinburgh (1900), No. 131 Lee Road, Blackheath, London (1900), Ogle Road, Southampton (1900, roof altered) [154], Nos 57–59 London Wall, City of London (1904), Gerrard Street, Soho, London (1904, destroyed) [121], Reform Row, Tottenham, London (1906), Nos 2–3 Alexandra Street, Cambridge (1907), Minster Street, Reading (1908), No. 273 Bon-Accord Street, Aberdeen (1908), Kingsland Green, Dalston, London (1908, top storey altered); 1901 Brompton Oratory Boys' School, Cale Street, Kensington, London; 1901 Church of England School, Maltravers Street, Arundel, Sussex; 1902–04 Littleshaw, Camp Road, Woldingham, Surrey; 1903–05 Lincoln Grammar School, Minterne House, Wragby Road, Lincoln; 1904–06 Minterne House, Minterne Magna, near Cerne Abbas, Dorset; 1904–08 Chelsea Town Hall extension onto King's Road, Chelsea, London (original 1885 part at back by Stokes's close friend J. M. Brydon); 1907–09 Convent of the Poor Clares, Main Street, Lynton, Devon; 1907–11 School buildings, Downside School, Stratton-on-the-Fosse, near Bath, Somerset; 1909 Nansidwell Hotel, Mawnam Smith, near Falmouth, Devon; 1910 St Wilfrid's Hall, Brompton Oratory, Kensington, London; 1910–15 North Court, Emmanuel College, Emmanuel Street, Cambridge; 1913–14 Gagnière office block (now Granada), Nos 34–36 Golden Square, Soho, London [167]; 1914–25 Georgetown Cathedral, Demerara, Guyana.

Tapper, WALTER J. (later Sir Walter) (1861–1935). *Born in Devon, articled to Rowell and Sons in Newton Abbot. Worked for Basil Champneys and G. F. Bodley, started own practice 1900. Most of his work was ecclesiastical and Gothic, much of it restoration of great sensitivity.* 1899 Gothic font cover, St Wulfram's

Church, Grantham, Lincolnshire; *c.* 1901 Church of the Ascension, Malvern Link, Worcestershire; *c.* 1905 Restoration work, Penshurst Place, Kent; 1905 St Erkenwald's Church, Southchurch Avenue, Southend-on-Sea, Essex; 1911–14 St Stephen's Church, Roberts Street, Grimsby, Lincolnshire; 1913 Church of the Annunciation, Quebec Street, London; 1913–14 St Michael's Church, Little Coates, near Grimsby, Lincolnshire; *c.* 1914–16 St Mary's Church, West Cliffe Grove, Harrogate, Yorkshire.

Thomas, A. BRUMWELL (later Sir Alfred) (1868–1948). *Born at Virginia Water, Surrey, educated at Westminster Art School, own practice c. 1896. One of the most successful and flamboyant practitioners of High Edwardian Baroque for large public buildings. Knighted 1906.*
1897–1906 Belfast City Hall, Donegall Square, Belfast [*172–173*]; 1898–1901 Eye Infirmary, Royal Devon and Exeter Hospital, Southernhay, Devon; 1899–1908 Woolwich (originally Plumstead) Town Hall, Wellington Street, Woolwich, London; 1904–08 Stockport Town Hall, Wellington Road South, Stockport, Cheshire [*189*]; 1911–14 Public Library, Lewisham Way, Deptford, London; *c.* 1914 Fever Hospital, Huddersfield, Yorkshire.

Thomas, WALTER AUBREY (d. 1912). *Apparently worked in Aberystwyth, Wales, before starting practice in Liverpool 1876. One of the most prosperous architects of Liverpool in this period and a designer of much character.*
1892 Philharmonic Hotel, Hope Street, Liverpool (extension 1898); 1906 State Insurance Building, No. 14 Dale Street, Liverpool; 1906–08 Tower Buildings, behind Pier Head, Liverpool; 1907 The Vines public house, Lime Street, Liverpool; 1908–11 Royal Liver Building, Pier Head, Liverpool [*233*].

Thornely, ARNOLD (later Sir Arnold) (1870–1953). *Born in Cheshire, articled in Liverpool, own practice 1898, became a partner in firm of Briggs and Wolstenholme 1906 after winning two major competitions, and did most of their design work. The firm became Briggs and Thornely after c. 1918.*
1898–1905 Presbyterian Church, Warren Road, Blundellsands, north of Liverpool (with W. G. Fraser); 1903–07 Mersey Docks and Harbour Board Building, Pier Head, Liverpool (executed with Briggs and Wolstenholme) [*188*]; 1907–12 Fairhaven Congregational Church, South Clifton Drive, Lytham St Anne's, Lancashire; 1912–21 Police Court and Sessions House, Blakey Moor, Blackburn, Lancashire; *c.* 1910 The Homestead, Birch Howe and several other houses around

Pine Walks, Prenton, Cheshire; 1913 King George's Hall, Blakey Moor, Blackburn, Lancashire; 1913 Faculty of Arts Building, University of Liverpool, Ashton Street, Liverpool (with Briggs and Wolstenholme and with F. W. Simon); 1914–20 Wallasey Town Hall, Brighton Road, Egremont, Wallasey, Cheshire.

Townsend, CHARLES HARRISON (1851–1928). *Born at Birkenhead, Cheshire, son of a solicitor and of the daughter of a Polish violinist. Articled to Walter Scott in Liverpool, worked for T. L. Banks in London 1883, in partnership with him 1884–88, then own Arts and Crafts practice. From 1892–1902 Townsend was the most successful of the English Free Style architects of larger buildings.*
1890 Tourelle, Salcombe, Devon; 1892 Rebuilt west front of All Saints' Church, Ennismore Gardens, Knightsbridge, London (Romanesque); *c.* 1892–95 St Martin's Church, Blackheath, near Guildford, Surrey (Townsend also built the Voysey-like Congregational chapel *c.* 1893 and many of the small houses in the new village, including Blatchfield *c.* 1894 and others; see below); 1892–94 The Bishopsgate Institute, Bishopsgate, City of London [*42*]; 1896 Linden Haus, Dusseldorf, Germany; 1896–1901 Horniman Museum, Forest Hill, south London [*45*]; 1899–1901 Whitechapel Art Gallery, Whitechapel, east London [*43–44*]; 1900 Dickhurst, near Haslemere, Surrey (possibly designed *c.* 1895); 1902–04 St Mary the Virgin, outside Great Warley, near Brentwood, Essex [*half-title, 143*]; 1902 Village cross, West Meon, Hampshire; *c.* 1902–07 Blatchcombe, Theobalds, Vicarage, and Cobbins (for himself), Blackheath, near Guildford, Surrey; 1904 Union Free Church, off the High Road, Woodford Green, Essex; 1906 Arbuthnot Institute Hall, Shamley Green, Surrey; 1906 House in The Glade, Letchworth, Hertfordshire; 1909–10 Schools at Penn in Holmer Green, Buckinghamshire; *c.* 1910 Peerie Hame (originally The Wakes), Guildane, near Guildford, Surrey; 1910 Village Hall, Panshangar, Hertfordshire; 1910–11 Library and lecture room, Horniman Museum, Forest Hill, south London; *c.* 1910 Restoration, Compton Wynyates House, Tysoe, Warwickshire; *c.* 1912 House, No. 2 Temple Fortune Lane and probably houses Nos 135–141 Hampstead Way, Hampstead Garden Suburb, London.

Treadwell and Martin. Henry J. Treadwell (1861–1910) and Leonard Martin (1869–1935). *Martin was trained by John Giles and at Royal Academy Schools. The partnership, which produced some of the most original office buildings*

and public houses of c. 1900, lasted from 1890 until Treadwell's death. Martin later built a cathedral at Onitsha, Nigeria.
1890s Rebuilding and later additions, St John's School, Leatherhead, Surrey; 1890s St Mary's Hospital (now Children's Hospital), Carshalton, Surrey; 1892–94 Scott's Restaurant, Nos 18–19 Coventry Street, London (now moved); 1890s Cottage Hospital, Cobham, Surrey; 1897–1904 St John's Skin Hospital, Lisle Street, north of Leicester Square, London (erroneously attributed to Frank Verity by Pevsner); 1897 Rising Sun public house, Tottenham Court Road, London; 1898 Old Shades public house, Westminster, London [*119*]; *c.* 1900 Furness office building, No. 60 St James's Street, London; *c.* 1900 No. 7 Hanover Street, London; *c.* 1900 Panton House, Haymarket, London; *c.* 1900 Office building, No. 74 New Bond Street, London; 1904 Whitehall House, Whitehall, Westminster, London (office building) [*119*]; 1905–06 Sandroyd School, Cobham, Surrey; 1906 No. 78 Wigmore Street, London; 1906 Office building, No. 106 Jermyn Street, St James's, London; *c.* 1906 Nos 78–81 Fetter Lane, Holborn, London; 1907 Office building, Nos 55 and 20 Conduit Street, Mayfair, London; 1907 Office buildings, No. 23 Woodstock Street and No. 7 Dering Street, off Bond Street, London.

Troup, FRANCIS W. (1859–1941). *Born in Aberdeenshire, articled to Campbell Douglas and Sellars, worked for J. J. Stevenson in London, then own practice 1890. Arts and Crafts architect, a disciple of Lethaby and designer of the Art Workers' Guild premises in Queen Square, London.*
1896 Almshouses, Farnley, south-west Leeds, Yorkshire; 1897–98 Mansfield House Club, Barking Road, Canning Town, Essex; 1901–03 Sandhouse (now Kingwood), Sandhills, southwest of Witley, Surrey; *c.* 1905 Pavilion, Bank of England sports ground, Priory Lane, Roehampton, London; 1909 House, No. 20 Queen Anne's Gate, Westminster, London; 1913 Blackfriars House, New Bridge Street, Blackfriars, London (office block); 1913 Hall of the Art Workers' Guild, Queen Square, Bloomsbury, London.

Turner, H. THACKERAY (1853–1937). *Son of a clergyman. Articled to Sir George Gilbert Scott. A leading figure in the Arts and Crafts movement and the first secretary of the Society for the Protection of Ancient Buildings. In partnership, as Balfour and Turner, with Eustace Balfour.*
1894 Wycliffe Buildings, Portsmouth Road, Guildford, Surrey (flats); 1895 Mead Cottage, Buryfields, Guildford, Surrey; 1900–03 Westbrook, north of the railway station, Godalming, Sur-

rey; c. 1900 Goodwins Place, Rose Hill, Dorking, Surrey; c. 1902 The Court, Buryfields, Guildford, Surrey (15 houses around a court); 1909 National Scottish Church, Crown Court, Russell Street, London; c. 1910 Northern side of Wilton Crescent, Belgravia, London (Balfour and Turner); 1910 Railways Convalescent Home, Shottendane Road, Margate, Kent.

Unwin, RAYMOND (later Sir Raymond) (1863–1940), in partnership with Barry Parker (1867–1947) from c. 1902 onwards. *Unwin trained as an engineer but became interested in building design and social conditions, which led to the formation of the partnership with Parker, who had trained as an architect, and of the first notable British town-planning firm. Unwin was knighted 1932 and awarded Royal Gold Medal 1937.*

1895 St Andrew's Church, Barrow Hill, near Staveley, Derbyshire (Unwin); 1895 Woodcote, Church Stretton, Shropshire (Parker); 1902–04 Town plan of New Earswick, north of York, and the early houses there (Unwin); 1903 Kildare Lodge, Minehead, Somerset (Parker). 1903–06 Co-operative housing, St Botolph's Avenue, Sevenoaks, Kent; 1903 Town plan of Letchworth Garden City, Hertfordshire, and houses there [*114*]; 1905–07 Folk Hall (originally called the Institute), New Earswick, north of York (Unwin); 1906 Town plan of Hampstead Garden Suburb, London, and, in following years, shops at Temple Fortune, Heath Close, Reynolds Close and The Orchard; 1907 Oakdene, Rotherfield, Sussex; 1911–12 Primary School, New Earswick, north of York (Unwin); 1913–14 The Clock House, Cowfold, Sussex (Parker).

Verity, FRANK T. (1864–1937). *Son of Thomas Verity, a successful architect. Articled to his father with whom he went into partnership c. 1890, and studied in Paris and with R. Phené Spiers. Became an advocate of French Classicism, especially after c. 1904, when the Beaux-Arts influence became fashionable. By this time, his buildings were being detailed largely by the young A. E. Richardson. Verity built flats, theatres and cinemas in London and Paris. His Scala Theatre, Charlotte Street, London (1904), has been destroyed.*
1890 The Pavilion, Lord's Cricket Ground, Marylebone, London; 1891 Club Building, Nos 96–97 Piccadilly, London (with his father); 1899 The French Hospital, north-east end of Shaftesbury Avenue, London; 1903 Flats, No. 12 Hyde Park Place, Bayswater Road, London; 1904 Flats, No. 25 Berkeley Square, Mayfair, London; 1905 Sudan House, No. 7 Cleveland Row, St James's, London

(flats) [*209*]; 1907–11 Polytechnic of Central London, Upper Regent Street, London; 1908–09 Nos 169–201 Regent Street, London.

Voysey, CHARLES FRANCIS ANNESLEY (1857–1941). *Born near Hull, Yorkshire, son of a clergyman and grandson of an engineer-architect. Father dismissed from Church of England c. 1871 for heresy and started Theistic Church in London. C. F. A. Voysey educated at Dulwich College, articled to J. P. Seddon, then worked for Saxon Snell and for George Devey. Own practice 1882, designed wallpapers etc., first architectural commission 1888.*
1888 The Cottage, north-east of Bishop's Itchington, Warwickshire (additions 1900); 1890 Additions to The Cliff, No. 102 Coventry Road, Warwick; 1890 Walnut Tree Farm, Castlemorten, Malvern, Herefordshire; 1891 Studio house, No. 17 St Dunstan's Road, West Kensington, London; 1891 Studio house, No. 14 South Parade, Bedford Park, London (lower wing added 1894) [*21*]; 1891–92 Houses, Nos 14 and 15 Hans Road, Knightsbridge, London; 1893–94 Perrycroft, above Colwall, Malvern Hills, Herefordshire [*22–23*]; 1894–1903 Cottages etc. at Ockham Park, Ockham, Surrey, and Lovelace monument in Ockham Church 1907; 1894 Lowicks, south-east of Frensham, Surrey (cottage); 1895–96 Wentworth Arms public house and 6 cottages, Elmesthorpe, near Hinckley, Leicestershire; 1896 Annesley Lodge, Platt's Lane, Hampstead, London [*24*]; 1896 Greyfriars (also known as Merlshanger or Wancote), near Puttenham on the Hog's Back hills, Surrey [*25*]; 1897 Norney, north-west of Shackleford, Surrey [*26*]; 1897 New Place, off Polecat Lane, north of Haslemere, Surrey; 1898–99 Broadleys, Gill Head, Windermere, northern Lancashire; 1898–99 Moor Crag, Gill Head, Windermere; 1899 Spade House, Radnor Cliff Crescent, Sandgate, Kent; 1899 Winsford Cottage Hospital, Halwill Station, south-east of Holsworthy, Devon; 1900–01 The Orchard, Shire Lane, Chorley Wood, Hertfordshire (for himself) [*104–105*]; 1902–03 Sanderson Wallpaper Factory (now Alliance Assurance), Barley Mow Passage, off Turnham Green, Chiswick, London [*153*]; 1902–04 Vodin (now Little Court), Old Woking Road, Pyrford Common, near Woking, Surrey; 1904 Miners' housing and Institute, Whitwood Colliery, Normanton, Yorkshire; 1905 White Horse Inn, Stetchworth, near Newmarket, Cambridgeshire (now a private house); 1905 The Homestead, Second Avenue, Frinton-on-Sea, Essex; 1909 St Winifred's Quarry, Coombe Down,

near Bath, Somerset; 1912 Lilycombe, Porlock Hill, west of Porlock, Somerset; 1913 Lodge for Hill Close (also by Voysey 1896), south-west of Studland, Dorset.

Wade, FAIRFAX B. (1851–1919). *Wade produced several buildings of merit around the turn of the century which were, according to the historian H. S. Goodhart-Rendel, designed by architectural 'ghosts'; this assertion should be treated with caution unless there is firm evidence, since similar remarks were made about countless other architects of the period. Wade's largest building, the Royal School of Needlework, on the corner of Exhibition Road and Imperial Institute Road, Kensington, London (1903), was demolished c. 1960. Early in his career, he did some Gothic church work, including St Mary, Overleigh Road, Handbridge, Chester (1885–87).*
1893 Compton House, Vicarage Lane, Denton, Northamptonshire; 1896 House, No. 64 Sloane Street, Knightsbridge, London; c. 1905 House, No. 54 South Audley Street, Mayfair, London; 1906 Arborfield Court, south of Arborfield, Berkshire; c. 1908 Angrove House, north-west of Crowborough, Sussex; c. 1910 Restoration and additions, Ockwells Manor House, south-west of Bray, Berkshire.

Walton, GEORGE (1867–1933). *Born in Glasgow, son of an artist. Trained as bank clerk, taking evening classes at Glasgow School of Art, the only formal art education he had before starting own practice 1888 as designer and interior decorator, later developing an architectural practice as well. Interest in Arts and Crafts movement and his friendship with C. R. Mackintosh were influences in the style of his individualistic work. His early works have been destroyed. Moved to London 1898. (Research by Nikolaus Pevsner.)*
1897–98 Interiors of houses at York and at Leadcameroch, Scotland; 1899 onwards Interiors of Kodak shops in London, Glasgow and overseas (probably destroyed); 1901 The Leys, Barnet Lane, east of Elstree, Hertfordshire (now a council home, some interior work survives); 1902 Interiors, The Philippines, near Brasted Chart, west of Sevenoaks, Kent; 1905 Interiors, Alma House, Cheltenham, Gloucestershire; 1905 Additions to Finnart House, on the road to Walton-on-Thames, Weybridge, Surrey (only the lodge appears to survive of Walton's work); 1907–10 Wern Fawr, Harlech, north-west Wales; 1908 The White House, near Shiplake, Oxfordshire (interiors destroyed).

Waterhouse, ALFRED (1830–1905). *Born in Liverpool, articled to Richard Lane in Manchester, own practice in Manchester 1853, later in London where he became one of the best-known architects* *of the second half of the nineteenth century. He won many competitions. Royal Gold Medal 1878. Many of his most famous buildings (e.g. Manchester Town Hall 1868–77) were done before the period covered by this book and in 1891 his son Paul became his partner. His subsequent buildings include the school at Yattendon, Berkshire (1891), where he owned the local manor. Also the Royal Institution of Chartered Surveyors, Parliament Square, London (1896–98), University College Hospital, Gower Street, London (1897–1906), Prudential Assurance, Holborn, London (1899–1906), Prudential Assurance, North Street, Brighton (1904).*

Watt, RICHARD HARDING (1842–1913). *A wealthy building patron and amateur architect who built many individualistic works at Knutsford, Cheshire. Watt employed one or another of the architects Walter Aston, John Brooke, H. S. Fairhurst and W. Longworth for these buildings, but appears to have designed most of the elevations himself. (Research by David McLaughlin and Julia Beck.)*
1895 The Old Croft, Legh Road, Knutsford, Cheshire (tower 1907); 1898 Moorgarth and other houses in Legh Road, Knutsford; 1899–1902 Ruskin Rooms and cottages behind (1904), King Street, Knutsford; 1902 Swinton Square, Knutsford; 1907–08 King's Coffee House with Gaskell Memorial Tower, King Street, Knutsford.

Webb, ASTON (later Sir Aston) (1849–1930), *mostly in partnership with E. Ingress Bell (1837–1914). Aston Webb was born in London, son of an artist. Articled to Banks and Barry, own practice 1873 onwards grew into the largest in England at the turn of the century. Knighted 1904. Royal Gold Medal 1905.*
1887–91 Victoria Law Courts, Corporation Street, Birmingham; *c.* 1890–97 Restoration and additions, St Bartholomew-the-Great, Smithfield, City of London; 1891–1909 Victoria and Albert Museum, Cromwell Road, Kensington, London; 1893 French Protestant Church, No. 9 Soho Square, London; 1893–95 Royal United Services Institute, Whitehall, Westminster, London [72]; 1893–1902 Christ's Hospital School, south-west of Horsham, Sussex; 1894–96 St Alban's Church, Margravine Road, Fulham, London; 1897 Mumford's Flour Mills, east end of Greenwich High Road, Greenwich, London; 1899–1905 Royal Naval College, on the hill above Dartmouth, Devon [180]; 1900–09 University of Birmingham. Edgbaston, Birmingham; 1900–06 Imperial College of Science and Technology, Imperial Institute Road, Kensington, London; 1901–13 Lay-out of The Mall and *rond-point* in front of Buckingham Palace, London (Queen Victoria

Memorial by the sculptor Sir Thomas Brock); 1901 Thames Warehouse, Stamford Street, Southwark, London; 1903 St Michael's Court, Gonville and Caius College, Cambridge; 1908–09 Admiralty Arch, between Trafalgar Square and The Mall, Westminster, London; 1909–13 Royal School of Mines, Prince Consort Road, Kensington, London; 1912–13 Buckingham Palace, east frontage to The Mall, London [205].

Webb, PHILIP (1831–1915). *The architectural father-figure of the Arts and Crafts movement. Born at Oxford, articled to John Billing in Reading, worked for G. E. Street 1852–56, where he met William Morris. Own practice 1856. Joined and designed for Morris's firm and, with him, founded the Society for the Protection of Ancient Buildings. Webb's Red House (1859) started a long line of domestic commissions, mostly in rural surroundings, which were not published in the building press but were visited by idealistic young architects and had a profound influence on Lethaby's generation. Almost all of Webb's houses were on principle designed in the vernacular manner of their particular neighbourhood, so he evolved no identifiable style of his own.*
1890–94 Cottage and gatehouse, Liphook, Hampshire (not located); 1890 Bell Brothers offices, Zetland Road, Middlesbrough, Yorkshire; 1891 Additions and rebuilding, Forthampton Court, south-east of Forthampton, Gloucestershire; 1891–94 Standen, Saint Hill, near East Grinstead, Sussex [3]; 1896 Exning House, Newmarket, Suffolk; 1898 Warrens House, Lyndhurst, Hampshire; 1898 Village Hall, Arisaig, Scotland; 1898 Hurlands, east of the church, Puttenham, Surrey; 1902 Cottages at Lechlade, Gloucestershire (not located); 1902 Morris Memorial Cottages, Kelmscott, Oxfordshire.

Weir, R. SCHULTZ. See Schultz.

Wilson, HENRY or HARRY (1864–1934). *Born in Liverpool, son of a clergyman, trained at Kidderminster Art School, articled to E. J. Shrewsbury in Maidenhead. Worked for John Oldrid Scott, John Belcher and then, from 1888, for J. D. Sedding (who died in 1891). Wilson carried on Sedding's practice, but with diminishing financial success, although he was arguably the most inspired architect-designer-craftsman of the Arts and Crafts movement. Wilson was the first editor of The Architectural Review 1896–1901. A close friend of Lethaby, the two men led a design team which submitted the most original of all the entries for the Liverpool Cathedral competition in 1903. After that, the greater part of his work was in church plate, with brilliant use of enamel, and other metalwork. Wilson taught with Lethaby and Pite at the Royal*

College of Art. In 1922 he went to live in Menton, France, where he spent the rest of his life.
1888–*c.* 1900 Holy Trinity Church Sloane Street, Chelsea, London (completion and furnishing of Sedding's commission) [38, 85]; *c.* 1890–96 Chapel and library, Welbeck Abbey, south-west of Worksop, Nottinghamshire; 1890–91 Public Library, Ladbroke Grove, North Kensington, London (his own commission while working for Sedding) [39]; 1892 St Peter's Church, Mount Park Road, Ealing, west London [40]; 1893 Tower of St Clement's Church (by Sedding 1871), St Clement's Road, Boscombe, Bournemouth, Hampshire; *c.* 1895 Lychgate and vestry, Holy Trinity Church, Ilfracombe, Devon; *c.* 1895 Tower of Holy Redeemer Church (by Sedding 1887), Exmouth Street, Finsbury, London; *c.* 1895 Furnishing and decoration of St Augustine's Church (by Sedding 1885), Archway Road, Hornsey, London; 1895–96 North chapel and *c.* 1909 north aisle and decoration, St Martin's Church, Brabyn's Row, Marple, Cheshire; 1895–97 St Mark's Church, Brithdir, Merionethshire; 1897–1908 Furnishing of St Bartholomew's Church, Ann Street, Brighton, Sussex (includes altar with baldacchino 1899–1900 [90], Lady altar 1902 with crucifix *c.* 1900, pulpit 1906, giant candlesticks *c.* 1908 and font 1908 as well as plate etc.); 1901 (attributed) Walmsgate Hall chapel (reconstructed 1960 as St Hugh's Church, Langworth, Lincolnshire); 1905 Chancel, St Mary's Church, Lynton, Somerset (Wilson had executed Sedding's design for the nave in 1893–94); *c.* 1905 Tower screen and font, St Mary's Church, Norton-sub-Hamdon, Somerset; 1913 Pulpit, Ripon Cathedral, Yorkshire; 1912 The Elphinstone Tomb, King's College, University of Aberdeen (cast 1914, erected 1925) [152].

Wood, EDGAR (1860–1935), *in partnership with J. Henry Sellers (1861–1954) from c. 1905 onwards. Born at Middleton, north-east of Manchester, son of a mill-owner. Articled to James Murgatroyd in Manchester, own practice 1885. The most important Arts and Crafts architect of northern England. Founder of the Northern Art Workers' Guild. (Research by John Archer.)*
1892 Manchester and Salford (later Williams and Deacons) Bank, Market Place, Middleton, near Manchester; 1893 Silver Street Chapel, Rochdale, Lancashire; 1894 Westdene, Archer Park, Middleton; 1895 Redcroft and Fencegate, Rochdale Road, Middleton (semi-detached); 1895–97 Cottages, Nos 2–4 Schwabe Street, Rhodes, Middleton; 1897 Victoria Hotel, Spot-

land Road, Rochdale, Lancashire; 1899–1902 Methodist church with school and cottage in courtyard, Long Street, Middleton [*54*]; 1900–01 Banney Royd (now Fire Services offices), Halifax Road, Edgerton, Huddersfield, Yorkshire; 1900–02 Lindley Clock Tower, corner of Lidget Street and Daisy Lea Lane, Lindley, Huddersfield, Yorkshire; 1901 onwards 14 houses on Richardson's Estate, Park Road etc., Hale, Cheshire; 1903–08 First Church of Christ Scientist, Daisy Bank Road, Victoria Park, south Manchester (interior derelict, currently being repaired) [*144*]; 1905 Holly Cottage, Holly Road, Bramhall, Stockport, Cheshire; 1906–07 Dronsfield Bros office building, King Street, Oldham, Lancashire (by Sellers) [*159*]; 1906 House, No. 36 Mellalieu Street, Middleton (Wood's first flat-roofed design); 1907 Dalny Reed, Barley, near

Royston, Hertfordshire; 1908 Upmeads, up a lane off Newport Road, Stafford [*111*]; 1908–10 Durnford Street School, Durnford Street, Middleton (with Sellers); 1908–10 Elm Street School, Elm Street, Middleton (with Sellers) [*160*]; 1908 3 shops, Nos 33–37 Manchester Road, Middleton; 1912 Semi-detached houses, Nos 165–167 Manchester Old Road, Middleton; 1913–20 39 houses on an estate, Fairfield Avenue and Broadway, Fairfield, Droylsden, near Manchester (probably designed by Sellers); 1914–16 Royd House, No. 224 Hale Road, Hale, Cheshire (for himself).

Young, WILLIAM (1843–1900). *Born in Scotland, Young moved to London c. 1870 and started his own practice, mostly in country houses. His Glasgow Municipal Chambers (1882–88) made him well known. After that he did much country house work in England, often for aristo-*

cratic clients, and in 1898 was selected on the advice of an R.I.B.A. committee as architect of the new War Office in Whitehall, London. Young had to work to a ground plan already prepared by government architects. He died after completing the English Baroque design, but before the building had risen above ground level. It was completed by his son Clyde Young.
c. 1890 Sefton Lodge, Newmarket, Suffolk; c. 1890 Interiors, Chevening Park, north-west of Sevenoaks, Kent; 1895–98 Rebuilt exterior and designed new interiors of Duncombe Park, south-west of Helmsley, Yorkshire; c. 1895 Rebuilding and extensive additions for Lord Cadogan at Culford Hall (now Culford School), north of Bury St Edmunds, Suffolk; 1898–1906 The War Office, Whitehall, London [*179*]; 1899–1903 Extensive additions and estate buildings for Lord Iveagh at Elveden Hall, near Brandon, Suffolk.

Index

For a further list of architects and buildings, see pp. 197–213

Numbers in italics refer to illustrations
ABERDEEN, Elphinstone Tomb, 127, *152*
Adams, H. Percy, 109, 178
Aesthetic Movement, the, 16, 17, 18, 28, 36
Anderson, R. Rowand, 62, 81
Archer and Green, 10
Architectural Association, 13, 21, 40, 62, 68, 79, 100, 102, 108, 128, 142, 149
Art Deco, 135
Art Nouveau, 38, 51, 60, 102, 112, 161
Art Workers' Guild, 13, 19–24, 27, 38, 40, 41, 43–4, 46, 48, 50, 51, 54–5, 62, 64, 68, 72, 78, 82, 127, 145, 164, 170, 175
Arts and Crafts Exhibition Society, 13, 20, 33, 58, 113
Arts and Crafts Movement, 8, 10–13, 14, 17–28, 31, 32, 33–7, 38, 40, 41, 43, 45, 48, 57, 58, 60, 64, 65, 70–3, 78, 79–80, 82, 83–4, 87, 88ff., 102, 106–13, 114, 118ff., 130, 131–2, 133, 140, 150–1, 170, 174
Ashbee, Charles Robert, 33–4, 35, 38, 51, 71, 94, 102, 109, 180, *27–9*
Atkinson, Frank, 148, 168, *208*
Aumonier, W., 175
Ayrshire, St Sophia's, Galston, 81
BAILLIE SCOTT, M. H., 27, 35–6, 90, 93–4, 96, 100, *30–1*, *106–7*, *116*
Baker, Herbert, 187
Barclay, H. and D., 60
Barnsley, Ernest, 122; Sydney, 82
Baroque, English, 8, 13, 21, 24, 44, 45, 58, *65*, *171*; High Edwardian, 140–52, 154–7, 185; revival, and public buildings, 60ff., 106, 114, 132

Bateman and Bateman, 95, 131, *155*
Bates, Harry, 44, 65
Bath, Guildhall, 65–6, *66–7*; Municipal Art Gallery and Museum, 66, *68*; buildings surrounding Roman Baths, 66
Bauhaus, 58, 139, 187
Beaux-Arts Classicism, 8, 13, 60, 68, 69, 151, 158, 160–9
Bedford, Francis, 172, *217*
Bélanger, F.-J., 160, *196*
Belcher, John, 17, 19, 44, 45, 64–5, 66, 67–8, 70, 71, 82, 83, 140, 145–6, 152, 156–7, 178–9, 181–2, *59*, *64*, *69*, *174–5*, *185*, *194*, *226*, *229–31*
Belfast City Hall, 52, 143–4, 145, 154, *172–3*
Bell, E. Ingress, 67, 70, 82, 149, *72*
Bell, Robert Anning, 50, *45*
Bentley, John Francis, 44, 74, 81–2, 83, 84, *78–9*, *87*
Berenguer, F., 48
Berkshire, Caversham Public Library, 106; Deanery Gardens, Sonning, 88–90, *98*; Luckley, Wokingham, 175, *220–2*; Shooter's Hill House, Pangbourne, 170–1, *210*; Wellington College, 60; White Lodge, Wantage, 35, 36, *30–1*
Bidlake, W. H., 80, 95, 125, *86*
Birmingham, Bishop Latimer Church, Handsworth, 125; Bournville village, King's Heath, 99, *113*; Eagle Insurance Buildings, 53–4, 130, *49–50*; Garth House, Edgbaston, 95; Redlands, Four Oaks, 95; St Agatha's, Sparkbrook, 80, *86*; Small Arms factory, Small Heath, 135, *163*; University, 82, 149; Victoria

Law Courts, 149
Blashill, Thomas, 100, 101
Blomfield, Reginald, 8, 13, 68, 144–5, 156, 164–7, 169, 170, *203–4*
Blow, Detmar, 28, 90–1, 92, *17*, *100*
Bodley, G. F., 8, 17, 44, 74, 77–8, 83, *91–3*
Bodley and Garner, 86
Bradshaw and Gass, 105
Brewer, Cecil, 56–7, 106, 113, 138, *55*, *168*
Brewill and Bailey, 131
Briggs and Wolstenholme, *188*
Brisbane Cathedral, 77
Bristol, Central Reference Library, 110–12, 116, 131, *130*; Everard's factory, 104; Royal Infirmary buildings, 112, *131*
Brock, Thomas, 167
Brodrick, Cuthbert, 60
Brooks, James, 17, 74
Browne, George Washington, 184
Bryce, David, 62
Brydon, John, 13, 60–3, 65–6, 68, 142, 144, 147–8, 170, *60*, *66–8*, *178*
Buckinghamshire, Five Bells, Iver Heath, 94; Wittington, 68
Burges, W., 8, 74
Burn, William, 22
Burne-Jones, Edward, 12, 80
Burnet, John J., 69, 76, 83, 114, 115, 116, 132, 135, 137–9, 152, 158, 167–8, 181, 184, 70, 80, 135, 157, *165–6*, *169*, *206–8*
Burnham, Daniel, 137, 168, *208*
Butterfield, William, 8, 14, 74
Byzantine style, 54, 74, 81–3, 87, 126–7
CALCUTTA, Victoria Memorial, 154
Cambridge, Humphry Museum and

Medical Schools, 73, 76; Westminster College, 52–3, 48
Cambridgeshire, White Horse Inn, Stetchworth, 107
Campbell, John A., 69, 76, 114–15, 135–7, 70, 80, 164
Canning, 100
Cardiff City Hall, 146–7, 151, 160, 176–7
Carfrae, J. A., 184
Caröe, W. D., 86, 87, 101
Century Guild, the, 18, 19
Champneys, Basil, 17, 19, 42, 77, 80, 82
Cheshire, Eaton Hall, 8, 2; Port Sunlight, 99; Stockport Town Hall, 155, 189
Classicism, 8, 10, 44, 46, 60, 76, 112; and see Baroque, High Edwardian
Clutton, Henry, 74
Cockerell, C. R., 60, 169
Cole, Henry, 10
Collcutt, Thomas, 8, 44, 72, 81, 1
Comper, J. Ninian, 86–7, 96–7
concrete, use of, 92, 97, 114, 115, 128, 130, 133–5
Cooper, Edwin, 185–6, 237
Cornwall, Truro Cathedral, 77, 81
Crane, Walter, 20, 43–4
Creswell, H. Bulkeley, 108, 126
Crewe, Bertie, 164, 186
Cross, Alfred, 106, 123
DAVIS, Arthur J., 13, 160, 161–3, 169, 185, 195, 197–200, 236
Dawson, Matthew, 100
Day, Lewis F., 20, 102
De Morgan, William, 95, 175
Denbighshire, Kinmel Park, 60
Devey, George, 14, 17, 21, 22, 28, 5
Devon, The Barn, Exmouth, 25–6, 90, 14–15; Castle Drogo, Drewsteignton, 98, 112; Fleet Lodge, Holbeton, 20; Royal Naval College, Dartmouth, 148, 149, 166, 180
Dorset, Bothenhampton Church, 78–9, 118, 84; Bryanston, Blandford Forum, 44, 64, 72, 61; Minterne House, Minterne Magna, 97–8; Pier Terrace, West Bay, 24, 51–2, 55, 51; St Osmund's, Parkstone, 126–7, 150
Douglas, Campbell, 17, 62
Doyle, J. Francis, 70, 178
Dressler, Conrad, 225
Dunbartonshire, The Hill House, Helensburgh, 95–6, 108, 110
Durham, St Andrew's, Roker, 123–4, 145–6
EDINBURGH, Barclay Church, 76; Boroughmuir School, 184; Civil Service and Professional Supply, 114, 132, 184, 157; Colinton, cottages at, 37; Edinburgh Life Assurance, George Street, 184, 235; Midlothian County Buildings, 184; R. W. Forsyth's department store, 114, 184; St Giles's Cathedral, Thistle Chapel, 185; St Peter's, Falcon Avenue, 126, 148
Edis, Colonel, 10
education, architectural, 40, 128,

158–60, 169
Elizabethan style, 21, 22, 41, 46, 52, 90
Emerson, Sir William, 154
Epstein, Jacob, 112
Essex, Colchester Town Hall, 70, 145–6, 160, frontispiece, 73, 174–5; St Mary the Virgin, Great Warley, 122–3, 143, half-title
Everard, J. B., 72
FIELD, Horace, 172, 213
Fife, New Library, St Andrews University, 184–5, 234; Wemyss Hall, 175, 223
Fleming, Owen, 100, 101
Flintshire, University College of North Wales, Bangor, 113, 132; Willens and Robinson factory, Queensferry, 108, 126
Ford, E. Onslow, 20
Forsyth, William, 139
Free Style, 6, 13, 21, 25, 26, 30, 32, 37, 38, 40, 41–2, 44, 45, 46–51, 57–8, 73, 104–5, 105–8, 109–13, 114–15, 115–16, 145, 150–1
Fuller Clark, H., 104, 117
GARDEN CITIES, 88, 93–4, 99–100
Garnier, Charles, 160
Gaudí, A., 48, 51
George, Ernest, 8, 88, 172, 215–16
Gibson, James, 114
Gibson, John, 60
Gibson and Russell, 142, 152
Gillespie, John Gaff, 115, 134–5, 156, 161
Gimson, Ernest, 17, 27–8, 80, 92, 95, 102, 112, 122, 124, 127, 175, 17–18
Glasgow, 8, 69; Athenaeum Theatre, 69, 70; Barony Church, Castle Street, 76–7, 80; Clyde Trust, 152; Edinburgh Life Assurance, St Vincent Street, 135–7; Glasgow Herald building, 45, 69; 157 Hope Street, 115; Lion Chambers, Hope Street, 115–16, 132, 156; McGeoch's store, 115, 116, 139, 133; Municipal Chambers, 60, 148; National Bank, 72, 184; Northern Insurance, St Vincent Street, 115, 135–7, 164; Queen's Cross, church, 122; Royal Insurance, 69, 71; 142 St Vincent Street, 51; School of Art, 57–8, 71, 116, 131–2, 56–8, 135–6; Scotland Street School, 115, 134; Wallace Scott Tailoring Institute, 138–9, 169
Gloucestershire, St Edward the Confessor, Kempley, 121–2, 140
Godwin, Edward, 16, 17, 20, 34, 38, 41, 71, 98–9, 6
Gothic style, 21, 87; late, 74, 76–80, 83, 84–7; Victorian, 8, 10, 12, 14, 17, 38, 45, 46, 60
Guernsey Public Buildings, 148
Guild and School of Handicraft, 33, 94
Guimard, Hector, 51
HAMES, F. J., 60
Hampshire, Avon Tyrell, Thorney Hill, 22, 64, 11; Gosport Public Library, 148, 123; High Coxlease, Lyndhurst, 88, 99; Marshcourt, Stockbridge, 90, 101; Portsmouth

Guild Hall, 60; St Andrew's and St Clement's, Boscombe, 46, 41; Telephone Exchange, Southampton, 131, 154
Hare, Henry, 42, 52–3, 70, 105–6, 113, 151, 48, 73, 122, 132
Harvey, Alexander, 99, 113
Henry, J. Macintyre, 184
Herefordshire, All Saints', Brockhampton, 92, 118–21, 123, 133, 137–9; Perrycroft, Colwall, 22, 31, 22–3
Hertfordshire, All Saints' Convent, London Colney, 52, 46; Church of the Holy Rood, Watford, 74, 81, 79; Dalny Reed, Royston, 97; Holwell House, 172, 215; The Lees, Elstree, 96; Letchworth Garden City, 93, 94, 99, 106, 114; Lululand, Bushey, 43; The Orchard, Chorley Wood, 93, 104–5
Hill, William, 60
Hiorns, 100
Hoffmann, Joseph, 96, 112
Holden, Charles, 38, 97, 108–12, 113, 116, 131, 133, 139, 178, 180–1, 183, 185, 186, 128–31, 225, 227–8
Holiday, Henry, 20
Honeyman and Keppie, 44, 57
Horne, Herbert, 18
Horsley, Gerald, 17, 40, 72, 78, 77
Howard, Ebenezer, 99
Huxley, T. H., 24
IMAGE, Selwyn, 18
JACKSON and Sons, Messrs George, 162
Jackson, T. G., 40, 41–2, 52, 142, 33–4
Jacobean style, 21, 41–2, 52, 68, 106, 131, 142
Joass, J. J., 145, 166, 178–9, 181–3, 204, 229–31
Jones, Owen, 10
Jourdain, Frantz, 133, 158
KENT, How Green, Hever, 91; St Alban's Court, Nonington, 21, 5
Kitson, Sydney, 172, 217
LANCASHIRE, Ashton Memorial, Lancaster, 156–7, 181, 194; Broadleys, Windermere, 32; Dronsfield Bros offices, Oldham, 133, 159; Durnford and Elm Street Schools, Middleton, 133–6, 160; Lancaster Town Hall, 156, 193; Methodist church and schools, Middleton, 57, 54
Lanchester, H. V., 146–7, 151, 152, 154, 155, 160, 169, 176–7, 190–2
Lawson, G. A., 66
Lee, Stirling, 122
Leicestershire, Leicester Town Hall, 60; National Westminster Bank, Leicester, 72; Papillon Hall, 90; Stoneywell Cottage, Ulverscroft, 27–8, 17–18; Wentworth Arms, Elmesthorpe, 55–6
Leiper, William, 76
Lethaby, William, 8, 12–13, 17, 19, 21–4, 28, 36–7, 38, 40, 42, 46–8, 49, 53–4, 56, 58, 64, 68, 78, 79, 80, 81, 84, 88, 92, 95, 99, 108, 110, 112, 113, 114, 118–21, 122, 125, 126, 127, 130, 133, 135, 145, 170, 174, 11–12, 32, 49–50, 137–9, 141

Liverpool, Anglican Cathedral, 46, 83–6, 122, 126, *91–3, 141–2*; Cotton Exchange, 152; Cunard Building, 185, *236*; Liver Building, 182, *233*; Mersey Docks Building, 154, *188*; Methodist Central Hall, 105, *106*; Royal Insurance, 70, 178, *226*; Technical School, 150; White Star Line building, 51
London, Admiralty Arch, 166; Albery Theatre, 164, *202*; All Souls' School, St Marylebone, 113; Ames House, Mortimer Street, 113; Annesley Lodge, Hampstead, 31, *24*; Battersea Town Hall, 68, 150; Bedford Park, 98–9; Belgrave Hospital for Children, Oval, 109–10, *128*; Bishopsgate Institute, 48–9, *42*; Blackfriars House, 138; Boulting and Sons offices, St Marylebone, 104, *117*; Boundary Street Estate, Shoreditch, 101; Bruce House, Covent Garden, 113; Buckingham Palace, 166, 167, *205*; Campbell Mausoleum, St James's Cemetery, Kensal Green, 82, *89*; Carlton Club, 105; Carlton Hotel, 161; Carnegie Public Library, Islington, 182; Central Hall, Westminster, 155, *190–1*; Central School of Arts and Crafts, Holborn, 113–14; Chelsea Polytechnic, 65; Chelsea Town Hall, 13, 60, 62, *60*; 37, 38–39, 72–73 Cheyne Walk, 33–5, 94, *27–9*; Christ Church, Brixton Road, 82, *88*; Christ Church, Newgate Street, 145; Claridge's, 8; 7 Cleveland Row, St James's, 169, *209*; Coliseum Theatre, 154, *186*; Country Life building, Covent Garden, 152; County Hall, 155–6, 185, *192*; County Insurance, Piccadilly, 166; Debenham House, 174–5, *219*; Deptford Town Hall, 152; Electra House, Moorgate, 152; Euston Road fire station, 108, *127*; Evelyn House, Oxford Street, 180; Gerrard Street Telephone Exchange, 104–5, *121*; 34–36 Golden Square, 138, *167*; Government Buildings, Parliament Square, 147–8, *178*; Hampstead Garden Suburb, 94, 99–100, *116, 147*; Hampstead Towers, 14–16, *4*; 37 Harley Street, 71, *74*; Heal's, Tottenham Court Road, 138, 177, 224, *168*; Holy Trinity Church, Kensington, 77–8, *83*; Holy Trinity Church, Sloane Street, 45, 79–80, *38, 85*; Horniman Museum, 50, *45*; Imperial College of Science, South Kensington, 148, 166; Imperial Institute, South Kensington, 8, *1*; Institute of Chartered Accountants, 44, 64–5, 68, 69, 140–2, *59, 64*; Inveresk House, Aldwych, 161, *195*; King Edward VII Galleries, British Museum, 167–8, *206–7*; Kodak Building, Kingsway, 137–8, *165–6*; Ladbroke Grove Public Library, 46, *39*; Law Society, Chancery Lane,

180, *225, 227*, Lloyd's Shipping Register building, 72; London, Edinburgh and Glasgow Insurance, Euston Square, 114, *182–3, 232*; The Mall, 166–7; Mappin House, Oxford Street, 181, *229–30*; Mary Ward House, Tavistock Place, 56–7, 106, 113, 138, *55*; Middlesex Guildhall, Westminster, 114; Millbank Estate, 101, *115*; 82 Mortimer Street, 71, *75*; 42 Netherhall Gardens, Hampstead, 21, *10*; New Scotland Yard, 44, 81, *37*; Norwich House, Holborn, 180; Old Bailey, 150–1, 160, *170, 181–2*; Old Shades, Whitehall, 51, *119*; Piccadilly Circus, 105–6, *204*; Piccadilly House, 154, 165, *187*; Port of London Authority headquarters, 185; Prudential Assurance, 8; Queen Alexandra's Court, Wimbledon, 172, *216*; 170, 180 Queen's Gate, 21, 64, *62*; Regent Street, 165–6, *204*; Rhodesia House, Strand, 112, 180–1, *228*; The Rising Sun, Tottenham Court Road, 51; Ritz Hotel, 161, *197–8*; Royal Automobile Club, 161–2, *199–200*; Royal Insurance, Piccadilly, 181–2, *231*; Royal London House, Finsbury Square, 152, *185*; Royal United Services Institute, Whitehall, 70, *72*; Sanderson Wallpaper Factory, Chiswick, 106, 131, *153*; St Cyprian's, Clarence Gate, 87, *96*; 7 St James's Square, 186–7, *238*; St Jude's, Hampstead Garden Suburb, 125–6, *147*; St Luke's, Hampstead, 80; St Marylebone Town Hall, 185–6, *237*; St Paul's Girls' School, Hammersmith, 72, *77*; St Peter's, Ealing, 46, *40*; St Peter's Hospital, Covent Garden, 62; Selfridge's, 168, *208*; 3 Soho Square, 104, *120*; Studio cottage, Bedford Park, 28, *21*; Sun Alliance, St James's Square, 152; Swan and Edgar's, Piccadilly, 166; 44 Tite Street, 16, 34, *6*; United University Club, 165, *203*; Victoria and Albert Museum, 8, 67, 102, 149, *69*; Victoria Memorial, The Mall, 167; Waldorf Hotel, 162, *201*; War Office, 60, 148, *179*; West End Lane fire station, 108, *125*; Westminster and County Insurance, Regent Street, 165–6; Westminster Roman Catholic Cathedral, 74, 81–2, 83, *78, 87*; White House, Chelsea, 16, *17*; Whitechapel Art Gallery, 49–51, 58, *43–4*; Whitehall House offices, *119*; Woolwich Municipal Buildings, 148
London County Council Architects, 57, 100–1, 107–8, 113, *115, 125*
Lorimer, Robert, 37, 98, 126, 175, *184–5, 148, 223, 234*
Lutyens, Edwin, 27, 88–90, 91, 97, 98, 100, 109, 125–6, 139, 152, 172–4, 184, 186–7, *19, 98, 101, 112, 147, 218, 238–9*
MACARTNEY, Mervyn, 17, 88, 95, 145,

170, 172, 175, *212*
McColl, D. S., 20
Mackenzie, A. G. R., 162, *201*
Mackintosh, Charles Rennie, 8, 13, 44–5, 48, 55, 57–8, 69, 71–2, 84, 90, 95–6, 97, 112–13, 115–16, 122, 131–2, 133, 135, *53, 56–8, 71, 108–10, 134–6, 142*
MacLaren, James, 17, 20, 21, 22, 34, 37, 43, 45, 54–5, 71, 106, *9, 36*
Mackmurdo, Arthur, 17–19, 20, 24, 28, 36, 48, 60, 144, 170, *7–8*
Manchester, Christian Science Church, Victoria Park, 123, *144*; New Theatre, 186; Rylands Memorial Library, 77, 80, *82*
Matcham, Frank, 154, 164, *186*
Matear and Simon, 152
Maufe, Edward, 138
Menin Gate war memorial, 165
Merioneth, St Mark's, Brithdir, 118
metal, use of, 132–3, 135–9, 161, 181
Mewès, Charles, 161–3, 181, *195, 197–200, 236*
Michelangelo, 62, 70–1, 152, 178
Micklethwaite, J. T., 40
Middlesex, Brooklyn, Enfield, 18–19, *8*; Frithwood House, Northwood, 172, *212*
Miller, Albert D., 168
Moira, Gerald, 151
Moore, Temple, 84, 86, *94–5*
Morris, William, 10, 12–13, 14, 17, 18, 20, 36, 48, 79, 81, 100, 107, 108, 164
Mountford, Edward, 61, 148, 150–1, 156, 157, *170, 181–2, 193*
Muthesius, Hermann, 37, 58, 106
NASH, Joseph, 41
Neo-Classical style, 60, 114, 158, 160, 182–3, 183–5, 185–7; *and see* Beaux-Arts Classicism
Neo-Georgian style, 24, 72, 114, 170ff., 224
Neo-Mannerism, 110, 178–82
Nesfield, W. Eden, 14, 60, 62
New Delhi, Viceroy's House, 187, *239*
Newton, Ernest, 17, 24, 88, 166, 172, 175, *13, 204, 214, 220–2*
Norfolk, Happisburgh House, 90–1, *100*; Home Place, Holt, 27, 91–2, *102–3*; Norwich Union head office, 152, *183*; Royal Arcade, Norwich, 104, *118*
Northamptonshire, St Mary's, Wellingborough, 87, *97*
Northumberland, Chesters, 24, 44, 64, *63*
Nottinghamshire, St Mark's, Mansfield, 86; Ram Hotel, Nottingham, 131
OLBRICH, Joseph, 112
Orkneys, Melsetter House, Hoy, 37, 88, 118, 125, *32*
Oxford, Brasenose College, New Quad, 42, *33*; Examination Schools, 42; Hertford College, 42; Mansfield College, 42; Town Hall, 52, *47*; Trinity College, Front Quad, 42, *34*
Oxfordshire, Henley Town Hall, 151
PARIS, La Bagatelle, 160, *196*; Humbert

de Romans auditorium, 51; Les Invalides, 63; L'Opéra, 160; Palais de Justice, 160; Petit Trianon, 160; La Samaritaine store, 132–3, *158*
Paris Exhibition 1900, 160, 161; Grand Palais, 160, 161; Petit Palais, 161; Pont Alexandre III, 161
Parker, Barry, 99–100, *114*
Pascal, Jean-Louis, 69, 167, 168
Paterson, Alexander, 184
Pearson, John Loughborough, 74, 76–7, *81*
Peddie, J. Dick, 184, *235*
Perthshire, Aberfeldy Town Hall, 54, 55; Farmer's House, Glenlyon estate, Fortingall, 20, 21, *9*; Hallyburton, Coupar Angus, 98
Pick, S. Perkins, 72
Pilkington, F. T., 76
Pite, A. Beresford, 17, 20, 44, 45, 64–5, 66, 67–8, 70–1, 82, 84, 113, 114, 126, 140, 178, 180, 181, 182–3, *59*, *64*, *74–5*, *88*, *151*, *226*, *232*
Playfair, William Henry, 76, 183
Pomeroy, F. W., 151
Prior, Edward, 17, 19, 22, 24–7, 28, 32, 40, 42, 50, 51–2, 58, 73, 78–9, 80, 84, 90–3, 102, 110, 118, 121, 123–5, 126–7, 133, 174, 175, *14–16*, *51–2*, *76*, *84*, *102–3*, *145–6*, *150*, *219*
Pugin, Augustus Welby, 8, 10, 14
'QUEEN ANNE' style, 8, 14, 38, 62
RANSOME, James, 172, *211*
rationalism in architecture, 128, 131, 137–9
Reilly, Charles, 112, 169
Renaissance, English, 140–2; Italian, 41, 62; *and see* Baroque, High Edwardian
Renfrewshire, Greenock Town Hall, 60
Reynolds-Stephens, William, 122–3, *143*
Ricardo, Halsey, 17, 25, 41, 52, 84, 95, 106, 127, 174–5, *47*, *219*
Richardson, A. E., 169, 186
Richardson, H. H., 20, 42–3, 49, *35*
Richmond, William, 151
Rickards, E. A., 146–7, 151, 152, 154, 155, 157, 160, 176–7, *184*, *190–2*
Riley, W. E., 101
Robertson, J. M., 42–3
Romanesque style, 43, 45
Royal Institute of British Architects, 40, 68, 158, 169
Ruskin, John, 10–12, 14, 17, 24
ST GEORGE'S GUILD, 12
St Helier, Jersey, Steep Hill, 172, *214*
Salmon, James, the younger, 51, 115–16, 132, 135, *156*
Salvin, Anthony, 21
Schultz, Robert Weir, 82, 91, 122, 126, *149*
Scott, George Gilbert, 8, 45, 74, 78, 84
Scott, George Gilbert, the younger, 74, 86
Scott, Giles Gilbert, 84–6, 87, *91–3*

Scott, John Oldred, 45
Seale, Gilbert, 151
Secessionism, 112, 113, 180
Sedding, John Dando, 13, 17, 19, 20, 44, 45, 46, 74, 79–80, 118, 125, *38*, *85*
Seddon, J. P., 17
Sellers, J. Henry, 97, 133–4, *159–60*
Shaw, John, 60
Shaw, Norman, 10, 14–16, 17, 19, 21, 22, 24, 33, 38, 40, 41–2, 56, 60, 62, 64, 68, 69, 70, 72, 78, 81, 83, 99, 118, 142–3, 144, 145, 152, 154, 165, 170, *4*, *10*, *37*, *61–3*, *187*
Simpson, John W., 56
Simpson and Milner-Allen, 148
Skipper, F. W., 152, *183*; G. J., 104, 152, *118*, *183*
Smith, Dunbar, 56–7, 106, 113, 138, 55, *168*
Society for the Protection of Ancient Buildings, 12, 100, 108
Spalding and Cross, 101
Spencer, Herbert, 17, 24
Spiers, R. Phené, 40, 68, 158
Sprague, W. G. R., 164, *186*, *202*
Staffordshire, All Saints', Leek, 78; Garrick Street Library, Wolverhampton, 105–6, *122*; Upmeads, Stafford, 97, *111*; Walsall Town Hall, 151–2
Stevenson, J. J., 17
Stewart, J. A., *176*, *177*
Stirling High School, 43, *36*
Stokes, Leonard, 17, 20, 22, 26, 44, 52, 62, 68, 97–8, 104–5, 131, 138, 147, 170, *46*, *121*, *154*, *167*, *210*
Street, G. E., 8, 12, 14, 17, 74
Sudan, All Saints' Cathedral, Khartoum, 126, *149*
Sullivan, Louis, 48, 112, 114, 137
Sumner, Heywood, 20
Surrey, Blackheath village, 32–3, 55, 96; Cobbins, Blackheath, 96–7; Dickhurst, 26; Greyfriars, Puttenham, 31–2, 33, 35, *25*; Hatchlands, 165; Norney, Shackleford, 32, *26*; Redcourt, Haslemere, 24, 170, *13*; Sandhouse, Witley, 95; Tigbourne Court, Witley, 27, 88, *19*; Westbrook, Godalming, 95
Sussex, Bill House, Selsey-on-Sea, 94; Christ's Hospital School, 149; King Edward VII Sanatorium, Midhurst, 110, *129*; Little Thakeham, 172–4; Minsted, Midhurst, 95; Roedean School, Brighton, 56; St Bartholomew's, Brighton, 82, 127, *90*; Standen, East Grinstead, 22, 108, *3*
Swales, Francis, 168, *208*
TAIT, Thomas, 137
Tanner, Henry, 147
Taylor, John, 148
Taylor, Minton, 100
Thomas, A. Brumwell, 143–4, 145, 148, 154–5, 172–3, *189*
Thomas, Walter, 182, *233*

Thomson, Alexander, 60, 76, 183
Thornely, Arnold, 154, *188*
Thornycroft, Hamo, 20, 44, 65
town planning, 98–101
Townsend, Charles Harrison, 13, 22, 26, 27, 32–3, 36, 38, 43, 48–51, 55, 58, 80, 84, 96–7, 102, 104, 122–3, 125, *20*, *42–5*, *143*
Treadwell and Martin, 51, 104, *119*
Troup, F. W., 95, 122, 138
Turner, H. Thackeray, 55, 95
UGANDA, Namirembe Cathedral, Kampala, 126, *151*
United States of America, Buffalo, Guaranty and Larkin buildings, 112; Illinois, Unity Temple, 112, 180; Massachusetts, Crane Memorial Library, 43, *35*; *and see* Richardson, H. H., *and* Sullivan, Louis
Unwin, Raymond, 99–100, *114*
VARLEY, F. C., *29*
Verity, Frank, 160, 168–9, *209*
Verity, Thomas, 10
Verstage, A. Halcrow, 100, 113
Voysey, C. F. A., 8, 17, 18, 20, 21, 22, 25, 26, 28, 32, 34, 35, 36, 37, 48, 51, 54–5, 84, 96, 97, 106–7, 110, 122, 131, 132, 134, 135, *21–6*, *104–5*, *124*, *153*, *162*
WALTON, George, 96, *109*
Warwickshire, The Hurst, Sutton Coldfield, 22, 170, *12*
Waterhouse, Alfred, 8, 67, 160, *2*
Webb, Aston, 8, 67, 70, 82, 148, 149, 166–7, 72, 180, 205
Webb, Philip, 10, 12, 14, 17, 20, 22, 24, 41, 54, 84, 100, 101, 107, 108, 112, 149, *3*
Wells, Randall, 80, 92, 121–2, *140*
White, William, 74, 158
Williams, Henry, 104
Willink and Thicknesse, *236*
Wills and Anderson, 148
Wilson, Henry, 17, 20, 22, 36, 38, 45–6, 48, 49, 79, 80, 82, 84, 102, 109, 112, 118, 122, 125, 126, 127, 131, 150–1, *38–41*, *85*, *141*, *152*
Winmill, Charles, 100, 107–8, *125*
Wood, Edgar, 36, 57, 97, 123, 125, 133–4, *54*, *111*, *144*, *159–60*
Worley, R. J., 104, *120*
Wright, Frank Lloyd, 112, 180
YEATES, A., 172, *215–16*
Yorkshire, Cartwright Library, Bradford, 148; County Buildings, Wakefield, 142; Heathcote, Ilkley, 174, *218*; Hull Central Library, 148; Hull School of Art, 154, *184*; Leeds Town Hall, 60; New Earswick garden suburb, 99; Red House, Chapel Allerton, 172, *217*; St Cuthbert's, Middlesbrough, 86, *94*; St Wilfrid's, Harrogate, 86, *95*; Saltair, 98; Sheffield Town Hall, 68, 150
Young, Clyde, 148
Young, William, 60, 148, *179*